Social Imaginaries in a Globalizing World

Religion and Its Others

Studies in Religion, Nonreligion, and Secularity

Edited by
Stacey Gutkowski, Lois Lee, and Johannes Quack

Volume 5

Social Imaginaries in a Globalizing World

Edited by
Hans Alma and Guido Vanheeswijck

DE GRUYTER

ISBN 978-3-11-064405-0
e-ISBN (PDF) 978-3-11-043512-2
e-ISBN (EPUB) 978-3-11-043415-6
ISSN 2330-6262

Library of Congress Cataloging-in-Publication Data
Names: Alma, Hans, 1962- editor.
Title: Social imaginaries in a globalizing world / edited by Hans Alma and Guido Vanheeswijck.
Description: 1 [edition].. | Boston : De Gruyter, 2018. | Series: Religion and its others: studies in religion, nonreligion and secularity, ISSN 2330-6262 ; Volume 5
Identifiers: LCCN 2018017858| ISBN 9783110441833 (print) | ISBN 9783110434156 (e-book (epub) | ISBN 9783110435122 (e-book (pdf)
Subjects: LCSH: Religion and sociology. | Postsecularism. | Globalization--Religious aspects.
Classification: LCC BL60 .S6143 2018 | DDC 306.6--dc23 LC record available at
    https://lccn.loc.gov/2018017858

Bibliographic information published by the Deutsche Nationalbibliothek
The Deutsche Nationalbibliothek lists this publication in the Deutsche Nationalbibliografie;
detailed bibliographic data are available on the Internet at http://dnb.dnb.de.

© 2020 Walter de Gruyter GmbH, Berlin/Boston
This volume is text- and page-identical with the hardback published in 2018.
Printing and binding: CPI books GmbH, Leck

www.degruyter.com

Table of Contents

Hans Alma and Guido Vanheeswijck
Introduction to Social Imaginaries in a Globalizing World —— 1

Section 1: Social Imaginaries. A Historical and Conceptual Analysis

Guido Vanheeswijck
On the Philosophical Genealogy of the Concept Social Imaginaries —— 21

Stijn Latré
Social Imaginaries
   A Conceptual Analysis —— 47

Stijn Latré and Michiel Meijer
Retrieving Realism in Social Imaginaries —— 73

Section 2: Social Imaginaries as Meaningful Spaces

Christa Anbeek, Hans Alma, Saskia van Goelst Meijer
Contrast Experiences and Social Imaginaries as Spaces for Truth-Seeking —— 95

Laurens ten Kate
The Play of the World
   Social Imaginaries as Transcending Spaces: From Taylor to Nietzsche —— 119

Joeri Schrijvers
'Plus de Biens': Jacques Derrida and Charles Taylor —— 141

Section 3: Human Rights and Migration — (Post-)Secular Social Imaginaries in Contemporary Perspective

Robin Vandevoordt, Noel Clycq and Gert Verschraegen
Studying Culture through Imaginaries
    Some Reflections on the Relevance of Imaginaries for the Social Sciences —— 167

Nicole L. Immler
Human Rights as a Secular Social Imaginary in the Field of Transitional Justice
    The Dutch-Indonesian 'Rawagede Case' —— 193

Christiane Timmerman, Gert Verschraegen, Kenneth Hemmerechts, Roos Willems
Europe and the Human Rights Imaginary
    The Role of Perceptions of Human Rights in Europe and Migration Aspirations —— 223

Ernst van den Hemel
Post-Secular Nationalism
    The Dutch Turn to the Right & Cultural-Religious Reframing of Secularity —— 247

List of Contributors —— 265

Index —— 267

Hans Alma and Guido Vanheeswijck
Introduction to Social Imaginaries in a Globalizing World

1 Background

How to study the contemporary dynamics between the religious, the nonreligious and the secular in a globalizing world? Obviously, their relationship is not only an empirical datum, liable to the procedures of verification, let alone to those of logical deduction. In order to study the dynamics between the religious and the secular in depth, we are in need of alternative conceptual and methodological tools which are complementary to sheer empirically verified research. In this volume, we will argue that the concept of *social imaginary* is of utmost importance as a heuristic tool to understand these dynamics.

This concept can be traced back to the writings of Benedict Anderson (1983), Cornelius Castoriadis (1987) and Charles Taylor (2004, 2007). From different perspectives, they seek to understand (late) modern societies. In our volume we will focus on the way Charles Taylor uses the concept. His *A Secular Age* (2007), which is widely recognized as a seminal work in the field of secularization theories and in the long tradition of genealogies of secularization, not only elaborates on the notion of social imaginary, it is also an original application of this notion's influence on the social dynamics between the religious and the secular in a changing world.

This volume is one of the results of research conducted in the context of the international and interdisciplinary consortium SIMAGINE, dedicated to the study of social imaginaries between secularity and religion in a globalizing world.[1] The central research question of the consortium is: What can the concept of social imaginaries contribute to the analysis – in current cultural theory, religious studies and globalization theory – of societies that are interculturally super-diverse and display complex blends of existential frameworks, with both secular and religious features? Starting from this question the consortium will develop its research along theoretical and empirical lines. The present volume clarifies our

---

[1] Participating research groups and departments are located at the following universities: University of Humanistic Studies, Utrecht, the Netherlands; VU University Amsterdam, the Netherlands; University of Groningen, the Netherlands; Utrecht University, the Netherlands; University of Antwerp, Belgium; VUB Brussels, Belgium; University of Cambridge, UK; University of Vienna, Austria; University of Colorado at Boulder, USA; University of California, USA.

use of the concept social imaginaries and its promise as an analytic tool for understanding central issues in contemporary (Western) societies.

2 Social Imaginaries: A Complex Term

Today, many people are struggling to find an appropriate language to understand what a modern western culture consists of. According to a widespread understanding, modern western culture has drastically transformed its 'traditional' cultural predecessors thanks to the rise of modern science and the overall use of scientific rationality. In his introduction to the volume of essays, *Philosophical Arguments* (1995), Charles Taylor concedes that this might be the case on a superficial level, but that on a deeper level this understanding is at least biased and only gives a very partial explanation. He holds that modern society could not have developed into its contemporary shape without the occurrence of other, often neglected, changes:

> The intuition behind this [view] is that modern society is different from those of preceding ages not just in the novel institutions and practices of representative democracy, the market economy, institutionalized scientific discovery, and steady technological advance; it is different not just in moral and political principles, in authenticity, rights, democratic legitimacy, equality, non-discrimination. The notion is that alongside these changes, connected with these and in a relationship of mutual support, is an asset of changes in the way we have come to *imagine* society. That is, the repertory of means available to understand how we relate to others in society has altered in a fundamental way. (Taylor 1995, x)

In the quote above, it was the very first time that Taylor stresses the complementary and even indispensable function of *imagining* the world, alongside *theorizing* it, in terms which announce his later use of social imaginaries. Obviously, his use of the term 'imagining' and later of the term social imaginaries still shows the traces of Cornelius Castoriadis's coinage of the concept "as an enabling but not fully explicable symbolic matrix within which a people imagine and act as world-making collective agents" (Gaonkar 2002, 1). Taylor defines social imaginaries as incorporating "a sense of the normal expectations that we have of each other; the kind of common understanding which enables us to carry out the collective practices which make up our social life. This incorporates some sense of how we all fit together in carrying out the common practice." (Taylor 2007, 172)

To clarify the importance of social imaginaries in understanding our contemporary culture and the differences with other cultures, he often relates the meaning of imaginaries to that of a *picture*. Explicitly referring to Ludwig Wittgenstein's critique of Cartesian epistemology, Taylor wishes to underline with the use of the word picture that the way we imagine our world is something utterly different and much deeper than a theory:

> It is a largely unreflected-upon background understanding which provides the context for, and thus influences all our theorizing in this area. The claim could be interpreted as saying that mainline epistemological thinking, which descends from Descartes, has been contained within and hence shaped by this not fully explicit picture; that this has been a kind of captivity, because it has prevented us from seeing what is wrong with the whole line of thought. At certain points, we are unable to think 'outside the box,' because the picture seems so obvious, so commonsensical, so unchallengeable. (Taylor and Dreyfus 2015, 1–2)

Precisely because imaginaries and pictures are situated at the paradigmatic level, underlying and presupposing theoretical constructs, they have such a deep, albeit often surreptitious and tacit influence. Due to that precarious status, the ramifications of this specific use of the concept social imaginaries are manifold and complex. By way of introduction, we focus on four of them.

First, the concept social imaginaries functions as a collective noun which contains – among others – secular, religious, political and economical imaginaries. In application to our topic of the contemporary dynamics between the religious, the nonreligious and the secular in a globalizing world, it is to be noted that secular imaginaries inherent to our contemporary society relate to what Taylor defines as the *immanent frame* we are currently living in. At the same time, they make that immanent frame possible, which means that traditional sources of transcendence have been eclipsed or even dispelled from our views on man and nature. So, the social imaginary of an immanent frame has become "a picture that holds us captive", as Taylor rephrases Wittgenstein (Taylor 2007, 549). Moreover, this immanent frame is not related to one single social imaginary, but can only be understood by reference to social imaginaries in the plural, since contemporary Western culture showcases a super-diversity which does not allow for one single picture or social imaginary.

Second, social imaginaries are characterized by a high level of *inarticulacy*: they escape full theoretical articulation, and since they cover a wider grasp that has no clear limits their range is somewhat indefinite or even undefinable. Therefore, whereas social imaginaries are primarily background understandings that enable certain practices, they only become real in and manifest themselves through these practices. Consequently, social imaginaries are as it were as much lived as they are understood. They are enshrined in the use of 'expressivist' words, gestures and practices.

Third, in his latest book, *The Language Animal*, Taylor borrows from Bourdieu and Calhoun the distinction between *orthodoxy* and *doxa* to elucidate the complex status of social imaginaries as distinguished from theories and beliefs. Whereas orthodoxy is related to beliefs that we maintain to be correct in the awareness that others may have different views, doxa is interwoven with felt reality: "the operations of selecting and shaping new entrants (rites of passage, examinations, etc.) are such as to obtain from them that undisputed, pre-reflexive, naïve, native compliance with the fundamental presuppositions of the field which is the very definition of doxa. (...) All these feed together into what I have called elsewhere the 'social imaginary' of a given society." (Taylor 2016, 273)

Fourth, contrary to adherents of Cartesian (and naturalist) epistemology, Taylor considers full transparency out of reach with regard to social imaginaries. Here, he is parting ways with Hegel, in whose synthesis "the unclear consciousness of the beginning is itself made part of the chain of conceptual necessity. The unclear and inarticulate, just as the external and contingent, is itself shown to have a necessary existence. The approximate and incompletely formed is itself derived in exact, articulate concepts." (Taylor 1975, 569) Taylor, instead, follows the line of Herder and his descendants, "for whom the unreflective experience of our situation can never be fully explicated" (Taylor 1975, 569). Still, he remains indebted to the Oxford philosophers Robin G. Collingwood and Isaiah Berlin, who stress the importance of articulating the contents of our hidden background so as to understand the changes in our understanding of the place of man in society.

Therefore, Taylor defines his main books and articles as 'essays in retrieval,' i.e. essays in articulating the often forgotten background functioning as an imaginary or a picture that holds us captive. In *The Language Animal*, he even underlines that "our compliance [with the fundamental presuppositions of the field which is the very definition of doxa] never depends, at least in a modern society, solely on habitus-induced doxa. The rules of our institutions, the canonical forms and scripts of various roles and footings, are also spelled out and justified. (...) This includes an articulation of the doxa, but may also incorporate various critical stances toward this." (Taylor 2016, 273)

Hence, we have to cope with the following questions: What does Taylor exactly mean by articulating our social imaginaries, incorporating various critical stances toward them? What does he exactly understand by making explicit their implicit background? What do *we* exactly mean by articulating our social imaginaries and being critical toward them? What do *we* exactly understand by spelling out their implicit background and justifying them? To what extent is it possible for social imaginaries, inherently implicit, to be made explicit?

3 Social Imaginaries, Religion and its Others

These very questions are of high relevance when it comes to the specific topic of 'religion and its others'. The fact that religious and secular imaginaries work largely in an implicit way and come to expression in social practices, raises questions with regard to those social scientific endeavors which aim at making them explicit mainly through surveys based on explicit statements regarding a religious or secular outlook on life. What exactly do these surveys measure? Or would it be possible to gain a better understanding of modern worldviews through methodological tools that do justice to the inarticulate character of social imaginaries on the one hand and their expression in images, narratives, rituals and practices that people share in daily life on the other? Would it be possible, making use of social imaginaries as heuristic devices, to reconsider the allegedly clear-cut boundaries between the 'religious' and the 'secular' as they might come together in modern social imaginaries? And would it then be possible to get a more nuanced view of the 'nonreligious,' that is treated as an undifferentiated category in the majority of social scientific studies? The present volume deals with these questions in three sections.

The first section is dedicated to the conceptual clarification of Taylor's notion of social imaginaries both through a historical study of their genealogy and through conceptual analysis. Since Taylor's use of the term is highly evocative and allows for different interpretations, conceptual clarification is needed. From the start, we want to make it very clear how we use the term and how we relate it to questions regarding the dynamics between the religious, the nonreligious and the secular in our globalizing world. In this regard, the question of the ontological nature of social imaginaries arises – a question which has generally escaped attention in the field of Taylor-scholarship.

In the second section, we proceed with the conceptual analysis by clarifying the relation of social imaginaries to the concepts of (religious) worldview, 'worldplay', sense-making and to Taylor's emphasis on the diversity of 'goods'. Social imaginaries are driven by a deep longing for a meaningful and valuable life, rooted in bodily experiences (Alexander 2013). This longing inspires people to make use of their imagination so as to create images of the 'good life' (seen for example in stories of paradise). Imagination is a social process: inspired by collective imaginaries of what is good and valuable in our social context, it allows us to take the perspective of other people. Such imaginaries can flow together into a more or less coherent (religious) worldview. Consequently, understanding worldviews in terms of often implicit images, pictures, stories, expectations and anticipations does more justice to their pervasiveness and social impact than seeing them as a mere cognitive frame of reference.

A worldview is no fixed frame people hold, but a practice they engage in. At the same time, worldview practices like rituals, narrating, community building are important ways of articulating social imaginaries, making them explicit and in principle (though not always in practice) open to critical reflection. Therefore, relating (religious) worldviews to social imaginaries opens promising roads for the study of both concepts. It allows us to understand worldview dynamics that are not dependent on a presumed dichotomy between the religious and the secular. Furthermore, it has implications for our better understanding of people's search for existential meaning, of conflicts in which diverging images of the good are implied, and of possibilities for religious or worldview pluralism.

Since modern societies are characterized by encounters, confrontations and sometimes conflicts between highly divergent imaginaries of the good, in secular states neutrality in the public sphere is seen as an indispensable condition for a peaceful way of coping with religious diversity. One of this neutral stance's consequences is that political choices are not evaluated in terms of their commitments to their underlying social imaginaries, even more, that the existence of social imaginaries is bluntly neglected. To give one illustration: although the (neo) liberal emphasis on economic growth and market forces is definitely rooted in a background imaginary of man and world, it is usually taken for granted without articulating the worldview stance that is taken. There is, however, one imaginary of the good that is broadly accepted and explicitly used in secular states: human rights.

Human rights can be understood as 'the last utopia' (Moyn 2010), the last global framework that came to the fore as other ideologies collapsed (cf. Joas 2004, 2017). Joas (2015) even understands the Western belief in human dignity as the result of a process of sacralization, in which each individual human being was perceived more and more as being sacred. At the same time, he discusses Western transgressions of human rights during the same period of time (e.g. slavery, torture) and points out that the West cannot claim human rights as its sole merit. This raises important questions when it comes to the modern Western social imaginary, in which dedication to human rights seems to be taken for granted as a sign of cultural superiority.

We think that actual debates regarding both the universality versus cultural relativity of human rights and the hypocrisy of the Western self-satisfaction in light of its own inhuman practices can gain from applying the perspective of social imaginaries. In this respect, Steele (2013) argues that we must articulate the ways human rights are embedded in Western historical identity. He points out that "reasoning about rights and self-governance through the social imaginary opens resources of public debate that have been blocked by modernity's disengaged epistemological and moral reasoning" (Steele 2013, 99). An implication of such public reasoning may be that it demands changes in our self-understanding. Therefore, social imaginaries offer both a powerful and self-critical perspective on topical societal questions around migration, transitional justice and populism. These very questions will be addressed in the third and final section of this book.

4 Social Imaginaries among the Disciplines

The worldview diversity we are facing today and which is situated on the operative level of tacit imaginaries/pictures raises urgent challenges when it comes to living together in groups and societies. As scholars, we carry the responsibility to offer appropriate conceptual tools and adequate methodologies to study these challenges in ways helpful for dealing with them. We are convinced that the concept of social imaginary might be such a conceptual tool, but we believe that it needs to be developed in an interdisciplinary way.

In this volume philosophers, religious scholars and social scientists (cultural psychologists, sociologists and cultural anthropologists) co-operate in an endeavor to clarify, elaborate and apply Charles Taylor's fruitful thought on social imaginaries to the dynamics between religions and secularity. To this end, we not only aim for theory-building, but also wish to relate this specific philosophical concept to practices of e.g. coping with existential questions, education, and social justice. We think that a thorough understanding of social imaginaries and the practices they allow for, contributes to a form of active pluralism in which differences are not just tolerated, but in which people actively search for understanding and mutual respect. Social imaginaries point both to coherence and diversity, to sharing and conflict. Research on social imaginaries allows us to do justice to the super-diversity of our era (Vertovec, 2007) which challenges us to reconsider 'religion and its others' and offers a platform for practice related analysis.

5 An Exemplary Case Study

To gain a more vivid understanding of how the concept of social imaginary can be applied to a concrete societal situation, we present a case study from the Netherlands (for a more elaborate discussion of the example, see Alma 2015). Since the last decade, there has been a debate about one of Dutch favorite festivities, Saint Nicholas (*Sinterklaas*), an annual ritual of gift-giving culminating on the evening of December fifth (see for more information Helsloot 2012). The main issue is that Saint Nicholas has a black-faced assistant, Black Pete (*Zwarte Piet*). Black Pete arrives with Saint Nicholas on a boat from Spain and is typically portrayed with colorful attire, curly black hair, full red lips and golden earrings. He is merry and sometimes a bit simple-minded. This tradition that went unquestioned for centuries has been criticized by the United Nations' Working Group of Experts on People of African Descent and is now the locus of fierce debates regarding its roots in colonialism and its racist undertones. Many interpretations are brought to the fore with a dynamic interchange between diverse cultural perspectives.

Although referring to a Roman Catholic saint in a predominantly Protestant country, the festival of Saint Nicholas has become a secular happening. Hence, the secular-religious divide as commonly used, is fully inadequate to understand what is happening here. It is much more the case that the Black Pete discussion is about different social imaginaries in which strong evaluations are at stake. For instance, we see at work here how a national identity, becoming "enchanted" (Gergen 2009, 179) or "sacralized" (Droogers and Harskamp 2014, 2), clearly leads to sharp conflicts and to threats of violence, especially on the social media platforms.

As we have seen, social imaginaries are background understandings enabling certain practices, in which people create images of their being and are created by these images alike. In this very process, people's deepest values are guiding their daily practices and are exemplified in the stories they are telling. Only by acting, by telling stories and by performing rituals may these deepest values find expression. In a way, they are even constituted by these practices. Articulating these values does not just give expression to what already exists, it is also an act of creation. Hence, precisely in these articulating-constitutive practices of coping with our world, social imaginaries' flexible boundaries are challenged, negotiated and reconstructed.

All this can be related to the Black Pete discussion in the Netherlands. From time immemorial, the festival of Saint Nicholas has been a taken for granted part of the Dutch social imaginary. Not related to explicit theories or rules, it has become an expression of an implicit sense of belonging in songs, (historical) narratives, collective and home-made rituals, dressing up and jokes. Because all these are embodied practices, challenging them may result in mental or even physical disgust (Helsloot 2012, 12). In other words, the festival of Saint Nicholas implies a deep felt notion that it is 'good' to be Dutch and to belong to a country where people can participate in such a festival of gift-giving and mild playful criticism. That a significant part of the Dutch population feels excluded or discriminated by this type of bonding is perhaps too painful to realize.

In this sense, the Black Pete discussion helps to articulate implicit notions of moral and spiritual order that people would never have become conscious of if they had gone unchallenged. As Taylor and Dreyfus argue in their book *Retrieving Realism:* "We can no longer relate to our way of doing or construing things 'naïvely,' as just too obvious to mention" (2015, 125). What's more, we have to realize that our way of doing is not innocent but maintains and even corroborates a social reality in which people are excluded. The Black Pete discussion makes it clear that challenging, negotiating and reconstructing imaginaries is not to be thought of lightly and that social imaginaries are truly spaces of contestation.

Obviously, the festival of Saint Nicholas is very much a work of the imagination. Saint Nicholas and Black Pete are imaginary figures and the whole festival – lasting from November until the beginning of December – is a play of the imagination. Young children are convinced of the real existence of the saint and his assistants, while adults and older children do their best to make the performances of Saint Nicholas as convincing as possible. In this imaginary play, Dutch adults convince themselves of its innocence, that has been part and parcel of an old Dutch tradition. In this imagined world, there is no room for thinking that Black Pete is a caricature of a black person, let alone that this portrayal is rooted in our colonial past and is reflecting the status of black people in contemporary Dutch society (see Helsloot 2012). Acknowledging this would confront their imagined self with racist inclinations.

Migration, however, generated a plurality of imagined worlds and emerging interest in the black pages of Dutch history. The commemorations of slavery and discussions about compensation measures for Jewish, Indonesian and Surinamese victims of violence and oppression are cases in point. Confronted with these attacks on the Dutch self-image, many people react by denying these critical views' validity and regarding them as blasphemous. In complex ways, the Black Pete discussion also relates to the feelings of anxiety that Islam and Muslims are taking over Dutch culture with 'their strange ways.' Consequently, Black Pete has become a symbol of Dutch perseverance (see Helsloot 2012).

Yet, the imaginary landscape of the Netherlands in this era of super-diversity has changed irrevocably. Next to fierce conflicts, there has been a search for imagining alternatives to Black Pete as well (e.g. Rainbow Pete), even if they are heavily contested in this clash of imaginaries where symbolic power relations are at play and the media have become an important battlefield. What is actually at stake is a (re)negotiating of what it means to have a Dutch identity. There has arisen the inescapable challenge of coping with the question how to give voice to divergent imagined selves and worlds that articulate deeply felt values, convictions and aspirations. Whatever the outcome of this debate, the social imaginary of Sinterklaas/Saint Nicholas has irrevocably changed.

To conclude: the concept of social imaginaries helps us to go beyond the religious-secular divide and to see strong evaluations and deep values at stake in so-called secular issues. Even if we can forsake organized religions, we can't forsake our search for belonging through shared imaginations of what we value most deeply (Haidt 2012, 307). Furthermore, the concept of social imaginaries helps us to go beyond the individual freedom versus social determinism divide. People, imaginatively engaging with collective stories, open a social space for creativity and transformation.

We see all this happen in the case of Black Pete as well. Polarized though this contest between social imaginaries may be, it testifies to the health of Dutch (and every) democracy when critical voices may challenge the dominant social imaginaries and search for collective expressions arguing for social change. Today, democracy is in need of this critical exchange of diverging social imaginaries so as to prevent one implicit and taken for granted imaginary from becoming a fixed blueprint of what our social life ought to look like.

6 Presentation of the articles

Section 1: Social imaginaries. A Historical and Conceptual Analysis

In the introductory article, *On the Philosophical Genealogy of the Concept 'Social Imaginaries,'* Guido Vanheeswijck states that the deepest sources of Taylor's use of the concept social imaginaries are not found in the realm of political philosophy or social anthropology, but are related to his life-long struggle to overcome the pre-eminence of epistemology in modern philosophy and modern culture. To justify that statement, his article traces the philosophical genealogy of Taylor's concept of social imaginaries in three steps. First, he shows that Taylor's use of the term social imaginaries is deeply indebted to the influence of the so-called German meta-critics of Kant (Hamann, Herder, Humboldt), especially to their emphasis on the *historical* and *linguistic* character of the transcendental background of our daily experiences. Next, he gives a short presentation of the influence exerted by the continental phenomenological tradition on Taylor's concept, focusing on how Heidegger, Merleau-Ponty and Wittgenstein have helped Taylor to understand the depth of our embedded nature as agents in the surrounding world. Finally, he highlights the role of the largely forgotten heritage of two Oxford philosophers of history's position (Collingwood, Berlin) in the development of Taylor's notion of social imaginaries, in particular their stressing the philosophical and cultural importance of *articulating* the contents of our hidden background so as to understand the changes in our understanding of the place of man in society.

In chapter 2, *Social Imaginaries: A Conceptual Analysis*, Stijn Latré amplifies the historical genealogy of the concept social imaginaries with a conceptual analysis. To that end, he focuses on Taylor's description of the immanent frame, a term Taylor employs as the title for the fifteenth chapter of *A Secular Age*. Latré points out that even if the immanent frame may at first glance seem to be an alternative wording for the secular age, this wording immediately imposes a certain descriptive and interpretive scheme on the concept of secularization. That scheme consists of the binary opposition immanence-transcendence, which is essential to Christian theology. Nevertheless, the immanent frame does not just refer to intellectual, philosophical *views* on man and nature. That is why Taylor prefers the Wittgensteinian term *picture* in relation to the immanent frame, a term strongly related to the pivotal concept social imaginary, or rather social imaginaries in the plural. Latré first describes the use of the concept of social imaginaries by Castoriadis, then explores how Taylor's conception of social imaginaries is intertwined with other essential concepts in his oeuvre, such as transcendental framework, strong evaluation, expressivist culture and cross pressures, and finally turns back to the immanent frame as a social imaginary so as to make clear how these concepts frame our contemporary understanding and experience of the immanent frame.

In Chapter 3, *Retrieving Realism in Social Imaginaries*, Stijn Latré and Michiel Meijer elaborate on the issue developed in the previous chapter. Once admitted that social imaginaries are closely related to implicit moral orientations and that these implicit orientations are constitutive for our strong evaluations, difficulties arise concerning their (ontological) nature. Is there any objective ground for our constitutive goods or are they the result of our subjective projection of value on our actions and onto the world? Based on Taylor's provisionally penultimate book, *Retrieving Realism*, Latré and Meijer argue that Taylor defends what he and Hubert Dreyfus have recently called *pluralistic robust realism*, holding the middle between a naive and supposedly natural form of realism on the one hand and projectivism on the other. In order to elucidate that position, they first take a closer look at how Taylor distinguishes scientific reality from moral reality and then proceed on how this dichotomy testifies to the tension between ontology and phenomenology throughout Taylor's work. Finally, they explicitly connect the role of strong evaluation in our moral experience with the impact of social imaginaries.

Section 2: Social Imaginaries as Meaningful Spaces

In chapter 4, *Contrast Experiences and Social Imaginaries as Spaces for Truth-Seeking*, Christa Anbeek, Hans Alma and Saskia van Goelst Meijer introduce the concept of *worldviewing* to do justice to the fluidity characteristic of the way many people relate to existential issues. The central question of their article is whether social imaginaries can be helpful in understanding contemporary processes of worldviewing. The authors argue that social imaginaries find partial articulation when people are confronted with contrast experiences: positive or negative experiences that question everyday interpretations of existence. These experiences call for moral re-orientation and an articulation of constitutive goods, made possible by what Taylor calls strong evaluation. Articulation or expression will always be partial and plural but is nonetheless a claim or aspiration to truth. The authors argue that articulation is an inter-human activity and that truth can only be thought of in terms of relation, process, inter-being. The process of truth-seeking is driven by the 'human eros': the urge toward full, embodied experience of meaning and value. It is helped by the imaginative ability to see the actual in light of the possible. Eastern philosophy has important insights to offer when it comes to understanding truth-seeking. The Jain doctrine of *anekantavada*, understood as "the many sidedness of all phenomena" (Steger 2006, 342), is explained and makes clear that many different, even contradicting viewpoints are necessary in the process of truth-seeking. Clarifying pluralism without reducing it to relativism, this perspective contributes to understanding social imaginaries as shared spaces for the dynamics of truth-seeking. The authors introduce a case-study to further explore this conception of social imaginaries. The case-study points to important aspects of truth-seeking – imagination, embodiment, ritualizing and intersubjectivity – that can be further explored not only theoretically, but also with regard to professional practices.

In chapter 5, *The Play of the World*, Laurens ten Kate relates social imaginaries to our globalizing world and argues that the concept of social imaginaries serves as a tool to describe, analyze and understand the fundamental condition of global pluralism on an existential level, understood as super-diversity. This condition asks for a new perspective on sense-making: sense as a direction, perspective and aspiration taking place in the unstable, temporary spaces social imaginaries offer. To come to a deeper understanding of these spaces, Ten Kate makes use of Nietzsche's concepts of play and world-play. He points out that a logic of imagination replaces the logic of foundation: humans are left to their own devices when it comes to visualizing why the world is a worthy place and what its destination could be. This happens in *playful worlds*, in which humans enter into a creative relation to the world. The anthropological structure of play is characterized by a strange coincidence of acting and being acted, of creating and being created. The dynamic of playing with and in, of imagining and being imagined, is called world-play by Nietzsche. Play means that humans lose themselves in the world-spaces – or social imaginaries – they have created, and find themselves because of this. Imaginary worlds form our finite homes. This process is strongly influenced by the digitalization of the present world, as it creates new possibilities for people to create playful worlds and temporarily live in these worlds. Ten Kate briefly describes computer games as spaces of hybrid world-viewing and social media as spaces of transcendence, as social imaginaries that invite us to experience what lies beyond our limits. Finally, Ten Kate points out that the play of the world involves a transcending movement on a fundamental level, characterized by a strange and playful interaction between absence and presence, between what is and what is not. Far from being neutralized in a secular age, transcendence turns out to be the kernel of social imaginaries.

In chapter 6, *'Plus de Biens': Jacques Derrida and Charles Taylor*, Joeri Schrijvers emphasizes Taylor's statement that "further secularism involves *more than one good.*" He argues that this statement is the best summary available for the practice of deconstruction and he even considers Taylor's emphasis on the diversity of 'goods' – liberty, equality, fraternity – as an invitation to a genuine dialogue between Taylor and Derrida. To that end, even if Taylor himself has often been dismissive of Derridean deconstruction, Schrijvers's aim is to examine the convergences between Derrida and Taylor in more than one respect. Although he is fully aware that most commentators have been critical of Taylor's so-called theological take on modernity and his dismissal of Derrida, Schrijvers's aim is not polemical but he rather seeks to show that what Taylor so dismisses, is actually much more worthy of our attention than Taylor himself seems to think. To see to where the cross-pressures of our secular age extend, he therefore tries to falsify all points that Taylor advances *against* Derrida: first, that Derrida is an anti-humanist; second, that there is no transcendent hope beyond history in Derrida; third, that the universality of rights is defended by Derrida without being grounded in the nature of things; finally that Derrida would lack all access to an effective healing action in history.

Section 3: Human Rights and Migration – (Post)secular Social Imaginaries in Contemporary Perspective

In chapter 7, *Studying Culture through Imaginaries*, Robin Vandevoordt, Noel Clycq and Gert Verschraegen explore the conceptual and heuristic relevance of social imaginaries for cultural analysis. They refer to a number of relevant debates among scholars of culture on what they should study and how they should go about. They compare the influence of Emile Durkheim with that of Max Weber and discuss the rise of a more historically oriented debate revolving around the relative coherence of cultural systems, pointing to the serious limitations of the traditional concept of culture in contemporary complex global conditions. The central question of the authors is how social imaginaries can contribute to the debates and problems in the social-scientific study of culture. To answer this question, they don't limit themselves to Charles Taylor's specific reading of the term, but look also at more empirically grounded variants, like those of Cornelius Castoriadis, Benedict Anderson and Arjun Appadurai. They point out specific contributions of Taylor's social imaginaries: his reconnecting of the flexibility of recent practice theories with an intellectual background; his hermeneutic focus on the historical path of particular cultural horizons; the substantial fluidity of the concept which renders it a useful heuristic tool for cultural analysis in the face of contemporary complexities; the focus on the creative capacities of individual agents to deal with imaginaries of different, overlapping institutions and social fields. Vandevoordt et al. argue that social imaginaries may help to theoretically integrate a number of apparently unrelated case studies, such as human rights, refugees, education and migration. They explore social imaginaries' contribution more empirically through the particular case of human rights.

In chapter 8, *Human Rights as a Secular Social Imaginary in the Field of Transitional Justice*, Nicole Immler analyses how human rights function as a social imaginary on the individual level and how they impact the political, social and cultural realm. She argues that human rights not only have a legal nature, but also a utopian character: Immler's aim is to reveal the implications of a legal human rights framework on imagining justice from an actor's perspective. She explores what the concept of social imaginaries has to offer for a critical, bottom-up approach in the Transitional Justice field, maintaining that using the lens of social imaginaries helps to emphasize the aspirations of the people involved and allows us to identify deeply embedded (moral) assumptions that shape societies. The chapter gives a historical overview of the development of human rights discourse into a global moral and secular imaginary and shows how the changed imaginaries of human rights developed into a right to compensation. This is studied empirically in the Dutch-Indonesian case of Rawagede, in which the Civil Court in The Hague obliged the Dutch government to apologize and pay compensation to some of the victims of its colonial policy in Indonesia. Using the concept of social imaginaries to understand this case, Immler shows that it is less a negotiation process about the *past* between the Dutch state and its former colonial 'subjects' in Indonesia, but more an inquiry into *present-*

day post-colonial Netherlands. Zooming in on some actors, the author comes to the conclusion that compensation claims are increasingly a frame in which present-day injustices are negotiated and in which legacies of discrimination and inequality, misrepresentations and gaps in history books are made explicit. From the perspective of the imaginative character of human rights, compensation should not be considered foremost as an instrument of acknowledgment, addressing the past, but as an instrument of dialogue that gives voice to all members in a pluralized society.

In chapter 9, *Europe and the Human Rights Imaginary*, Christiane Timmerman, Gert Verschraegen, Kenneth Hemmerechts and Roos Willems refer to debates on the meaning of Europe in its current social, cultural and religious heterogeneity and the politicized role religion acquires in these debates. Drawing on the international EUMAGINE research project, the chapter addresses the question of how migrants and non-migrants from non-EU countries perceive human rights and democracy-related issues both in their home country and in Europe, and how these perceptions affect their migration aspirations. The authors conceive of human rights as a global secular imaginary that emerged after World War II and sketch how Europe and the European Union became associated with ideas of human rights and secular democracy. The actual enjoyment of many human rights presupposes a well-functioning state and public institutions. For this reason, migration can be considered as a legitimate channel to gain access to cultural and religious freedom, job opportunities, social security and decent education. Nevertheless, non-European migration is often considered as an unforeseen and largely unwelcome side-effect of the attractiveness of European welfare states. Against this background, the EUMAGINE project did empirical research on the relation between perceptions of human rights and democracy, and migratory aspirations of potential migrants and non-migrants in Morocco, Turkey, Senegal and Ukraine. The hypothesis was formulated that migration aspirations are affected by perceptions of democracy and human rights, while controlling for other relevant factors. This hypothesis was confirmed on the basis of the analyses of data collected in accordance with quantitative and qualitative methodologies. It is concluded that men and women are motivated not only by the economic opportunities that may come with migration, but that the global imaginary of human rights, which has by now diffused all over the globe, fuels the aspiration to migrate to countries where rights are well-protected.

In chapter 10, *Post-Secular Nationalism: The Dutch Turn to the Right & Cultural-Religious Reframing of Secularity*, Ernst van den Hemel focuses on the role of religion in populist constructions of secular national identity, in particular on the role of the term 'West's Christian heritage,' often used by populist right wing parties in the process of garnering electoral and popular success in the Netherlands, Great Britain, Belgium, France and in the United States of America. These parties challenge classical divides between progressive and conservative politics but also between secular and religious divides. Van den Hemel argues that a major aspect of populist discourse in Western Europe is not its theoretical or ideological coherence, but rather its attempt to reframe the backdrop against which religiosity and secularity are imagined. His major hypothesis is that Taylor's notion of the social imaginary offers a productive approach to analyze this dimension of populist discourse. This hypothesis is developed in five steps. He first describes some paradoxical effects of populist discursive practices. Then he addresses how Taylor's notion of the social imaginary might be better suited to approach the reframing of religion and secularity than so far dominant approaches in the analysis of populist discourse. After having crafted a conceptual definition of 'post-secular nationalism,' he elaborates on the two parts of this equation ('post-secular' and 'nationalist'), illustrating how populist discourse challenges certain assumptions behind Taylor's approach to secularity. Finally, he specifies the freshly coined definition of 'post-secular nationalism' by comparing it to civil religion and speculating on the effects this discourse has for the imagination of national communities.

Bibliography

Alexander, Thomas M. 2013. *The Human Eros: Eco-ontology and the Aesthetics of Existence.* New York: Fordham University Press.
Alma, Hans. 2015. "Religious Pluralism as an Imaginative Practice." *Archive for the Psychology of Religion* 37:117–140.
Anderson, Benedict. 1983. *Imagined Communities: Reflections on the Origin and Spread of Nationalism.* London: Verso.
Castoriadis, Cornelius. 1987. *The Imaginary Institution of Society* (translation by Kathleen Blamey). Cambridge, MA: MIT Press.
Droogers, André, and Anton van Harskamp, eds. 2014. *Methods for the Study of Religious Change: From Religious Studies to Worldview Studies.* Sheffield: Equinox.
Gaonkar, Dilip Parameshwar. 2002. "Toward New Imaginaries: An Introduction." *Public Culture* 14:1–19.
Gergen, Kenneth J. 2009. *Relational Being: Beyond Self and Community.* Oxford: Oxford University Press.
Helsloot, John. 2012. "Zwarte Piet and Cultural Aphasia in the Netherlands." *Quotidian* 3(1). Retrieved from http://www.quotidian.nl/vol03/nr01/a01
Joas, Hans. 2004. "Der Glaube an die Menschenwürde als Religion der Moderne?" In *Braucht der Mensch Religion? Über Erfahrungen der Selbsttranszendenz* von Hans Joas, 151–168. Freiburg: Herder Spektrum.
Joas, Hans. 2015. *Sind die Menschenrechte westlich?* München: Kösel.

Joas, Hans 2017. *Die Macht des Heiligen: Eine Alternative zur Geschichte von der Entzauberung.* Berlin: Suhrkamp.

Moyn, Samuel. 2010. *The Last Utopia: Human Rights in History.* Cambridge, MA: Harvard University Press.

Steele, Meili. 2013. "The Social Imaginary as a Problematic for Human Rights." In *Theoretical Perspectives on Human Rights and Literature*, edited by Elizabeth Swanson Goldberg and Alexandra Schultheis Moore, 87–102. London: Routledge.

Steger, Manfred B. 2006. "Searching for Satya through Ahimsa: Gandhi's Challenge to Western Discourses of Power." *Constellations* 13(3):332–353.

Taylor, Charles. 1975. *Hegel.* Cambridge: Cambridge University Press.

Taylor, Charles. 2004. *Modern Social Imaginaries.* Durham and London: Duke University Press.

Taylor, Charles. 2007. *A Secular Age.* Cambridge, MA: The Belknap Press of Harvard University Press.

Taylor, Charles. 2016. *The Language Animal.* Cambridge, MA: Harvard University Press.

Taylor, Charles, and Hubert Dreyfus. 2015. *Retrieving Realism.* Cambidge, MA: Harvard University Press.

Vertovec, Steven. 2007. "Super-diversity and its Implications." *Ethnic and Racial Studies* 30 (6):1024–1054.

Section 1: **Social Imaginaries. A Historical and Conceptual Analysis**

Guido Vanheeswijck
On the Philosophical Genealogy of the Concept Social Imaginaries

> *The proponents and developers of the Romantic theory have been among the most passionate critics of the epistemological tradition, from Hamann's review of Kant's Critique of Pure Reason to the writings in our century of Heidegger, of the later Wittgenstein, and of certain postmodernists.*
>
> Charles Taylor

1 Introduction

The notion of social imaginaries is one of the central concepts in Charles Taylor's opus magnum *A Secular Age*. He defines them as "incorporating a sense of the normal expectations that we have of each other; the kind of common understanding which enables us to carry out the collective practices which make up our social life. This incorporates some sense of how we all fit together in carrying out the common practice" (Taylor 2007, 172). Furthermore, he explicitly distinguishes social imaginaries from social theories. Unlike theories, imaginaries are shared by large groups of people and they are articulated in images, stories and legends, rather than expressed in theoretical terms (Taylor 2007, 171–2).

The notion 'social imaginaries' comes up rather late in Taylor's writings. He first used the concept in his 2003 essay, *Modern Social Imaginaries*, within the context of his earlier reflections on the theme of 'multiple modernities.' His major claim was that even if all modern societies eventually develop a modern state and a market economy, the specific outcome of this process will always be (partly) dependent on what went into the change. Put differently, even if cultures are being transformed in analogous directions, it does not follow that they will ultimately converge. Hence, to account for the differences among multiple modernities, Taylor coined the concept of social imaginaries, clearly indebted to Benedict Anderson's famous phrase 'imagined societies' (Taylor 1995, xi–xii) and borrowing from Castoriadis's influential book, *The Imaginary Institution of Society*.[1]

However, the deepest sources of Taylor's use of the concept social imaginaries are not to be found only in the realms of political philosophy or social anthropology. Rather, they are related to Taylor's life-long struggle to overcome the

---
[1] Cf. Anderson 1983, Castoriadis 1987. See also the next article by Stijn Latré.

https://doi.org/10.1515/9783110435122-002

pre-eminence of epistemology in modern philosophy and modern culture. What does it exactly mean for Taylor to overcome epistemology and how does he challenge its primacy? Before answering these questions, we must first take into account his clear-cut distinction between epistemology in a narrow and in a broad sense.

In its narrow conception, epistemology is seen as a foundationalist philosophical discipline that could test the validity of all truth claims. In a broader sense, however, the focus is less on epistemological foundationalism and more on the understanding of knowledge that made this foundationalism possible. In the latter conception, modern epistemological tradition represents a tradition in which "knowledge is to be seen as correct representation of an independent reality (...) as the inner depiction of an outer reality" (Taylor 1995, 3). For Taylor, this wider epistemological position is neither innocent nor neutral: since it functions as the condition of possibility for ontological, anthropological and religious stances, it is the main, albeit often unconscious, source of our deepest convictions. In his view, the modern epistemological tradition has given rise to the central anthropological and social beliefs of modern Western culture: beliefs in what he describes in *Sources of the Self* and *A Secular Age* as the 'disengaged subject,' the 'punctual self' and an 'atomistic view of society.'

Taylor rejects this epistemological stance (which he relates to the rationalist and empiricist traditions of Descartes, Locke and Hume) as an illusion: "it assumes wrongly that we can get to the bottom of what knowledge is, without drawing on our never-fully-articulable understanding of human life and experience" (Taylor 1995, vii–viii). To overcome this illusory epistemological stance, to which our modern culture has been so strongly susceptible, Taylor puts forward a form of argumentation whose origins lie in Immanuel Kant's philosophy and which has become known as "the argument from transcendental conditions". What transcendental arguments try to do is to bring to articulacy the background that makes our experience of the surrounding world intelligible to us" (Taylor 1995, 69).

Therefore, it is no coincidence that Charles Taylor has located the concept social imaginaries in the Kantian tradition, by identifying their role as analogous to that of the Kantian transcendental schemes. When a theory penetrates and transforms the social imaginary,

> this process isn't just one-sided; a theory making over a social imaginary. The theory in coming to make sense of the action is 'glossed,' as it were, given a particular shape as the context of these practices. Rather like Kant's notion of an abstract category becoming 'schematized' when it is applied to reality in space and time, the theory is schematized in the dense sphere of common practice. (Taylor 2007, 176)

Yet, there remains a central difference between Kant's transcendental schemes and Taylor's social imaginaries. Whereas Kant's transcendental schemes are universal and mainly tailored to the use of concepts in positive sciences, Taylor's social imaginaries are historical and for the most part applied to our understanding of concepts in the humanities.

To elucidate that difference, this article will trace the philosophical genealogy of Taylor's concept of social imaginaries in three steps. Our starting point is the influence of the so-called German 'meta-critics' of Kant (Hamann, Herder, Hegel) on Taylor's use of social imaginaries. Taylor has often hinted at their influence, but never elaborated this issue. I would like to show that Taylor is deeply indebted to this meta-critical tradition, especially to its emphasis on the *historical* and *linguistic* character of the transcendental background of our daily experiences. The next step presents the influence of the continental phenomenological tradition on Taylor's concept. Since Taylor himself has explicitly underlined the strong influence of phenomenological authors on his own philosophy, I limit myself to a concise summary of how Heidegger, Merleau-Ponty and Wittgenstein, by stressing the transcendental conditions of *intentionality* of our daily experiences, help Taylor to understand the depth of our embedded nature as agents in the surrounding world.

Finally, I focus on the largely forgotten heritage of two Oxford philosophers of history's position (Collingwood, Berlin). Because Taylor hardly mentions their influence (he refers, of course, to Isaiah Berlin as his former teacher, but never mentions R.G. Collingwood except in his vey latest book, *The Language Animal*) and even neglects their explicit reactions against the epistemological tradition, my presentation of their positions will be more extensive. Moreover, both authors, making use of terminology compatible with the concept of social imaginaries, stress the philosophical and cultural importance of *articulating* the contents of our hidden background so as to comprehend the changes in our understanding of man's place in society.

If I am right about all this, then it is only against that threefold background that the specificity of Taylor's concept of social imaginaries and in particular the role of 'religious and secular imaginaries' in our contemporary society can be clarified so as to evade possible misunderstandings as to its applications.

2 Hamann's Meta-Critical Demolition of Kant's Eternal Aspirations

Since Immanuel Kant was the very first to reflect on the necessary conditions of our everyday experiences and scientific knowledge claims, Taylor considers him to be a key figure in his project of overcoming epistemology (Taylor 1995, 82). Kant claimed that neither our daily experience nor our scientific knowledge is made intelligible on the basis of the modern epistemological construal, in either its rationalist variant (Wolff, Leibniz) or its empiricist variant (Locke, Hume). With that perspective in mind, he made a crucial distinction between the contents of concrete data of experience on the one hand and the concepts and categories by which we organise and interpret these data on the other. Whereas the data of experience are constantly changing, the fundamental categories by which we order the data of experience remain eternal and invariable. In relation to Hume's empiricism and scepticism, Kant asserted that we cannot have experience of the world, let alone scientific knowledge of it, if we must start with nothing but atomic, raw data. If our mental states are to constitute genuine experience or knowledge of an objective reality, then the raw data must be bound together to form a coherent whole. Only if these raw, atomic data are related to eternal a priori-structures (time, space) and subsumed under eternal a priori-categories (unity, causality,…), could fundamental truths on man and world be established once and for all.

According to Taylor, Kant's 'Copernican' revolution showed the inadequacy of the modern epistemological construal. Without the apparatus of a priori-structures, he argued: "it would be possible for appearances to crowd in upon the soul and yet to be such as would never allow of experience. (…) They would not then belong to any experience, consequently would be without an object, merely a blind play of representations, less even than a dream" (CPR, A 111–112).[2]

Consequently, Kant's basic intuition was that transcendental philosophy does not deal with ever-changing raw data, but rather with the transcendental structure of experience (a priori-structures of time and space) and knowledge (twelve a priori categories) within which the ever changing data can appear as knowable and interpretable. This transcendental structure forms an indispensable background or framework, a shared context of significance without which all

---

[2] Quoted by Taylor 1995, 10. CPR: abbreviation for Kant, Immanuel. 1987. *The Critique of Pure Reason* (translated by Norman Kemp Smith). London: MacMillan.

data we receive are nothing but "a blind play of representations, less even than a dream".

Kant claimed that these a priori structures and categories through which we experience and interpret the external world, were permanent and unalterable and hence identical for all human beings. It was due to their permanence and universality that we were able to experience our world as an organised whole, to formulate universal scientific laws governing the world and to communicate with each other about that world. This very central presupposition was attacked by Johann Georg Hamann, Kant's friend and philosophical opponent, in his posthumously published essay *Metakritik über den Purismum der Vernunft*.[3]

Hamann's idea of a meta-critique is, as the term itself suggests, an enquiry into the foundation of Kant's critical theory. If the duty of reason is to criticize all our arguments and beliefs, as Kant claimed, then one may wonder, Hamann retorted, whether reason can evade any form of self-critique. So, unless a critical theory is inconsistent, it must become meta-critical, that is to say, it must examine critically the status of its own criticism. Frederick Beiser brilliantly summarizes the quintessence of the meta-critics' stance:

> If the meta-critical problem is the point where Kant's philosophy ends, it is also the point where much post-Kantian philosophy begins. Kant's successors were willing to accept his contention that the authority of reason depends on the possibility of criticism; but, unlike Kant, they looked critically at the possibility of criticism itself. In questioning this possibility, they were taking the criticism of reason a new and important step beyond Kant. They were no longer content to examine the first-order claims of reason as Kant had – the claims of physics to know the laws of nature, or the claims of metaphysics to know things-in-themselves. Rather, they insisted upon questioning its second-order claims – its claims to be a sufficient criterion of truth and to be in possession of self-evident first principles. (Beiser 1987, 7)

In his *Metakritik über den Purismum der Vernunft* Hamann was the very first philosopher to undermine Kant's view that reason has universal and impartial aspirations. To that end, he focused on an aspect of Kant's transcendental a priori apparatus that so far had never been doubted: its universal, eternal and impartial character. To be sure, Hamann accepted the existence of an a priori background – in this sense he remained indebted to Kant's 'Copernican Revolution' – but he made that background or framework historical by underlining its temporal and cultural character. By so doing, Hamann did not only undermine one

---

[3] Although Hamann had drafted his meta-critique by July 1781, it was not published until 1800. Hamann decided not to publish his review of Kant's CPR, because he feared that his critique would offend Kant (cf. Beiser 1987, 38).

of the central presuppositions of Enlightenment's philosophy, he also laid the foundations of what is traditionally described as the romantic Sturm-und-Drang movement or as the Counter-Enlightenment.[4]

Moreover, Hamann reminded Kant of the fact that thought never precedes language nor concepts precede words. On the contrary, he underlined in his idiosyncratic style that thought remains always indebted to language and not vice versa:

> Then it does not take a deduction to prove the genealogical priority of language over the seven holy functions of logical propositions and inferences and their heraldics. Not only the entire ability to think rests on language, according to the unknown prophecies and slandered miracles of the meritorious Samuel Heinke; but language is also the crux of the misunderstanding of reason with itself, partly because of the frequent coincidence of the greatest and smallest concept, its emptiness and fullness in ideal propositions, partly because of the endless figures of speech before the conclusions, and much more of that kind. (SW, N III, 286)[5]

Due to Kant's false image of the aspirations of reason because of its disregard of its linguistic dependence, he had – Hamann believes – unduly imposed a threefold 'purification':

> The *first* purification of philosophy consisted basically in the partly misconceived, partly unsuccessful attempt to make reason independent of all custom, tradition, and belief in the latter. The *second* is still more transcendental and aims at nothing less than an independence of experience and its everyday induction – for, after reason sought who knows what? – beyond experience for 2000 years, it suddenly not merely despairs of the progressive course of its ancestors, but also promises its impatient contemporaries, with so much defiance – and this in a short time – that universal and infallible Philosopher's Stone, so indispensable for Catholicism and despotism, to which religion with its sanctity and legislation with its majesty are swiftly subjected, especially in the wane of a critical age, where empiricism on both sides, struck with blindness, makes its own nakedness more suspicious and ridiculous day by day. The *third*, most sublime and as it were empirical purism therefore concerns language, the single, first and last organon and criterion of reason, without any other credentials than tradition and use. But one gets on with this idol too almost as that ancient did with the Ideal of Reason. The longer one reflects, the more deeply and inwardly one is struck dumb and loses all breath to speak. (SW, III, 284–285)

Hamann wants to undo this threefold purification by putting reason back within the linguistic, historical and cultural context to which it properly belongs. But

---

[4] I borrow this term from Berlin 1980, 1–24.
[5] SW: abbreviation for Hamann, Johan Georg. *Sämtliche Werken*, edited by Josef Nadler. Vienna: Herder Verlag, 1949–1957. Translated by Gwen Griffith Dickson. In Dickson 1995, 519–525.

prior to that, Hamann first attacks Kant's tendency to dichotomize between sensibility and understanding:

> But if sensibility and understanding spring as two stems of human knowledge from one common root, so that through the one objects are given and through the other thought; to what end such a violent, unwarranted, obstinate divorce of what nature had joined together! Will not both stems wither and corrupt through such a dichotomy and division of their common root? Would not a single stem better serve as an image of our knowledge, with two roots, one above the air and one below in the earth? The first is revealed to our sensibility; the latter on the other hand is invisible and must be thought by our understanding, which agrees better with the priority of the thought and the posteriority of the given or taken, as well as agreeing with the favourite inversion of pure reason in its theories. (SW, III, 286)

Of course, Kant himself was aware of the problem of the dichotomy between sensibility and understanding and had elaborated a solution to bring the two together. He had raised the question as well *how* a posteriori concrete sense perceptions could be subsumed under priori abstract concepts of understanding. And it is common knowledge that, to answer that question, he had introduced the level of transcendental schemata as an intermediary between the abstract level of understanding and the concrete level of sensibility. That is to say, transcendental schemata are rules for the application of pure concepts to the sense impressions we receive (CPR A, 138–139).

However, if one accepts the priority of language to thought, as Hamann does, then the introduction of the level of transcendental schemata is fully superfluous. Since words have both an aesthetic and logical capacity and so form a third mediating procedure that connects sensibility and understanding, they make the introduction of transcendental schemata redundant. Therefore, Hamann's terminology to illustrate the mediating function of words may be read as an ironical parody on Kant's terminology to describe the mediating function of transcendental schemata:

> Words therefore have an aesthetic and logical capacity. As visible and audible objects they belong with their elements to sensibility and intuition, but according to the spirit of their employment and meaning, belong to understanding and concepts. Consequently words are as much pure and empirical intuitions, as they are pure and empirical concepts: empirical, because the sensation of sight or hearing works through them; pure, in so far as their meaning is determined by nothing that belongs to those sensations. (SW, III, 288)

By making words into the mediating factor between sensibility and understanding, Hamann explicitly emphasized the social, historical and cultural dimensions of reason, aspects that were neglected by Kant and the majority of the Enlightenment. Because for Hamann language is the instrument and the criterion of reason and language varies with a nation's or people's customs and traditions, a universal form of reason can never occur. Therefore, reason is not capable of going beyond the level of particular cultures and of judging them from a 'view from nowhere.'

Given that Taylor admits to being strongly influenced by the meta-critics' position, his identification of the role of social imaginaries with that of Kantian transcendental schemata is rather confusing. Although Taylor stresses the historical character of social imaginaries, his comparison with the role of transcendental schemata gives rise to underestimating their historical and cultural character. This comparison is even more surprising since Hamann's emphasis on the priority of language over thought has had an enormous, albeit indirect impact not only on the further evolution of post-Kantian philosophy, but on Taylor's thought as well. It was through Hamann's emphasis on the role of language that Johann Gottfried Herder, the other meta-critic of the Kantian position, originated his expressivist theory of language which proved to be of central importance in Taylor's anthropology and philosophy of culture.

3 The Decisive Role of the Phenomenological Tradition

Although Hamann had launched a bitter polemic against his former student Herder on the issue of the origin of language, it was through Herder's work that Hamann's ideas were handed down to subsequent generations and to Charles Taylor himself.[6] Taylor's central claim is that, even if Herder and Hamann were not the most rigorous of all thinkers which probably made it easier for many contemporary philosophers to ignore them, they were the hinge figures to have originated a new, 'expressivist' view of language and meaning.[7]

---

6 "Ironically, it was the fate of Herder, who was Hamann's original target, to transmit Hamann's teachings to the post-Kantian generation. In his *Ideeen zur Philosophie der Geschichte der Menschheit* Herder admitted the point behind Hamann's criticisms and assimilated Hamann's teaching into his own philosophy of history. Through his work, Hamann's ideas were handed down to the next generation." (Beiser 1987, 140–141)

7 "(…) deeply innovative thinkers don't have to be rigorous in order to originate important ideas. The insights they capture in striking images can inspire other, more philosophically exigent minds to more exact formulation. This was exemplified, I believe, in the relation of Herder to Hegel. The consequence has been that the earlier thinker drops out of sight, and the later becomes the canonical reference point for certain ideas." (Taylor 1995, 79)

Moreover, in the context of his struggle against the dominance of the epistemological construal, Taylor sees the debates around the 'expressivist' nature of language as closely interwoven and even overlapping with his endeavour to overcome epistemology. Since the Renaissance, two understandings of the role of language have been competing each other. Hobbes and Locke, like Hamann and Herder, saw the place of language as dependent on and circumscribed by their epistemological theory of knowledge. Whereas Hobbes and Locke defended an instrumentalist view of language, analogous to their instrumental view of knowledge, the Romantic proponents of the expressivist theory of language and art, who were for the most part all descendants of the Haman-Herder revolution, were among the passionate opponents of the epistemological construal.

Since *The Explanation of Behaviour* in 1964, Taylor has been elaborating an alternative position in contemporary philosophy for these disengaged views of knowledge and language. To that end, he has been drawn mostly to continental major thinkers from the phenomenological tradition, such as Martin Heidegger, Maurice Merleau-Ponty, Michael Polanyi and later Hubert Dreyfus. Analogous to the view that neither knowledge nor language can be understood within the a-cultural confines of Cartesian epistemology or Lockean theory of language, Taylor believes that our subjective experiences are related to an indispensable background of cultural and historical surroundings as well. In other words, following the major continental phenomenological philosophers, Taylor proclaims that the essence of human selfhood is always situated in a historical, cultural and practical context and that 'human selves' are never isolated 'punctual,' 'atomistic' individuals but must be seen as 'beings-in-the world.'

In the wake of Heidegger and Merleau-Ponty, Taylor urges us to see that our status as being-in-the-world is both social and practical and that the background we are dependent on consists of evaluations and social norms, most of which remain implicit and are only seldom formulated as explicit beliefs. They manifest in the way we handle things and cope with our concrete affairs, as it were embodied in our daily practices. The same notion of background re-appears in Wittgenstein's argumentation against the possibility of private language and in his remarks in *Philososophical Investigations* and *On Certainty* that human meaning is always constructed against the background of a form of life. Taylor's view of engaged and embodied agency has made him an ally of Hubert Dreyfus and a critic of the widespread faith that our intelligent performances can be understood in terms of sheer formal operations or calculi, devoid from a background of significance (Taylor 1995, 6). Borrowing Michael Polanyi's terminology, he contends that every form of engaged agency is made intelligible only when placed in a context of the kind of agency that serves as the subsidiary horizon within which the engaged agency is the focal object of our explicit attention (Taylor 1995, 68–69).

Moreover, Taylor emphasizes the strong link between his positions for the disengaged views of knowledge and language on the one hand and his alternative view of the political and social culture of modernity on the other. Analogous to the culturally unindexed Cartesian theory of knowledge and the homogenizing effect of Lockean theory of language, there is a widespread understanding that modernization is transforming all cultures in more or less the same direction, making societies everywhere more or less alike (Taylor 1995, xi–xii). Taylor, by contrast, believes that a modern society not only differs from its predecessors in making novel political institutions, creating a market economy, inventing new technologies and propounding new moral and political principles. Alongside these explicit changes is a rather implicit set of changes in the way we have come *to imagine society* (Taylor 1995, x). These changed social imaginaries in the realm of society and politics, analogous to the embodied and culturally embedded aspects in the domains of language and thought, form the quintessence of what Taylor defines as the phenomenological idea of a social 'background.'

> It is that of which I am not simply unaware, as I am unaware of what is now happening on the other side of the moon, because it makes intelligible what I am uncontestably aware of; at the same time, I am not explicitly or focally aware of it, because that status is already occupied by what it is making intelligible. (Taylor 1995, 69)

Social imaginaries operating in that social background, are thus basically different from social theories and can never be adequately expressed "in the form of explicit doctrines, because of their unlimited and indefinite nature. That is another reason for speaking here of an 'imaginary,' and not a theory." (Taylor 2007, 173)

Yet, it is the very task of a philosopher (and of a sociologist as well) to bring that background of social imaginaries to articulacy. But how is it possible to articulate that background of imaginaries, while that background is simultaneously defined as precisely inarticulate, subsidiary and implicit. Already since he wrote his monograph on Hegel in 1975, Taylor has been struggling with this issue of the (im)possibility of articulating our subsidiary background of imaginaries. His point of departure is that our explicit consciousness is surrounded by a horizon of the implicit. Hegel tried to articulate that implicit horizon in conceptual statements so as to come to explicit clarity of that implicit background as the embodiment of the Absolute Spirit. What makes this final victory of conceptual clarity and articulacy impossible for Taylor, is Hegel's ontology, the thesis that what we ultimately discover as the general background of everything is the necessary, conceptual evolution of the Absolute Spirit (Taylor 1975, 569).

Once he discarded the Hegelian belief in that kind of ontology, it became clear for Taylor that the relation between the articulacy and the inarticulacy of our implicit background of social imaginaries is extremely complex and complicated. Therefore, he sought subtler words to grasp that complex state of being simultaneously aware and unaware of our background of imaginaries. To articulate that complexity, he often refers, as already stated, to terminology used by Wittgenstein and Polanyi, or he defines that implicit background of human experience in Heideggerian terms as 'pre-ontology' or 'pre-understanding':

> Another way of stating (…) that I am not simply unaware of it, is to say that the background is what I am capable of articulating, that is, what I can bring out of the condition of implicit, unsaid contextual facilitator – what I can articulate, in other words. In this activity of articulating, I trade on my familiarity with this background. What I bring out to articulacy is what I 'always knew,' as we might say, or what I had a 'sense' of, even if I didn't 'know' it. We are at a loss exactly what to say here, where we are trying to do justice to our not having been simply unaware.
>
> But if the background is brought to articulacy, doesn't it then lose the second feature, that of not being the focal, explicit object? This seemingly plausible inference is based on a misunderstanding. The background is what makes certain experiences intelligible to us. It makes us capable of grasping them, makes them understandable. So it can be represented as a kind of explicit understanding, or 'pre-understanding' in Heidegger's term. To bring it to articulacy is to take (some of) this and make it explicit. But the reason for the two words in parentheses in my preceding sentence is that the idea of making the background completely explicit, of undoing its status as background, is incoherent in principle. (Taylor 1995, 69)

Taylor's wavering attitude – "we are at a loss exactly what to say here" – with regard to this issue is striking. Dissatisfied with Hegel's conceptual and ontological solution to the relation between articulacy and inarticulacy of our implicit background, he resorts to phenomenologist positions like that of Heidegger and others. But the Heideggerian term 'pre-ontology' or 'pre-understanding' has created a lot of confusion, particularly regarding the ontological status of social imaginaries.[8] To clarify what Taylor exactly has in mind, I will, therefore, focus on two authors of the Anglo-Saxon philosophy, Robin George Collingwood and Isaiah Berlin. Notwithstanding Taylor's neglect of their explicit reactions against the epistemological tradition (cf. Taylor 1995, 1), my purpose in this

---

[8] Cf. Gordon 2008, 647–673 and my response to Gordon's position in Vanheeswijck 2015: 69–85. See for a further discussion on the ontological impact of social imaginaries, the article in this volume on this topic by Stijn Latré and Michiel Meijer.

final section is to elucidate, with the help of both authors' terminology, Taylor's balanced position on the philosophical and cultural importance of *articulating* the contents of our hidden background so as to comprehend the changes in our understanding of the place of man in society.

4 The Hidden Influence of Collingwood and Berlin

In the opening paragraphs of his seminal essay, *Overcoming Epistemology*, Taylor claims that in the Anglo-Saxon world the dominance of the modern epistemological tradition remained more or less unchallenged until the publication of Richard Rorty's *Philosophy and the Mirror of Nature* in 1979. For seventy years, during the heyday of logical empiricism and positivism, its theory of knowledge had been the undisputed centre of philosophy. While this was true of the Anglo-Saxon world, Taylor continues, on the Continent the challenge to the epistemological tradition was already in full swing and Heidegger and Merleau-Ponty exerted a wide influence in that same period (Taylor 1995, 1–2).

However, in drawing such a sharp distinction between the Continental and the Anglo-Saxon philosophy, and in underlining only the arguments of continental thinkers in the demise of logical empiricism, Taylor neglects the importance of two Oxford philosophers with whose work he was familiar: Robin George Collingwood (1889–1943) and Isaiah Berlin (1909–1997). That neglect is rather strange, since Berlin had been Taylor's teacher and colleague in Oxford for many years and it is generally known that Collingwood fostered Berlin's interest in the philosophy of history.

4.1 Collingwood's 'Absolute' Presuppositions

As Taylor has been reacting against sheer behaviourist and rationalist models of explanation throughout his philosophical career, so Collingwood has been criticizing empiricist and logical positivist models that were predominant in the thirties. That critique culminated after 1935, the year that Collingwood had been appointed professor of metaphysics on the prestigious Waynflete Chair of Metaphysics in Oxford. In that period, Collingwood elaborated his doctrine of absolute presuppositions, mainly as a rebuttal of the basic principles of logical empiricism that were being popularized by the publication of Alfred J. Ayer's *Language, Truth and Logic* in 1936.⁹

In that so called bible of logical empiricism and positivism, Ayer divided meaningful propositions into two categories: only empirical verifiable and analytic propositions are meaningful and have truth value. All other propositions – among which metaphysical propositions take a prominent place – he called pseudo-propositions or meaningless statements. Metaphysics is therefore regarded as an unscientific and unfruitful description of a pseudo-reality supposedly lying behind perceivable reality.¹⁰ Hence, Ayer's main objective was to demonstrate the impossibility of metaphysics and to promote its elimination.

According to Collingwood, Ayer's logical positivism is closely related to propositional logic, based on a realistic epistemology.¹¹ Epistemological realists state that reality is *only* knowable through comparing concepts and propositions with reality itself. Within this epistemological framework, only verifiable and tautological propositions are accepted as significant statements whereas the significance of (absolute) presuppositions is rejected. Here Ayer was indebted to the anti-Kantian tenor that is so typical of figures like Moore and Russell.¹²

Collingwood rejected both epistemological realism and propositional logic. As an alternative, he began to work out a logic of question and answer, in which no single propositions but question/answer complexes are the 'locus' of truth.¹³ This logic of question and answer implies a view of knowledge not as a direct mirror of reality, but rather as an activity in which question and answer are indissolubly related. The meaning and truth of a statement can, therefore, only be discovered by starting from the question to which that statement is meant as an answer. It is only within the context of this logic of question and

---

9 In a letter to the Clarendon Press (dated 14 November 1938) Collingwood writes: "I have been for a long time contemplating a short book which should explain to the public what Metaphysics is, what it is for, how it works, and why the various people who clamour for its abolition ought not to be listened to" (see Johnson 1998, 26).
10 Cf. Ayer 1974, 45–61. Ayer's first publication on the (im)possibility of metaphysics was: Ayer 1934, 335–345.
11 Cf. Collingwood 2013, 52.
12 See Hylton 1993, 461: "The fundamental anti-Kantianism of Russell and Moore can be articulated into a number of interrelated doctrines that played a fundamental role in Platonic Atomism. The first is perhaps the most directly related to the Kantian issues discussed: the idea that the objects at which our knowledge aims are wholly independent of the knowing subject."
13 Collingwood states that he already in *Truth and Contradiction* started to elaborate that logic of question and answer (Collingwood 2013, 42). Only the second chapter of the manuscript *Truth and Contradiction* has been preserved. See Martin 1998, 126–128.

answer, that Collingwood's concepts of history and metaphysics can be understood.

Collingwood agreed with Ayer and the logical positivists that metaphysical statements are neither empirically verifiable nor tautological propositions. But within Collingwood's logic of question and answer, there are more than these two sorts of propositions in the domain of cognitive statements. Both empirically verifiable and tautological statements are answers to underlying questions or *presuppositions*. Those questions are themselves answers to further questions; the last question, finally, functions as an *absolute presupposition*. In other words, since metaphysical statements have the grammatical form of propositions but actually express absolute presuppositions, they do not manifest themselves at the level of empirically verifiable or tautological propositions, but at the level underlying those propositions. Because Ayer disregards this deeper level, he does not understand what metaphysics is really about.

Since logical positivism fails to recognize the role of presuppositions, it entertains a false concept of metaphysics: metaphysical propositions, as the expressions of absolute presuppositions, are reduced to propositions of which the truth or falsity has to be established through empirical verification or logical deduction. For Collingwood, such a concept of metaphysics has nothing to do with what metaphysics really is; it is pseudo-metaphysics. The danger, inherent in logical positivism, is not only that metaphysics is stigmatized as non-cognitive, but also that confused and rudimentary thinking is propagated as genuine science. Only by tracing the presuppositions underlying propositions, the meaning of those propositions can be explained. By not acknowledging the function of presuppositions, by preferring propositional logic to a logic of question and answer, logical positivism's scientific value is compromised from the very start.[14] If logical positivists really attempted to show the cognitive to full advantage, then, according to Collingwood, they failed greatly.[15]

It is to be noted that the term 'absolute' is confusing and even potentially misleading. Since different eras make different absolute presuppositions, Col-

---

[14] "But exactly by the unraveling of presuppositions, scientific thinking distinguishes itself from unscientific thinking; each attack on the starting point – that thinking has presuppositions – is a direct attack on science itself, and includes an attempt, consciously or unconsciously, to reduce each form of thinking to its most confused and unscientific level." (Collingwood 1998, 170–171)

[15] "I already suggested that a more or less orchestrated attack on reason itself is a characteristic of the present world. Maybe the 'logical positivists' do not really want to participate in that, but they have gone through a lot of trouble to manoeuvre themselves into a position in which they, intended or unintended, fight on the same side as the attackers." (Collingwood 1998, 171)

lingwood did not intend to imply that absolute presuppositions were eternal and immutable. On the contrary, absolute presuppositions are 'absolute' only in relation to a particular period in history.[16] Precisely the fact that Collingwood's 'absolute' presuppositions are seen as historical has led to the discussion among Collingwood scholars about whether his defence of metaphysics was tenable. I do not want to go here into this discussion, since the only focus here is on the historical relation between Collingwood and logical positivists, not on the cogency of his concept of metaphysics as a historical discipline.

In developing his logic-of-question-and-answer, in which presuppositions and the issue of the possibility of metaphysics play a central role, Collingwood obviously returned to the Kantian position. Like Kant, he situated the conditions of possibility for the understanding of reality in the transcendental structures of human subjectivity. By so doing, he moved his attention from the level of empirical or tautological propositions to that of relative or absolute presuppositions and so distanced himself from the epistemological paradigm of analytic philosophy.[17]

However, Collingwood – strongly influenced by the philosophy of history of among others Vico, Herder and Dilthey – was fully aware that the belief in one eternal transcendental subjectivity, subsuming all phenomenal data and so constituting 'all' laws of knowledge, was eventually untenable. As an heir of the Copernican Revolution but influenced by Vico and the work of the German metacritics as well, he subsequently undermined the universal claims of Kantian transcendental subjectivity: the historian and philosopher of history Collingwood was pre-eminently aware of the fragmentation and historicity of this 'transcendental' subjectivity.[18]

---

16 Cf. Skagestad 2005, 106.

17 Hylton 1993, 462: "(…) since Russell and Moore denied that there are necessary conditions or presuppositions to knowledge, they see the fundamental epistemic relation as presuppositionless. Knowledge, at least of the fundamental sort, is direct and unmediated. Both Russell and Moore take our knowledge of simply sensory qualities as the paradigm and the model of this kind of knowledge."

18 As far as I know, Collingwood refers only once to Hamann in Collingwood 1924, 58. It is possible that Collingwood knew Hamann's *Metakritik* through Benedetto Croce's translation 1906, 74–82.

4.2 Robin G. Collingwood and Isaiah Berlin

Thus in the same period that Heidegger's and Merleau-Ponty's reactions to the epistemological tradition were exerting a wide influence, Collingwood's reaction to logical empiricism was – pace Taylor – also exerting some influence in the Anglo-Saxon world. Isaiah Berlin, inspired by Collingwood's ideas, may be considered as the most influential representative of this reaction against the epistemological construction in the second half of the twentieth century. Because Berlin is foremost known as a historian of ideas, it may surprise many readers that he started his career as an analytic philosopher and had produced 'purely philosophical writings' as well.[19] Berlin began his philosophical career in Oxford as Fellow of All Souls College in an analytical environment. Through his friendship with J. L. Austin, A. J. Ayer and Stuart Hampshire he was initiated into logical positivism and his first publications (in journals as *Mind* and *Proceedings of the Aristotelian Society*) focused on epistemological issues.[20] For more than two years – between spring 1937 and summer 1939 – the so-called 'Brethren,' the most promising representatives of the logical positivists, met each week in Berlin's office at All Souls College to exchange their arguments and ideas about typically analytical problems such as personal identity and theories of perception. Austin, Ayer and Hampshire belonged to the group, Collingwood, then already ailing, was invited, but declined.[21]

Despite his frequent contacts with his analytic 'Brethren,' Berlin had never considered himself a full-fledged analytic philosopher. His philosophical approach was too historical, his method too synthetic and his cultural background too diverse and variegated. That was also the reason he felt attracted to Collingwood who, with his historical approach of philosophical problems, was rather seen as a 'lone wolf' in the Oxbridge-environment. Already since 1929 Berlin had been following Collingwood's course on the philosophy of history, from which he distilled two central ideas, which will re-emerge time and again in his later work. First, our thought and practice are always determined by histor-

---

19 See Bernard Williams, *Introduction*. In Berlin 1978, xi: "Isaiah Berlin is most widely known for his writings in political theory and the history of ideas, but he worked first in general philosophy, and contributed to the discussion of these issues in the theory of knowledge and the theory of meaning (...) In this selection from Berlin's *more purely philosophical writings* [italics mine], the three papers which represent the earliest period of his concerns (...)"
20 His 'analytic' articles are to be found in Berlin 1978.
21 Ignatieff 1998, 85: "The magic circle was small: Ayer, Berlin, Hampshire, Austin, Donald MacNabb, A.D.Woozley and Donald MacKinnon. R.G.Collingwood was invited but declined."

ically changing presuppositions and second, humans are finite and imperfect beings, incapable of constructing a complete system that reveals the whole truth.

The more he met with the 'Brethren', the more Berlin's scepticism toward logical positivism increased.[22] Along the way, he began to develop a philosophical concept of his own, the quintessence of which is presented in his essays *The Purpose of Philosophy* and *Does Political Philosophy still exist?*[23] In the latter essay from 1961, Berlin applies his concept of philosophy to problems in the field of the political science. In the former one, originally from 1962, he elaborates the same issue in more general terms, focusing on the specific task of philosophy as such and on the premises from which it starts.

Collingwood's influence is strikingly present in these essays. Berlin openly attacks logical positivism, making use of similar arguments and even terminology. His central claim, analogous to Collingwood's, is that there are meaningful statements that do not belong to Ayer's strict and too narrow collection of empirically verifiable and logical statements. Furthermore, Berlin believes it is impossible to make a clear-cut distinction between empirical and logical statements on the one hand and normative statements on the other and then to curtail the domain of philosophical research to the first category, as logical positivists do. It is impossible for the simple reason that empirical statements are always based on (mostly concealed) normative presuppositions. Even more, according to Berlin, all statements are always determined by underlying presuppositions, models, or paradigms and these very presuppositions form the genuine subject-matter of philosophy:

> Philosophy, then, is not an empirical study: not the critical examination of what exists or has existed or will exist – this dealt with by common sense knowledge and belief, and the methods of the natural sciences. Nor is it a kind of formal deduction as mathematics or logic is. Its subject-matter is to a large extent not the items of experience, but the ways in which they are viewed, the permanent or semi-permanent categories in terms of which experience is conceived and classified. (Berlin, 1978: 9)

In line with Collingwood, Berlin believes that the majority of these categories are transient and have a historical character. Put differently, our basic presuppositions – in Collingwood's terms, our 'absolute' presuppositions – are not logically necessary or eternal a priori categories. Rather, they function as historically variable points of departure for interpreting reality as it appears to us. In Taylor's

---

[22] See for a presentation of Berlin's relation to the 'Brethren': Ignatieff 1998, 77–96.
[23] Both essays are included in Berlin 1978, 1–11 and 143–172.

terminology, social imaginaries for interpreting (social) reality as it appears to us.

Against this backdrop, Berlin gives philosophy a twofold purpose.[24] Its first purpose is to elucidate the categories, concepts and models which, albeit often unconsciously, are at the basis of our thought and behaviour. Subsequently, a philosopher has to evaluate these categories, concepts and models and, if necessary, to amend or to replace them with more adequate variants. Moreover, the central place he assigns in his epistemological theory to the role of underlying, historically variable presuppositions in human thought and behaviour is related to his anthropological viewpoint that human beings are inherently finite and imperfect. In his courses on philosophy of history, Collingwood often referred to the famous quote of Kant that "out of the crooked timber of human nature, nothing straight could be made." Struck by this passage, Berlin makes that quote his own favourite one.[25]

It was Collingwood as well who stimulated Berlin to read the work of the Napolitan philosopher Giambattista Vico (1668–1744).[26] Actually Vico, investigating the historical succession of cultures, was the very first to remark that each culture develops a view of reality of its own. That common view is embodied in all various aspects of what people do, think and feel in a specific cultural era and it is transmitted by the language and the customs people make use of, by the ideas, metaphors and institutions which give voice to their interpretation of reality. Moreover, since all these views are different from era to era and are mutually incomparable, Vico introduced a specific method for the humanities which is strongly related to this historical concept of human culture: in contrast to the natural scientist who describes nature from an external point of view so as to explain its structure, the scholar in the humanities has to describe the specific character of cultural manifestations from an internal point of view so as to understand its meaning and significance.

---

24 This description of philosophy's task is unmistakably influenced by Collingwood. See Ignatieff 1998, 58: "If there was any single source in Oxford for Berlin's later interest in the philosophy of history, (...) and in his evolving conviction that thinking historically was the best way to do philosophy, it was Collingwood. The two never became close – Collingwood gently rebuffing one of Berlin's invitations to join a seminar – but the influence was important."
25 See Berlin 1990, xi–x.
26 *The Pursuit of the Ideal*. In Berlin 1990, 8: "Then I came across Giambattista Vico's *La scienza nuova*. Scarcely anyone in Oxford had then heard of Vico, but there was one philosopher, Robin George Collingwood, who had translated Croce's book on Vico, and he urged me to read it. This opened my eyes to something new."

His study of the ideas of Vico led Berlin to the romantic Kant-critics of the late eighteenth century; he devoted special attention to the work of the two major meta-critics, Hamann and Herder. His first article on Johann Georg Hamann dates from 1956 and is later reprinted as a short chapter in his selection of eighteen-century authors.[27] In the years that followed, he devoted other essays to Hamann and in 1993 he published the monograph, *The Magus of the North: J. G. Hamann and the Origins of Modern Irrationalism*.[28] As a historian of ideas, Berlin saw even stronger similarities between Herder and Vico.[29] Like Vico, Herder had focused on the comparison between national cultures in different countries during similar periods. Herder's investigations made Berlin realize that each culture has an identity of its own and that the compilation of its customs and habits is the multi-coloured expression of that identity. The way people live, think, feel and speak, the clothes they wear, the songs they sing, the gods they worship, the food they take, the ideas and habits which are fundamental to them, all this forms the foundation of different cultural communities in developing their own 'life-style.'

In Berlin's interpretation of the two major romantic meta-critics' writings it becomes clear how the customs, habits, metaphors and ideas that define different cultural communities' particularities, function as their basic or 'absolute' presuppositions. It is precisely at this level of basic presuppositions – a level largely neglected in British analytic philosophy for a long time – that, according to Berlin and Collingwood, the philosopher's task and philosophy's purpose are located.

4.3 'Fighting in the Daylight'

Through his close contact and friendship with Isaiah Berlin – they first met in 1956 in Oxford where Taylor has been his pupil and later became his successor as Chichele Professor in Oxford – Charles Taylor got acquainted with the writings of the two romantic meta-critics. Particularly Herder's philosophy of culture and language – and indirectly that of Hamann – exerted an enormous influence on Taylor's interpretation of modernity.[30] But Taylor inherited from Berlin as well an

---

27 Berlin 1956, 270–275.
28 See for more information on Berlin's study of Hamann's oeuvre: *Editor's Preface*. In Berlin 1993, ix–xiii.
29 Berlin 1976 (last enlarged edition as Berlin 2000).
30 See Taylor 1995, 79: "Isaiah Berlin helped to rescue Herder from his relative neglect by philosophers. His seminal role in the creation of post-Romantic thought and culture has gone un-

interest in the broader perspective of Western Modernity's complex genealogy. Therefore, Berlin and Taylor alike did not confine their studies in the history of ideas to the evolution of ideas within the history of speculative thought.

By contrast, they were looking for parallels between philosophical ideas on the one hand and congenial evolutions within literature, art, politics and society on the other. Moreover, their primary intention was not to retell the well-known stories of how great philosophers' systems made way for one another. They focused on dissident figures as well, in particular those who were the first to criticize and challenge time-honoured traditions and their basic presuppositions. In this sense, they were both practitioners of the historical analysis of absolute presuppositions, as proposed by Collingwood in *An Essay on Metaphysics:* "The metaphysician's business, therefore, when he has identified several different constellations of absolute presuppositions, is not only to study their likenesses and unlikenesses, but also to find out on what occasions and by what processes one of them has turned into another" (Collingwood 1998, 73).

Within that context, it is no coincidence that both Berlin and Taylor focused their attention on the post-Kantian, romantic thinkers of the end of the eighteenth century, who initiated the so-called Counter-Enlightenment.[31] Sensitive to the cultural community's indispensable role for the individual's self-realisation, they raised incisive questions regarding the rationalistic and universalistic ideals of Enlightenment. Beyond doubt, there are major differences between Berlin's and Taylor's outlooks, to which I return on the next pages. But these differences do not detract from their shared view that Western modernity is not reducible to either the Enlightenment or Romanticism, but constitutes a complex and potentially explosive mixture of the two strands.

Although Berlin considered himself a life-long 'liberal rationalist,' who rejected an excess of subjectivism and particularism and subscribed to the ideals of enlightened thinkers as Voltaire, Condorcet, Helvetius and Holbach according to which man was emancipated from obscurantism and fanaticism and he was able to oppose cruelty, oppression and superstition, he deemed their ideas as simultaneously too abstract and simplistic. How abstract and simplistic they really are Berlin had learned from their main critics and opponents: Vico, Hamann, Herder, but also de Maistre and Burke, who participated in what Berlin called

---

noticed, at least in the English-speaking world. The fact that Herder is not the most rigorous of thinkers probably makes it easier to ignore him. But deeply innovative thinkers don't have to be rigorous in order to originate important ideas."

31 An excellent presentation of Berlin's thought is to be found in Roger Hausheer, *Introduction to Berlin 1980*. It goes without saying that such an historical inquiry can in principle be applied to every period in western culture and to any culture and any period whatsoever.

the 'Counter-Enlightenment'. Larry Siedentop, a one-time pupil of Berlin's, once remarked that "his teacher liked to venture out into the Romantic irrational by day, but always returned to the Enlightenment at nightfall".[32] More or less the same description applies to Taylor. He believes that Enlightenment has been a great gain for humankind in certain aspects, but at the same time he confesses to being "a hopeless German romantic of the 1790s. I resonate with Herder's idea of humanity as the orchestra, in which all the differences between human beings could ultimately sound together in harmony." (Warner, VanAntwerpen, Calhoun 2010, 320)

Isaiah Berlin takes a mid-position between Collingwood and Taylor. Collingwood was the first to give a transcendental foundation of the specific status of philosophy as a history of ideas, without elaborating such a philosophy of its own. That was done by Berlin. His great merit was that, by focusing upon often forgotten or marginalized authors from the eighteenth or nineteenth century, he exposed the strains and tensions that occurred beyond the level of ideas that have shaped Western modern culture. As sensitive as Berlin to Enlightenment's vigour and one-sidedness, Taylor intended, by highlighting the complexity of its genealogy, to show the necessity of 'retrieval' – I borrow the term from Taylor – so as to amend the shortcomings of a too narrow, rationalistic interpretation of western modernity.

Unlike Berlin, who was first and foremost an author of short essays, Taylor has worked out his philosophical research in large studies with a panoramic scope. In both *Sources of the Self: The Making of the Modern Identity* and *A Secular Age*, Taylor tells a philosophical and historical story of ideas, going back to the deepest sources of western civilisation, showing how from the very start it developed within a field of tensions between different social imaginaries, becoming an equivocal culture, of which we experience, as it were simultaneously, its 'grandeur' and 'malaise.' To that end, Taylor, like Collingwood and Berlin mediating between the knockers and the boosters of modern culture, opts for re-articulating and making explicit the deeper sources of meaning and morality, the basic presuppositions we – albeit mostly unconsciously – are living by.

In *The Purpose of Philosophy* Isaiah Berlin defined the task of philosophy, which is often a difficult and painful task, in an analogous way:

> To extricate and *bring to light* [italics mine] the hidden categories and models in terms of which human beings think (that is, their use of words, images, and other symbols), to reveal what is obscure or contradictory in them, to discern the conflicts between them that

---

32 See Ignatieff 1998, 250.

prevent the construction of more adequate ways of organising and describing and explaining experience. (Berlin 1978, 10)

The principal causes of confusion, fear and misery, he continued, are blind adherence to outworn basic presuppositions, suspicion of critique and self-examination, and resistance to rational analysis of how we live. Therefore, "the goal of philosophy is always the same, to assist men to understand themselves and thus operate in the open, and not wildly, *in the dark*" (Berlin 1978, 11; italics mine).

Here, Berlin's definition of the purpose of philosophy and in particular his use of the dark/light metaphor are strongly indebted, even verbatim, to Collingwood's appeal to the philosophers of his age to combat Fascism by making explicit the absolute presuppositions of his own era. "I know that all my life I have been engaged unawares in a political struggle, fighting against these things *in the dark*. Henceforth I shall fight *in the daylight*. (Collingwood 2013, 167, italics mine)

4.4 Robin G. Collingwood and Charles Taylor

But, as stated earlier, how is it possible to articulate that background of basic presuppositions, while that background is simultaneously defined as precisely unconscious, inarticulate and implicit. At this point, Berlin and Taylor part ways, and the similarity between Collingwood and Taylor is much stronger. Unlike Berlin, Collingwood and Taylor have a Hegelian background. Even if the three authors, as they struggle with this issue of the (im)possibility of articulating our background of presuppositions or imaginaries, share the view that our explicit consciousness is surrounded by a horizon of the implicit, they differ in their respective attitudes towards the Hegelian solution.

Whereas Berlin designates his repudiation of Hegelian metaphysics as the chief difference with Taylor's position (Tully 2003, 1–2), Collingwood and Taylor follow Hegel in trying to articulate the implicit horizon so as to come to more clarity of that implicit background. Yet they reject Hegel's specific ontology, that is, the thesis that what we ultimately discover as the general background of everything is the necessary, conceptual evolution of the Absolute Spirit (Taylor 1975, 569).

Once the Hegelian belief in that kind of ontology is discarded, it becomes clear for Collingwood and Taylor alike that in order to articulate the implicit background of absolute presuppositions or social imaginaries, we need 'subtler words' to formulate an alternative, tentative ontology so as to grasp that complex relation between being aware and simultaneously unaware of that background.[33] Much more than Wittgenstein, Polanyi or Heidegger, Collingwood's emphasis of the need of articulacy against the background of an alternative ontology, is, in my view, akin to Taylor's position as developed in different essays, even if Taylor has mentioned Collingwood's writings only once in his whole oeuvre, in his latest book, *The Language Animal*. Admittedly, Collingwood's choice of the term 'metaphysics without ontology' and Taylor's choice of the term 'moral ontology' have evidently led to more confusion than to genuine understanding. But if my interpretation has some plausibility, then for Collingwood and Taylor alike it is still possible for philosophy to retrieve reality. By studying the historical process of changing absolute presuppositions or social imaginaries, the philosopher at once underlines the temporal character of every philosophical construct and emphasizes that the mystery of being remains a mystery. But it is the philosopher's task to understand, to the best of his ability, the emotion of wonder from within.

I would like to illustrate that commonality by one example. In the first part of *Sources of the Self*[34] Taylor contrasts the naturalistic view in which *frameworks* are superfluous with his own exposition of the place of indispensable *frameworks* in our lives. He selects four characteristics of these frameworks which he defines in a terminology strikingly similar to Collingwood's: they are incommensurable, because they themselves are the transcendental starting-point for making choices; they form the ultimate point of departure for the questions we raise; they mostly remain implicit, but can be rationally made explicit; they are liable to historical evolution. What Collingwood called absolute presuppositions, Taylor refers to as *frameworks*. The neo-positivism to which Collingwood objects undoubtedly shares its characteristics with naturalism that Taylor combats.

For Taylor, it is impossible to study the structure of reality apart from human experience. That is why Taylor uses the term 'human/moral ontology.' Precisely that study of reality Collingwood defines as historical metaphysics. Like Taylor, he repudiates ontology as a study of being or reality, apart from human experience. For Collingwood absolute presuppositions of human thought are related to reality; Taylor believes that our human *frameworks* or imaginaries have an ontological status: "We treat our beliefs, theories, as over against reality, to be related to these frameworks. But all this goes on within a larger context of presumed

---

[33] See Tully 2003, xiv–xvi.
[34] See Taylor 1989, Part I: Identity and the Good: Inescapable Frameworks, 3–25; The Self in Moral Space, 25–53.

contact with reality. The presumption can be erroneous, but never totally." (Taylor 2013, 76)

5 Conclusion

In his preface to *Philosophical Arguments*, Taylor himself recapitulated – in an anticipatory way – the philosophical genealogy of the term social imaginaries: "The proponents and developers of the Romantic theory have been among the most passionate critics of the epistemological tradition, from Hamann's review of Kant's *Critique of Pure Reason* to the writings in our century of Heidegger, of the later Wittgenstein, and of certain postmodernists" (Taylor 1995, ix).

By historicizing the Kantian a priori transcendental apparatus, they introduced the debate on the relation between rationality and culture (and in a derivative sense between Enlightenment and Counter-Enlightenment) which today plays such a central role in continental and in Anglo-Saxon philosophy of culture alike.

In this article, I tried both to elaborate on Taylor's recapitulation and to amend it by pointing out the inaccuracy of his identification of social imaginaries with Kantian transcendental schemata and by reminding the reader of the commonality between Taylor's project of articulacy and retrieval and that of Berlin and Collingwood. If there is some plausibility in all this, then this exposition of the threefold background may clarify the specificity of Taylor's concept of social imaginaries and in particular the role of 'religious and secular imaginaries' in our contemporary society so as to evade possible misunderstandings as to its applications.

Taylor's point in *A Secular Age* is that to be religious or secular is not primarily related to a difference in theories or doctrines, but rather to a shift in our fabric of social practices that embody the social imaginaries of our common lifeworld. The decline of religion and the rise of secularization can be understood only within the 'reform master narrative' of the transformation of our pre-modern social imaginaries into that of the currently default imaginary of 'The Immanent Frame' in religious affairs. But of course, all this needs much more clarification. To that end, Stijn Latré provides a conceptual analysis of the immanent frame in the next article, while in the third article Michiel Meijer and Stijn Latré focus on the possible ontological impact of social imaginaries.[35]

---

[35] This text is a revised version of Guido Vanheeswijck, "The Philosophical Genealogy of Tay-

Bibliography

Anderson, Benedict. 1983. *Imagined Communities: Reflections on the Origin and Spread of Nationalism*. London: Verso.
Ayer, Alfred J. 1974. *Language, Truth and Logic*. Harmondsworth: Penguin.
Ayer, Alfred J. 1934. "Demonstration of the Impossibility of Metaphysics." *Mind* 43:335–345.
Beiser, Frederick. 1987. *The Fate of Reason: German Philosophy from Kant to Fichte*. Cambridge, MA: Harvard University Press.
Berlin, Isaiah. 1956. *The Age of Enlightenment: The Eighteenth-Century Philosophers*. Boston and New York: New American Library.
Berlin, Isaiah. 1976. *Vico and Herder: Two studies in the history of ideas*. London: Hogarth Press. (Last enlarged edition as Berlin, Isaiah. 2000. *Three critics of the Enlightenment: Vico, Hamann, Herder*. Princeton: Princeton University Press.)
Berlin, Isaiah. 1978. *Concepts and Categories: Philosophical Essays*, edited by Henry Hardy. London: The Hogarth Press.
Berlin, Isaiah. 1980. *Against the Current*. London: The Hogarth Press.
Berlin, Isaiah. 1990. *The crooked timber of humanity: Chapters in the History of Ideas*, edited by Henry Hardy. London: John Murray.
Berlin, Isaiah. 1993. *The Magus of the North: J.G.Hamann and the Origins of Modern Irrationalism*, edited by Henry Hardy. London: John Murray.
Castoriadis, Cornelius. 1987. *The Imaginary Institution of Society*. Cambridge, MA: MIT Press.
Collingwood, Robin George. 1924. *Speculum Mentis*. Oxford: Clarendon Press.
Collingwood, Robin George. 1998. *An Essay on Metaphysics* (revised edition with an Introduction and Additional Material edited by Rex Martin). Oxford: Clarendon Press.
Collingwood, Robin George. 2013. *An Autobiography and Other Writings* (with Essays on Collingwood's Life and Work and an Introduction by David Boucher and Teresa Smith). Oxford: Oxford University Press.
Croce, Benedetto. 1906. "La 'Metacritica' di G.G.Hamann contro la Critica Kantiana". *La Critica* 4:74–82.
Dickson, Gwen Griffith. 1995. *Johann Georg Hamann's Relational Metacriticism*. Berlin: Walter de Gruyter.
Gordon, Peter. 2008. "The Place of the Sacred in the Absence of God: Charles Taylor's 'A Secular Age.'" *Journal of the History of Ideas* 69 (4):647–673.
Hamann, Johan Georg. 1949–1957. *Sämtliche Werken*, edited by Josef Nadler. Vienna: Herder Verlag.
Hylton, Peter. 1993. "Hegel and analytic Philosophy". In *The Cambridge Companion to Hegel*, edited by Frederick C. Beiser. Cambridge: Cambridge University Press.
Ignatieff, Michael. 1998. *Isaiah Berlin: A Life*. London: Chatto & Windus.
Johnson, Peter. 1998. *The Correspondence of R.G. Collingwood: An Illustrated Guide*. Swansea: R.G. Collingwood Society.
Kant, Immanuel. 1987. *The Critique of Pure Reason* (translated by Norman Kemp Smith). London: MacMillan.

---

lor's Social Imaginaries: A Complex History of Ideas and Predecessors". *Journal of the History of Ideas*, 78 (3), July 2017, 473–496.

Martin, Rex. 1998. "Collingwood's Logic of Question and Answer, its Relation to Absolute Presuppositions: A Brief History." *Collingwood Studies* 5:122–133.

Skagestad, Peter. 2005. "Collingwood and Berlin: A Comparison." *Journal of the History of Ideas:*99–112.

Taylor, Charles. 1975. *Hegel*. Cambridge: Cambridge University Press.

Taylor, Charles. 1989. *Sources of the Self: The Making of the Modern Identity.* Cambridge: Cambridge University Press.

Taylor, Charles. 1995. *Philosophical Arguments*. Cambridge, MA: Harvard University Press.

Taylor, Charles. 2003. "Ethics and Ontology." *The Journal of Philosophy* 100 (6):305–320.

Taylor, Charles. 2005. "The 'Weak Ontology' Thesis." *The Hedgehog Review* 7 (2):35–42.

Taylor, Charles. 2013. "Retrieving Realism." In *Mind, Reason, and Being-in-the-World: The McDowell-Dreyfus Debate*, edited by Joseph K. Schear, 61–90. Abingdon: Routledge.

Taylor, Charles, and Hubert Dreyfus. 2015. *Retrieving Realism*. Cambridge, MA: Harvard University Press.

Tully, James, ed. 2003. *Philosophy in an Age of Pluralism: The Philosophy of Charles Taylor in Question*. Cambridge: Cambridge University Press.

Vanheeswijck, Guido. 2015. "Does History Matter? Charles Taylor on the Transcendental Validity of Social Imaginaries." *History and Theory* 54 (1):69–85.

Warner, Michael, Jonathan VanAntwerpen, and Craig Calhoun, eds. 2010. *Varieties of Secularism in A Secular Age*. Cambridge, MA: Harvard University Press.

Stijn Latré
Social Imaginaries

A Conceptual Analysis

1 Introduction: The Immanent Frame

Taylor's *A Secular Age* (2007) is widely recognized as a seminal work in the field of secularization theory, and more specifically in the long tradition of genealogies of secularization. The book constitutes, in Taylor's own phrasing, a 'Reform Master Narrative' of the conditions of belief and unbelief in the West. Why is it so that belief in God was indisputable at the outset of the 16th century, whereas belief in God has become one option among many others in our contemporary Western society, and even an option which is hard to take? (Taylor 2007, 25) In our Western world – roughly speaking geographically defined as Western Europe and the North Atlantic – we all belong to 'the immanent frame,' a term Taylor employs as the title for the fifteenth chapter of *A Secular Age*.

'The immanent frame' may at first glance seem to be an alternative wording for 'the secular age.' However, this wording immediately imposes a certain descriptive and interpretive scheme on the concept of secularization. This scheme consists of the binary opposition immanence-transcendence, which is essential to Christian theology. By referring to our western cultural predicament as one of living in an immanent frame, Taylor clearly situates this predicament in the tradition of Christian theology, even if he traces the history of secularization back beyond Christian history to the axial age.[1] Living in a secular age is living in an immanent frame, which means that traditional sources of transcendence have been eclipsed or even dispelled from our views on man and nature.

However, the immanent frame does not just refer to intellectual, philosophical *views* on man and nature. Taylor rather prefers the word *picture* in relation to the immanent frame, so that the immanent frame is "a picture that holds us captive," as he rephrases Wittgenstein (Taylor 2007, 549). The immanent frame can indeed only be understood by reference to another pivotal concept of Taylor's more recent work, *social imaginary*, or rather *social imaginaries* in the plural,

---

[1] On the relation between secularization, the axial age and the dynamics of transcendence, see Latré 2014. On Taylor's historical narrative of secularization, see Cloots, Latré and Vanheeswijck 2013.

since contemporary Western culture showcases a super-diversity which does not allow for one single picture or social imaginary. In this chapter, I will first describe the use of the concept of social imaginaries by Castoriadis (2) and Taylor (3). I will then explore how Taylor's conception of social imaginaries is intertwined with other essential concepts in his oeuvre, such as 'transcendental framework,' 'strong evaluation,' 'expressivist culture' and 'cross pressures' (4). I will then turn back to the immanent frame as a social imaginary and see how these concepts frame our understanding and experience of the immanent frame (5).

2 Castoriadis and CTS on Social Imaginaries

In his influential book *The Imaginary Institution of Society* (1987), Castoriadis reacted "against the deterministic strands within Marxism, which he regarded as both dominant and unavoidable" (Gaonkar 2002, 1). As an alternative, Castoriadis developed the notion of social imaginaries, a concept that was to emphasize "the creative force in the making of social-historical worlds" (Gaonkar 2002, 1). In this respect, the concept bears close connections with notions as 'civil society' (Taylor 1995) and 'the public sphere' (Habermas 1989).

In 2002, *Public Culture* dedicated its winter issue entirely to the concept of social imaginaries. That issue was the result of more than a decade of reflection in the Center for Transcultural Studies (CTS), a Center counting, among others, Arjun Appadurai, Craig Calhoun, Charles Taylor and Michael Warner among its members. In the opening essay of this social imaginaries-issue, Dilip Parameshwar Gaonkar has developed a short but very useful summary of Castoriadis's thought on this subject.

As Gaonkar puts it, Castoriadis's orientation is ontological and "triggered by the basic question: How are a multiplicity of social-historical worlds, in all their novelty and alterity, possible?" (Gaonkar 2002, 6). Castoriadis noted that the nature of society and history had been consistently explained in the deterministic fashion of ancient Greek philosophy. To think of the nature of society and history, was to gain knowledge about the eternal essences behind sensory appearances, was to grasp "an immanent logic or law that governs the universe and the human endeavors within it." (Gaonkar 2002, 6) Against that view, Castoriadis wanted to see social change as something creative and contingent, and no longer as some marginal modification of an underlying logical or ontological form or *eidos*. According to Castoriadis, history is driven by "radical otherness, immanent creation, non-trivial novelty" (Castoriadis 1987, 184). As Gaonkar put it, "a social-historical world is created ex nihilo in a burst of imaginative praxis carried out not by conscious individuals or groups but by anonymous masses who constitute themselves as a people in that very act of founding" (Gaonkar 2002, 6). Castoriadis has qualified the ex nihilo rhetoric by recognizing some constraints: the external (our biology, for example the fact that we must eat), the internal (the need to transform solitary individuals into socialized individuals, for example family life), the historical (the inertia of an instituted society) and the intrinsic (need for coherence within the symbolic order). However, all this happens in a huge variety of ways, not in any deterministic or preordained way (Gaonkar 2002, 6).

Taking into account his distinction between deterministic and emergent views on the development of social reality, it is no surprise that Castoriadis's typology of social-historical formations revolves around the heteronomy-autonomy dichotomy. Two years after the French 'transcendental anthroposociologist'[2] Marcel Gauchet had described human history as a development from heteronomous to autonomous sociality in his unsurpassed *Le désenchantement du monde*, Castoriadis brings up the same dichotomy, with the same orientation as in Gauchet's work. Heteronomous societies belong to the era of so called 'primitive' religions and are characterized by laws, myths and meanings which are immutable, and derive their legitimacy from an extra-social, transcendent source. By contrast, "autonomous societies habitually call into question their own institutions and representations and the social imaginary that underwrites them" (Gaonkar 2002, 8).

For Castoriadis, autonomy and multiplicity constituted the counterpart for the deterministic views of heteronomous societies. But what is at stake in this multiplicity? And does this multiplicity not entail mixed forms along the heteronomy-autonomy divide, rather than classing all modern social imaginaries within the autonomy type? (Gaonkar 2002, 9–10)

These and other questions were addressed by the members of the CTS group. In 1999, they drafted a statement about *new imaginaries*, falling apart in a broad definition and four areas of application, though Gaonkar refers to all these features as "five key ideas" (Gaonkar 2002, 4). The definition reads as follows: "Social imaginaries are ways of understanding the social that become social entities themselves, mediating collective life" (Gaonkar 2002, 4). These 'ways of understanding' are not to be understood as intellectual, philosophical, so to speak 'objective' or 'third person' points of view. Social imaginaries are "implicit understandings that underlie and make possible common practices." They operate

---

[2] Gauchet refers to what he is doing in his work as 'antroposociologie transcendentale' (Gauchet 2003, 10).

at an institutional level (e.g. hoisting the flag of a nation) and at an individual level: the social imaginary functions implicitly as an orientation for personal identity, for finding one's place in the world (Gaonkar 2002, 4). To summarize, social imaginaries operate mostly at an implicit level, but notwithstanding this dimension of concealment, they are constitutive and transcendental for individuals and their social formations. I will return to this feature of transcendentalism below.

After this general definition, the CTS statement points to four specific modes of building a social imaginary. The first mode is about 'stranger sociability' (Gaonkar 2002, 5). We are all connected to strangers by the use of mass media. This is a case of what Taylor (2004, 86) would later call 'metatopical' common space. We do not need to assemble at the same specific location in order to be connected to all watchers of the same soccer game, readers of the same journal or followers of the same twitter account. Metatopical mass media may even engender revolutions, as we saw in the case of Tunisia and the so called Arab spring.

The construction of a national identity, reflected in the sovereignty of a national people, is a second example of a new, modern social imaginary. This imaginary construes a categorial 'we': you are either American, or you are not. Nationalism empowers a people with "agential subjectivity" (Gaonkar 2002, 5), making it the subject of history.[3] As Gauchet put it, it was only after the French Revolution that humanity really invented history (Gauchet 2007, 127–154). The flip side of this empowering of the people as the main actor of history is the possibility of an increase in categorical violence (Taylor 2011, 81–83): people in, say, the Balkans, have fought each other because of being Croat or Serb, that is: they slaughter one another without having any personal or 'real' conflict with the person they shoot.

The national social imaginary is transcended by more general, abstract imaginaries. We can see a shift here from the first person 'we' to 'third-person' objectifications of society: the market, the mainstream, census categories. These are modes of connectedness which do not necessarily entail subjectivity nor call for social action or reform. We all belong to the market economy as a 'system,' whether we actively try to do away with it, or try to improve this system, or just passively undergo its sway. A third-person objectification can, perhaps somewhat surprisingly, also take shape as a collective sentiment or affect. Gaon-

---

[3] Benedict Anderson's work has been trail-blazing with regard to the relation between social imagination and nationalism. For reasons of brevity I cannot dwell on it here. See Anderson 1983.

kar (2002, 5) gives the example of mass grieving after the death of Princess Diana. In this case, the collective sentiment did not inspire social action nor result in new social movements. By contrast, other collectively experienced affects may acquire agency. The Belgian public sentiment after the pedophilia case of Dutroux in 1996 provoked the 'White March' in Brussels, where 300.000 people gathered to denounce the mal functioning of politics, police and law systems. This 'White Anger' resulted in several local 'White Committees'.

The last but important feature of modern social imaginaries is that they realize their agency in secular temporalities, rather than that agency is "existing eternally in cosmos or higher time" (Gaonkar 2002, 5). Hence the original purpose of the concept social imaginaries by Castoriadis is paid tribute to. Nonetheless, the 'old' structure of these classic, 'cosmic' forms of agency may still haunt modern consciousness, as is the case in what Gauchet has called the secular religions of Marxism, fascism and Nazism. These ideologies still exhibit the 'old' structure of religion by articulating a perspective of ultimate salvation or *Endlösung*. But unlike, say, Christian theology, this perspective of ultimate redemption is now located *within this world,* on a secular plane, whereas Christianity connects ultimate salvation with a transcendent 'end of times,' and hence put in an eschatological perspective dependent on a transcendent God (Gauchet 2010; Löwith 1949). The potential totalitarianism of modern social imaginaries and the possible outburst of violence is, according to Gaonkar, contained by collective mass events such as sports, e.g. the Olympics, where nations may compete in a more friendly fashion (Gaonkar 2002, 5). This analysis reminds of René Girard's remarks on modern society and the containment of mimetic violence and rivalry, though we want to note that the mimetic structure of human desire is for Girard a perennial and essentialist anthropological feature concerning all individuals, but with potentially destructive social consequences in mob violence. In any case, it is clear that the potential violence within or between modern social imaginaries does not receive sufficient attention by the CTS group, though Taylor alerts of the dangers of "categorical violence" in later writings (Taylor 2011, 81–104).

3 Modern Social Imaginaries According to Taylor

Taylor published his book *Modern Social Imaginaries* only two years after the social imaginaries-issue in *Public Culture*. It was published in the Public Planet Books Series, edited by, among others, Dilip Gaonkar and Michael Warner. Thus the book is clearly continuous with CTS publications on social imaginaries in *Public Culture*.

In the introduction, Taylor argues that the modern moral order, of which he describes the genealogy in natural law theory (Grotius, Pufendorf and Locke) in the first chapter, has taken form in three distinctive social imaginaries of our days: the market economy, the public sphere and the sovereignty of the people. Taylor's impressive volume *A Secular Age* discusses the immanent frame as the often implicit social imaginary of our days when it comes to issues such as religion, quest for meaning or the good life. I will not dwell on any of these particular forms of social imaginaries, but will rather turn to Taylor's short defining chapter in *Modern Social Imaginaries*, logically entitled *What Is a "Social Imaginary"?*

In line with the statement described by Gaonkar in *Public Culture*, Taylor underlines the differences between social *imaginary* and social *theory*. As Taylor states, social imaginaries are about

(i) The way ordinary people 'imagine' their social surroundings, and this is often not expressed in theoretical terms, but is carried in images, stories, and legends. It is also the case that
(ii) Theory is often the possession of a small minority, whereas what is interesting in the social imaginary is that it is shared by large groups of people, if not the whole society. Which leads to a third difference:
(iii) The social imaginary is that common understanding that makes possible common practices and a widely shared sense of legitimacy. (Taylor 2004, 23)

So social imaginaries pertain to the imaginations of large groups, sharing certain assumptions that *make possible* and *legitimize* a range of common practices. The italics emphasize the transcendental aspect of these social imaginaries, and the normative dimension involved. I will shortly return to these features in my discussion of the relation between social imaginaries and other key concepts in Taylor's work.

Apart from these notable features of transcendentalism and normativity, Taylor points to another distinctive feature: that of *inarticulacy*. As Taylor writes in the same chapter, a social imaginary involves a "wider grasp of our predicament: how we stand to each other, how we got to where we are, how we relate to other groups" (Taylor 2004, 25). Social imaginaries thus clearly go beyond the level of practical knowledge. They are not about knowing how to fix the braking system of your bike, though, in a sense, they share the same structure of *Zuhanden* and *Vorhanden* Heidegger articulated in *Sein und Zeit* (1926). Social imaginaries are already understood and employed at an ontic level, just like the brakes of a bike. It is only when the brakes fail to fulfill their purpose of braking that the brake *qua* brake moves from the background of intentionality and consciousness of the biker to the foreground of thematic attention, from merely *Zuhanden* to *Vorhanden*. But unlike the practical knowledge of braking, social imaginaries are about a *wider grasp*, about which Taylor writes: "This wider grasp has no clear limits. That's the very nature of what contemporary philosophers have described as the 'background.' It is in fact that largely unstructured and inarticulate understanding of our whole situation, within which particular features of our world show up for us in the sense they have." (Taylor 2004, 25)

We may conclude that the level of inarticulacy which is involved in the use of social imaginaries bears two meanings: first, a social imaginary escapes full theoretical articulation, and second, a social imaginary is inarticulate in the sense that it covers 'a wider grasp that has no clear limits': its range is somewhat indefinite or even undefinable.

My analysis of Taylor's defining chapter on social imaginaries brought to light three important features. Social imaginaries are to some extent transcendental, normative and inarticulate. I will now delve deeper into these characteristics by relating them to other pivotal concepts in Taylor's work.

4 Relation to other Concepts in Taylor's Work

4.1 Expressivist Culture

I will start off with the last feature of inarticulacy, since it will turn out to be crucial for most concepts I will discuss in this section. In the previous section, it became clear that social imaginaries constitute the background understanding of certain social practices. About the connection between practice and background understanding, Taylor writes: "If the understanding makes the practice possible, it is also true that it is the practice that largely carries the understanding" (Taylor 2004, 25).

Here we get a closer glance of what Taylor means by the structural inarticulacy of social imaginaries. Since the practices largely carry the understandings involved in social imaginaries, the meaning of the latter can never be fully recuperated in any theoretical language. We learn to carry out certain social activities, ranging, for example, from engaging in a conversation to participation in general elections, without the need for a full a priori theoretical articulation of that practice.

The first meaning of the inarticulacy of social imaginaries thus leads us to Taylor's epistemological position, which can be summarized under the heading *expressivism*. Taylor articulates his criticism of classic modern epistemology most clearly in his essay *Overcoming Epistemology* (Taylor 1995, 1–19). In this essay,

Taylor chides the Cartesian requirement of gaining full certainty and transparency about the basic principles of knowledge before engaging in the world. To counter this hyperbolic requirement, Taylor refers to phenomenological analysis of experience, of our 'being-in-the-world,' of the 'background of Being' (Heidegger). Taylor also connects his position to the later Wittgenstein's adagio of 'meaning is use'. So one way to read the citation quoted above, is that we engage in certain practices which reveal a certain 'background' of 'tacit knowledge' (Polanyi), and that this background is still to be articulated more fully.

Taylor's criticism of Cartesian epistemology – and of all 'foundationalist' endeavors in this field – bears close connections to his conception of language as expressivist. Taylor has much sympathy with the romantic, post-Enlightenment views of Herder and Humboldt, who consider language as a medium of expression which is *constitutive* for what is expressed. Language is not just a tool to refer to an external world. The reduction of language to its function of denotation was predominant for some time, in the debates involving logicians and philosophers of language such as Gottlob Frege, Edmund Husserl, Bertrand Russell, and the young Ludwig Wittgenstein. By contrast, post-World War II philosophers like J.L. Austin turned to 'ordinary language' as constitutive for meaning, considering language to be far more than the externalization of an idea we first think most purely within the silent realm of our thoughts. Austin became famous for his 'performative' theory of language, in his celebrated article *How to do things with words* (Austin 1962).

Taylor incorporates this new tradition of the 'Oxford ordinary language school' into his own philosophy. The practice of language is itself constitutive of meanings and new realities. Of course, language also has a denotative function, by which conventions can quite easily be altered. We could all agree to use the sign 'POTS' instead of 'STOP' to denote the command we are all familiar with, though we might temporarily run the risk of an increase in traffic accidents. But it would be much harder to agree on changing certain words in a poem. A poem is the paradigmatic case of the expressivist use of language. The material bearer of meaning (a word, a stanza, the entire poem) evokes new meanings that cannot appear without it, which accounts for the difficulty of translating poetry. Imagine a die-hard Flemish nationalist objecting against the opening lines of the famous war poem by John McRae, *In Flanders Fields*. Suppose he would make the suggestion that 'the poppies blow' bears a reference to opium that spoils the soul of Flemish youth, and that he would suggest to rephrase this line as 'In Flanders fields, where flies the crow.' We can all see how this affects the poetic richness of the poem, not to mention the history of this poem that transformed the poppy into the symbol of World War I in Flanders and beyond.

So the meaning of 'practice that largely carries the understanding' has become more clear now. Social imaginaries are background understandings that enable certain practices, but they only become *real* in and through these practices. Social imaginaries are as it were as much *lived* as they are understood. Social imaginaries are enshrined in the use of expressivist practice. But there is another way in which social imaginaries refer to expressivism in Taylor's philosophy. Expressivism has itself become one of the most powerful social imaginaries of our times, in that we regard ourselves and other people as 'expressivist beings.' This idea is closely knit with the 'age of authenticity' Taylor refers to in *Ethics of Authenticity* (1992) and *A Secular Age* (2007). The age of authenticity is characterized by a certain individualism, that of 'being true to yourself.' But that should not necessarily be interpreted as the requirement that all truth about myself originates within my inner self, as some articulations of the idea of autonomy would have it. Authenticity, Taylor argues, entails self-referentiality of *manner*, but not necessarily of *matter*. To be an authentic person means to recognize and appropriate certain sources for my behavior or identity as *mine*, but this does not imply that the origin of these sources is also to be situated within myself. For example, I may confess to the intrinsic worth of nature or to belief in God as being *my* convictions, but refer to nature or God as external sources, as true realities existing *out there*, and inspiring me. According to Taylor, our secular age is deeply marked by this social imaginary of authenticity and thus expressivism: living my life means being true to an expression of sources within me or without.

To sum up, social imaginaries bear a double reference to expressivism. First, social imaginaries only come into being in certain social practices. There seems to be some circularity involved here: social imaginaries enable as background understandings certain social practices, but the latter in a way also constitute or carry these imaginaries. This circularity probably only poses a problem to adherents of Cartesian epistemology who strive for full articulacy and transparency, a goal Taylor considers out of reach with regard to social imaginaries.

Second, contemporary (Western) social imaginaries take shape in a culture of expressivism and authenticity, which serves as a frame to more specific imaginaries and practices, and in this respect seems to be inescapable.

4.2 Transcendental Frameworks

This brings us to our next point: Taylor's notion of transcendental frameworks which are to some extent *inescapable*. We have noted above that social imaginaries carry a transcendental aspect, in that they make possible certain social practices. However, as we learnt from the first chapter, these transcendental conditions of social practice are not to be understood in a Kantian fashion. It is not the case that human agency is framed by *universal* structures or categories, as Kant assumed. According to Taylor, we all make use of *some* framework or categories, because without categories, experience would be utterly impossible. We would be crushed by a multitude of stimuli, not knowing what to select or build on to gain further knowledge. That is why Kant postulated that we frame all incoming empirical data immediately within the a priori forms of space and time. Without these, we would be completely at loss in the field of perception.

But unlike Kant, Taylor argues that these transcendental frameworks, whatever their object may be (perception, moral agency), are to be considered as 'temporary best account' explanations why we experience what we experience. Transcendental frameworks are thus still shaping the conditions of possibility of 'something that exists': perception, or social practices. But they are fundamentally revisable, and hence historically contingent. We have learnt a lot about the historical reasons for this shift in thinking about transcendental arguments in the previous chapter, but I will now delve into Taylor's more analytical article about *The Validity of Transcendental Arguments* (Taylor 1995, 20–33) to see why Taylor still considers this mode of reasoning as valid in our days, and why this is so important with regard to social imaginaries.

In that article, Taylor articulates three distinctive features about transcendental arguments 'Kantian style.' First, they have an indubitable starting point in human experience. For example, for Kant, it was clear that all human beings have to agree that they have some experiences, so that experience exists. Another *Faktum* for Kant was that knowledge or science exist. In the context of Taylor's social imaginaries, we can agree that some forms of social practice simply exist.

The next question is: what makes these facts or these practices possible? The second feature of transcendental arguments is that they always ask for what Taylor calls indispensability claims. Transcendental arguments thus methodically scrutinize the limit conditions for the existence of a certain phenomenon. A sound method is to take the *via negativa:* under which conditions would the phenomenon considered (experience, social practice,…) cease to be what it is?

A third deterministic of transcendental arguments is that they claim to be apodictic, self-evident. The limit conditions or indispensability claims should be universally recognized as being self-evidently true, and prior to any experience in which they are involved (Taylor 1996, 27–28). Taylor logically concludes: "So transcendental arguments are chains of apodictic indispensability claims which concern experience and thus have an unchallengeable anchoring" (Taylor 1996, 28). Taylor continues with a set of questions: "But then what grounds the apodictic certainty or the self-evidence that these claims are supposed to enjoy? And if they are self-evident, why do we have to work so hard to demonstrate them? And why is there any argument afterwards, as there always seems to be?" (Taylor 1995, 28)

A first question is about the ground for apodicticity in transcendental arguments. Taylor illuminates this third feature of transcendental arguments by referring – somewhat circularly – to the second feature: apodictic claims are justified by looking at the indispensability claims they implicitly involve. To make this more concrete, Taylor gives the example of playing chess (Taylor 1995, 29–30). Suppose a child would accidentally move the tower three squares in a straight line, so that it does not make any mistake against the constitutive rules of chess. The child then asks: "Mummy, am I playing chess?" We immediately feel that the answer can only be negative. Playing chess does not just involve a random and accidental application of the constitutive rules of the game. The activity of playing chess involves some conscious knowledge of these rules. Only when the move with the tower is a conscious, intentional action, we would be able to say: "Yes, you are playing chess." So some knowledge or intentionality is presupposed in the activity of playing chess. (Which raises other philosophical questions as to whether computers can really *play* chess, but this would take us too far.) What we have gained now is a more full articulation of the limit conditions of what it is to play chess.

However, the example of playing chess is somewhat misleading. Playing chess is an activity we first have to acquire on a cognitive level, by very consciously memorizing the constitutive rules of the game. Engaging in experience or social practice is something we already do before gaining full articulation of the activity, as we explained in the previous section. But again, making a 'transcendental move' here involves reflection about the limit or indispensability conditions of the activity involved. The perceiver or social agent would be able to recognize failure of perception, or failure in carrying out, for example, rules of politeness. Social imaginaries can be regarded as being of this type: they involve shared practices. The question about their limit conditions often only arises in the case of conflict: when the practice stops to be what it is (as in the case of the brakes of the bike I described above), or when we meet other people challenging our social practice. In such cases, it is only by encountering a certain *contrast experience* that we start off thinking (imagining) about the 'transcendental conditions' of the practices we took for granted. This notion of contrast experiences is more deeply articulated in Chapter 4 by Christa Anbeek, Hans Alma and Saskia van Goelst Meijer.

To sum up, we may say that the touchstone for the indispensability and apodicticity of transcendental conclusions lies in the contrast with the limiting conditions or conditions of failure of the fact/practice under scrutiny. But Taylor's other questions about transcendental arguments remain open: "And if they are self-evident, why do we have to work so hard to demonstrate them? And why is there any argument afterwards, as there always seems to be?" (Taylor 1995, 28)

According to Taylor, the apodicticity of transcendental arguments relies on a correct formulation of the arguments. And this is a requirement which is hard to meet and causes continuous discussions. As Taylor states: "For although a correct formulation will be self-evidently valid, the question may arise whether we have formulated things correctly" (Taylor 1995, 32).

So Taylor eventually seems to consider transcendental arguments a more rich and creative description or formulation of things presupposed in our daily experienced, presuppositions of which we already had an implicit understanding or that were already applied in certain practices. In this respect, transcendental arguments are part of the so called hermeneutic circle. The human being articulates something more fundamental about what it is to be a human being. But he cannot do so from a distance. The ideal of disengaged reason is utterly impossible for sciences of man. This makes it particularly hard to arrive at some universally acceptable method which would generate true universals about human experience. Hence transcendental reasoning reaches its own 'limit conditions' by knocking at the door of ontology: is it still possible for transcendental reasoning to arrive at conclusions bearing some kind of ontological certainty? Taylor concludes in the style of Platonic *aporia:* "A valid transcendental argument is indubitable; yet it is hard to know when you have one, at least one with an interesting conclusion. But then that seems true of most arguments in philosophy" (Taylor 1995, 33).

For the purposes of this essay, one question remains open: why is Taylor's view on transcendental frameworks so important in our discussion of social imaginaries? To give the straightforward answer: the concept social imaginaries is Taylor's answer to critics judging Taylor's notion of transcendental framework too idealistic or too intellectual (Taylor 2004, 31–48). With the notion of social imaginaries, it becomes clear that we all engage in certain social practices, and that all people implicitly take some stance on the social map. Moreover, the task of articulating our transcendental presuppositions implied in our engaging in social practice is not limited to philosophers. Everyone may encounter a contrast experience that makes him or her ponder about the presuppositions of his or her moral and social engagements in life. This allows us to move from the collective level of social imaginaries, where specific group practices or practices of an entire nation or culture involve certain social imaginaries, to the level of individual persons and their strong evaluations.

4.3 Strong Evaluation

Why do moral agents act as they do? Why do certain moral actions seem to be natural and necessary to one person, whereas someone else may find these actions only optional or even unimportant to pursue? Taylor situates the origin of our moral choices in what he calls strong evaluations, which are inescapable for all human beings.

People tend to have various aspirations in their lives. Some aspirations are considered to be more important than others. Taylor considers certain aspirations as *qualitatively different* from others. We desire certain aspirations more strongly than others. These aspirations or objects of aspirations are then, in Taylor's language, strongly evaluated. Taylor is deeply indebted to Harry Frankfurt in his articulation of strong evaluation. Frankfurt used the concept of 'second-order desires' to denote the human capacity to order desires qualitatively and thus hierarchically, a capacity that distinguishes humans from animals. Taylor equally considers this capacity as a human universal (Abbey 2000, 18).

All this does not imply that every choice for a certain action is the result of strong evaluation. Whether I decide to wear a hat before I leave home in the morning, is inspired by certain practical needs – Is the weather cold or hot? Which people will I meet today? – rather than by moral principles. However, some choices in the sphere of daily routine may at some point become the object of strong evaluation, and become part of my moral identity. Whether I prefer to go to work by car or by train may initially depend on practical concerns: what is most easy to do, and what is fastest? But suppose I get convinced that the train is a more adequate means of transport from an ecological point of view. Then choosing the train would entail a moral principle, something I experience as intrinsically valuable or good. When asked about my moral motivation for taking the train, I will no doubt be able to refer to my ecological concerns as a moral principle.

This very articulation of my moral identity seems to presuppose that strong evaluation implies the willingness of individuals to reflect on their moral behavior, and the willingness to take this reflection as a ground for action. According to Abbey, Taylor does not want to push things that far.[4] We may be strong eval-

---

[4] Abbey 2000, 19. According to Abbey, Taylor's earlier writings are susceptible to the interpretation that strong evaluation presupposes rational reflection. This has provoked some criticism on Taylor's conception of morality as being too rationalist. If this were true, Taylor could not realize his own ambition, viz. to offer an account for moral experience, since it is hard to maintain that rational reflection on our values is a universal feature of the human condition (Abbey 2000, 19–20). In later writings, Taylor wants to avoid the pitfall of intellectualism by speaking of "a

uators on an intuitive and implicit level. Self-reflexivity nor articulation seem to be necessary (transcendental) conditions of strong evaluation. It is rather the other way around. Strong evaluation is a necessary condition of articulation: "The strong evaluator can articulate superiority just because he has a language of contrastive characterization. So within an experience of reflective choice between incommensurables, strong evaluation is a condition of articulacy, and to acquire a strongly evaluative language is to become (more) articulate about one's preferences." (Cited by Ruth Abbey in Abbey 2000, 20)[5]

Whether articulated on a reflexive level or remaining implicit, moral choices presuppose strong evaluations. But what then does inspire or scaffold our strong evaluations, implicitly or in a more articulate way? We have seen that strong evaluation involves the capacity to make qualitative discriminations. These discriminations are between different 'goods' or 'values' in our life. But what is the moral source for these discriminations? By articulating and justifying our moral sources, we delve deeper into the sources which motivate us to make that specific moral choice. We articulate our conception of the good. For Taylor, good is "designating anything considered valuable, worthy, admirable, of whatever kind of category" (Taylor 1989, 92). Taylor calls these goods *life goods*.[6] For example, you may think of the annual street party where all neighbors can meet as something valuable.

But what then is the source of these life goods? Taylor refers to a good which transcends all other goods by inspiring them, but also by constituting them: a hypergood or constitutive good. It is what we recognize, in the process of articulation, as the ultimate motivation for our moral conduct. For Plato, this was "the order of being, or perhaps the principle of that order, the Good" (Taylor 1989, 92–93). For Kant, this constitutive good was the moral law within us, to be discovered by the rational will. Taylor considers 'rational agency' as the 'constitutive good' of Kant's theory. (Taylor 1989, 94) According to Taylor, all such constitutive goods exercise an erotic power, comparable to the attraction of the idea of the Good in the philosophies of Socrates and Plato: "There is a sense in which knowing a constitutive good means loving, admiring or respect-

---

sense of a qualitative distinction: that is why I spoke above of acting within a framework as functioning with a 'sense' of a qualitative distinction. It can be only this; or it can be spelled out in a highly explicit way, in a philosophically formulated ontology or anthropology" (Taylor 1989, 21). The next chapter will deal with the issue of ontology.

5 See Charles Taylor 1976.

6 "I have been concentrating on qualitative distinctions between actions, or feelings, or modes of life. The goods which these define are facets or components of a good life. Let us call these 'life goods.'" (Taylor 1989, 93)

ing it. Because of this, one is moved by it and wants to move ever closer to it: loving the good and wanting to act in accordance with it are inextricably linked for Taylor." (Abbey 2000, 47)

It is clear that constitutive goods have a transcendental dimension: they are the conscious or hidden background of moral practice. Questions arise here as to the epistemological and ontological status of these constitutive goods. How can one get to know these goods, how can one be sure to have attained such a source in the process of articulation? And what is the ontological nature of these goods: are these goods objective, existing independently from our moral practice and our articulations of these practices, or are these goods themselves only constituted by our moral practice, hence depending on human will and creativity? In short, and applied to the functioning of constitutive goods in social imaginaries: does Taylor return to the ontological realism he was seeking to escape in congeniality with Castoriadis or does he really embrace human creativity and autonomy in social matters? We will come back to these questions about Taylor's ontology in the next chapter.

5 Cross Pressures

But one more thing needs to be said about constitutive goods. They are plural, and may thus cause dilemmas and conflict. Taylor often denounces moral projects of the modern moral order as being 'monomaniac.' They tend to neglect moral tragedy, caused by a plurality of human aspirations and constitutive goods, by reducing morality to a single cause or source (Taylor 2007, 52). Such would be the case for Kantianism and the human dignity of the rational agent as a single moral source, for utilitarianism and its 'greatest benefit for the greatest number of people,' and for hedonism in its reaching for pleasure and avoidance of pain.

As indicated above, we all live in what Taylor has called the 'age of authenticity.' Authenticity is indeed part of our imaginary when it comes down to questions of personhood and relations with significant others. Typical of authenticity is a certain fragility. What am I to be loyal to? The predicament of our days is that individual persons may experience various sources or constitutive goods as attractive. Which makes every source vulnerable and fragile when put in perspective with other sources. Why would I choose to live as a Christian, if the way of living as a Christian or an atheist can hardly be distinguished in everyday life? Christians and atheists own the same houses, wear the same clothes, take the same kind of jobs and raise their children in a similar fashion. Taylor has labelled this moral predicament of our days as that of the *cross pressured selves*, as different from *porous* and *buffered selves* (Taylor 2007, 38, 594–617).

The era of porous selves basically refers to the pre-modern era of mankind. Gods, spirits, half gods, men, animals and other creatures: all shared the same world or cosmos in a meaningful order, without strict boundaries between persons and their surroundings. A falling tree or lightning may be the work of a god. I may be the vehicle of certain divine spirits. This is the era in which one cannot speak yet of persons or selves. On the plane of social and moral order, distinctions between good and evil are equally opaque. But the meaningfulness of the order one lives in is never questioned as such, and all human aspirations and forces of nature take part in this meaningful unity.

The (anachronistic) concept of the porous self makes way for the buffered self in the evolution of culture to modernity. The project of Cartesian philosophy was to find an indubitable certainty within the self, before gaining knowledge about God or the world, and before engaging in them. Due to some challenges arising in Christian nominalist theology, on which I have written elsewhere,[7] the self has to buffer against both a capricious God with absolute power, and a whimsical nature which threatens the existence of the self. God is beyond human knowledge, but at least we can try to keep at bay the forces of nature. Hence the enormous success of science and technology, arising from some disengaged stance of neutral observation of nature, meant to increase our grip on the latter – the famous endeavour of man to become *maître et possesseur du monde*.

But this model of a disengaged, buffered stance to the world fails when applied to morals. As indicated above, our moral sources are plural, and cannot be reduced to one single aspiration, however hard some philosophers have tried to justify such reductionism. So we end up with a combination of two elements. On the one hand, human subjectivity is left on its own, finding no longer solace in a God whose creation (cosmic order) provides a solid and reliable access to divine will and reason. Any pre-given order or meaningfulness seems to be lost. On the other hand, moral life continues to be full of tragedy, conflict, multiple aspirations and interests that cannot be reduced or ordered by one moral principle. This is what Taylor calls the cross pressured self. We feel the attractiveness of different moral sources, which renders the endeavour to articulate our own moral sources fragile in a structural and ultimate way, since no pre-given framework containing a moral order is at hand.

---

[7] See again Cloots, Latré and Vanheeswijck 2013. See also Latré and Vanheeswijck eds. 2012.

Within this 'supernova' of life views and moral sources, Taylor discerns three basic positions.[8] One is the fruit of the optimistic embracing of modernity's epistemological turn to human subjectivity. Reducing pain and suffering, making this world a better place to live in are the basic themes of what Taylor calls humanism. It contains philosophies such as liberalism and socialism that strive for human freedom and equality for all people.

These Enlightenment ideals – one immediately thinks of the French revolution – were challenged by counter-Enlightenment philosophies, as we have seen in the previous chapter. Romantic strands in philosophy purported to reconnect the buffered self to nature, to close the ontological abyss between them. One of these strands took the road of showing how human nature is itself part of natural forces, including violence and suffering. The philosophy of Nietzsche is one such example which continues up to our days in what Taylor calls anti-humanism. The main objection to humanism is that it reduces differences between people to such an extent that all human creativity and aspiration to 'something higher' is stifled. Granting freedom to everyone on a basis of equality will in the long run end in the nihilism of the 'last man,' who no longer has any ideals to strive for, to sacrifice oneself for and thus loses all creative power. Taylor refers to these allegations coming from Romanticism and its specific Nietzschean mode as the "anti-levelling objection" (Taylor 1989, 355 – 367): if all are to be free and equal, there are no longer good and evil people, people we scorn or admire, ideals to pursue in our endeavour 'to become a gentleman.' A similar objection can be made at the level of culture. When social imaginaries of different cultures meet, one reaction could be to place all cultures on the same footing. 'Equal respect for all cultures' is a good point to start with, but the peril of some type of multiculturalism is that this starting point is also a kind of terminus. Some leftist forms of multiculturalism thus slide back in the very difference-blindness they wanted to avoid. Taylor made this point convincingly in his celebrated essay *The Politics of Recognition* (Taylor 1994). Instead of just keeping with the starting point of equal respect for all, Taylor suggest we engage in a real, substantive dialogue about what is to be praised and what ought to be rejected in the cultures involved in the dialogue. A real, substantial process of recognition which goes beyond the (necessary) attribution of certain rights always runs the risk of rejection, of a total or partial abdication or non-recognition. Value judgements cannot be excluded from a dialogue that is sensitive to cultural differences.

---

8 Taylor first articulated these positions in *A Catholic Modernity?*, an essay republished *in Dilemmas and Connections* (2011). He developed these positions more fully in *A Secular Age* (2007).

The anti-levelling objection can also be expected from religious perspectives that allow for some form of transcendence – which is denied in humanism and anti-humanism alike. The moral implications of embracing a transcendent perspective on human life are various, and revolves around the issue of 'fullness' or 'the good life.' A transcendent perspective poses the question of the possibility of an ultimate reconciliation or salvation which goes beyond – transcends – all human categories. Something of these transcendent aspirations gleans when we talk about justice and peace, for example. It is very hard to find a consensus about what humans may meaningfully say about ultimate justice or peace,[9] though many people would immediately embrace these as important goals to strive for, not just individually, but universally, as worthy to pursue for all of humanity. Believers in transcendence hope that such ultimate peace and justice exists, but expect it to come from some transcendent reality, since human categories or endeavours always seem to fall short of these ideals.

What we have here is a three-cornered debate between humanism, anti-humanism and transcendent perspectives where everyone can side with a partner against a third party, thus causing cross pressures between all parties. Anti-humanism and humanism are allies in rejecting transcendence. Transcendent perspectives on life side with the anti-humanist approach in the anti-levelling objection: there is more in life to aspire after than just reducing pain and suffering. And some perspectives on transcendence (e.g. Christianity) and humanism may join hands in trying to make this place a better place to live in, in embracing an optimistic view of human capacities, though they diverge on the ultimate issue about ontological transcendence.

Which perspective or social imaginary is the most promising? Despite the multitude of positions and the fragility of all sources of meaning ensuing from this plurality, Taylor does not give up hope for some integrative imaginary of fullness. I will come back to this issue of integrative fullness in my last section, where I deal with the social imaginary Taylor called the immanent frame.

6 The Immanent Frame Revisited

I set off by describing our age, in the words of Taylor, as an immanent frame, which is the social imaginary that 'holds us captive' in our days. I then offered a conceptual clarification about social imaginaries, departing from Castoriadis,

---

[9] See in this respect Taylor's discussion with Martha Nussbaum on horizontal and vertical transcendence in *A Secular Age*. (Taylor 2007, 625–629).

continuing with Taylor's articulations, and connecting these with other key concepts in Taylor's philosophy. We found that the three most conspicuous features of social imaginaries, viz. their dimensions of transcendentalism, normativity and inarticulacy, are closely linked to Taylor's concepts of transcendental frameworks, strong evaluation, moral sources and expressivist culture.

We now return to this expressivist culture, which seems increasingly to express its self-identity with reference to the immanent frame. As we have seen above, expressivist culture leans on the notion of authenticity, which does not preclude references to sources of meaning beyond the self. In the quest for meaning, the self may refer just to itself or humanity, as is the case for Kantian style affirmations of human dignity and human rights. Or we may see nature as a moral source with intrinsic value. Another stance one may adopt is that of utter meaninglessness, whether in some form of Nietzschean nihilism or in a blunt form of material reductionism. Within this spectrum, multiple variations are possible. For example, one can emphasize human dignity and secular reason, but at the same time grant liberties to religions which articulate in their traditions universal intuitions of the good still waiting for 'translation' into a secular language. The German philosopher Jürgen Habermas (Habermas 2005) is a representative of this position.

Habermas's position is what Taylor calls an 'open spin' on transcendence (Taylor 2007, 549–550). Taylor and Habermas affirm that we live (in the West) in a secular age, an immanent frame. But neither of them is prepared to affirm that the age of transcendence is permanently gone. Of course Taylor goes one step further in his adoption of transcendence than Habermas, as we will shortly see in our discussion of the difference between 'aspiration to fullness' and 'hunger for meaning.' Nonetheless one can see Habermas's recent position towards religion as an open spin. By contrast, a philosophical position such as materialism can be called a 'closed spin.' Matter as a physical reality is just all there is. It is just a matter of time before science can reveal the final truths about the cosmos and unmask all our religious, metaphysical and moral beliefs as illusions. This is what Taylor has called a 'subtraction story.' Take away or subtract all beliefs of the kind just mentioned, and you end up with the only truth remaining: that of materialism, of laws of nature to be studied by science.

It may seem as if we are discussing highly sophisticated intellectual and philosophical constructions here. But for all complexity involved, we are still dealing with social imaginaries. Take the example of naturalism just mentioned. The urge for scientific justifications is omnipresent in our world. Marketing directors are eager to label their product with the seal scientifically proved. And since our body and its experiences is all there is, we are tirelessly reminded of tips and tricks to keep it sane or to keep this or that organ in ultimate shape, by working out in the gym, eating the right food in the right proportions, and the like. Even if we are attracted to the view that there is something more than just sensory experience, we will not be immune to the messages of temporary consumerist society, based on the assumptions of science.

So it seems that we are stuck in the immanent frame with open and closed spins on transcendence. The closed spins even deny the reasonableness of any articulation of transcendence. But this closed world structure, as Taylor called it in an article published previously to *A Secular Age*, is not just the prerogative of unbelievers. Some strands embrace transcendence, but are closed in the sense that they assert to have found the perpetual truth about man, God and world, or that they scorn the world and every form of natural human experience and desire as low and base. The papacy of Benedict XVI tended to go in that direction, since Benedict repeatedly affirmed the eternal truth of the Church's dogmas over against the vices of the modern world, including relativism on an epistemological level and permissiveness in moral affairs. So the transcendent can eventually be as closed to the immanent as the immanent to the transcendent.

This possibility of exclusiveness is somewhat surprising from the perspective of both conceptual and cultural analysis. As we mentioned at the outset of this article, the concept of immanence makes no sense without the concept of the transcendent, and vice versa. Once transcendence is denied, it would be logical to equally dismiss of immanence as an old-fashioned, culturally shaped concept, and to invent something new. One might even wonder whether the immanent frame is an adequate concept for the purposes Taylor wants to use it for, since (conceptual) reference to transcendence seems to be equally inescapable as the immanent frame itself. The immanent frame defines itself as 'no longer bearing reference to transcendence,' which amounts to a logical paradox.

More importantly, if we look at the evolution of culture, it simply makes no sense to defend any form of the subtraction stories mentioned above. Science does not simply substitute for the illusions of religion, because science could only come about through the intermediary stages in the evolution of religion. It would take us too far to explore this thesis in full depth, so I will do with a sketchy account here. One could say that the longest period of human history held an almost closed spin on transcendence. It is the period of what Gauchet and others have called 'primitive' or 'primeval' religion. It ranges from the dawn of mankind to approximately 3000 BC or the Egyptian empires with the emergence of the State.[10] Within that long period of time of so called mythic cul-

---

10 For a more lengthy discussion, see *The Axial Age and the Dynamics of Transcendence*, Latré 2014.

tures, groups of hunter-gatherers were primarily concerned with repeating their rituals and continuing the world as it was delivered to them by their ancestors and ancestral gods. This period of time corresponds structurally to what Taylor has called the era of the porous selves, where there are no clear boundaries between nature, man and gods. In a way, this was also an immanent frame – leaving conceptual difficulties in using this term aside – in that gods and semi-gods inhabited our world just like all other 'creatures.' The only reference to transcendence in the mythic stories is about a past immemorial, a 'time out of mind' in which the gods established the rules of the world as they are now. So the only type of transcendence we find in primitive religion is a dim sort of temporal transcendence, not yet enshrined in a dualistic conception of reality.[11]

Subsequently, and for reasons too extensive to develop here, western 'axial' culture started to develop the notion of transcendence. Divine omnipresence in nature, in the sensory world gave way to a form of subjective transcendence: all divinity became concentrated in one super-subject, transcending nature and man as the Creator. This dualistic view of the world is present in Greek philosophy, but also in monotheistic religion. Only when we can think of the world as containing two layers: the invisible and the visible, the transcendent and the immanent, we may conceive of the gods as ultimately *one*, and locate the divine *outside* this world as absolute subjectivity. To make a long story short: science needed a religion disenchanting itself by its articulation of transcendence in order to become possible. That is what Gauchet means by depicting Christianity as "the religion for the departure from religion" (Gauchet 1997, 101–106).

But the full articulation of transcendence brings along an increasing engagement in the world as its mimetic twin. Since God stands now over against man and nature on a different ontological level, since the world is now devoid of gods, it is also open to human curiosity and scrutiny. A thesis of this kind has been advanced by Hans Blumenberg in his *Legitimacy of the Modern Age* (Blumenberg 1983). Our own human subjective capacities are the only reliable sources to deal with our nakedness in the face of indifferent nature. The result is modern science as we know it today, including its tendencies to eclipse any world view containing a form of transcendence. So we end up with an immanent frame that may again be closed to transcendence. But unlike the immanent frame of primeval religion, the gods are now nowhere, instead of everywhere. The world is now disenchanted. Western modern culture has pushed divine transcendence to such a level of absoluteness (e.g. in some strands of Protestantism

---

[11] For a more complete account, see again Latré 2014, 190–206.

and Deism) that we have lost sight of God altogether. This is what Taylor really means by the immanent frame of our days.

This accounts for the closed spin on transcendence in our days. But what about the open spin? Does it still make sense today when the social imaginary of the immanent frame holds us captive? Taylor believes it does, but to understand why, I will have to make one last conceptual distinction, between what he calls hunger for meaning as opposed to aspiration to fullness.

Taylor draws this distinction most clearly in the opening pages of Chapter 18 of *A Secular Age* (Taylor 2007, 676–680). Taylor considers our contemporary use of the expression quest for meaning as problematic insofar as it is hypostatized into a universal feature of human experience. According to Taylor, human beings do not seek for meaning as such. They always feel attracted to some concrete or specific meaningful tradition, narrative, person... People get moved or inspired by Socrates, Buddha, Jesus Christ, Mother Teresa and Nelson Mandela, to name just a few, but not by hunger for meaning as such. Not that our post-modern talk of individual quests for meaning is completely beside the point. It is a useful notion with great descriptive value. But it is also at best *one specific form* of a universal human feature.

This universal feature of human experience, as Taylor seems to suggest, is that we all have to define ourselves somewhere on the map when it comes to our *aspiration to fullness*. This term is more universal than hunger for meaning, because the supposed 'hunger' seems to presuppose that meaning is first experienced as completely absent, to be subsequently discovered or constructed to satisfy our hunger. But that interpretation precludes the possibility that meaning is already there, already given, mediated in manifold more or less traditional cultural forms and social imaginaries. In fact, during most of human history, meaning was experienced as embedded in some cosmic structure, and was never considered as lost or as something in need of (re)construction. The integrative framework of fullness was already pre-existent.

What Taylor means by this, comes to the fore in another of his interesting writings, namely in his *Varieties of Religion Today* (Taylor 2002). In this booklet written on the occasion of the centenary of William James's *Varieties of Religious Experience*, Taylor explains the difference between pre-modern and post-modern forms of melancholia. Of course melancholia is as old as humanity. But to describe the pre-modern form of melancholia as a total loss of meaning would be anachronistic. According to Taylor, meaning as such was never lost in pre-modern times. It might occur that a person went astray and lost its personal connection to the framework of meaning (Plato's ontology, the Christian tradition) predominant in society. Or the predominant framework could on a subjective level fail to deliver what it promised to, namely realizing some kind of integrative fullness. But in all of these cases, meaning was never lost. In a sense, one only had to reconnect to the framework to be on track again, and one could look for guidance by a priest or other shepherds of the given, meaningful order.

But post-modern individuals increasingly have to find their way without shepherds, as some versions of liberalism and its self-sufficient appraisal of autonomy have it. Meaning as such becomes an issue only when all imaginaries of fullness, religions, philosophies, stories, myths, inspiring persons... become ultimately fragile and unstable. This contemporary situation of fragility and 'cross pressures' explains why many post-modern individuals experience meaning as such as a problem in their lives, a form of melancholia which Taylor considers unprecedented in human history. Perhaps the issue of meaning can indeed only arise in the 'liquid modernity' and 'liquid times' Zygmunt Baumann described so adequately (Baumann 2000 and 2007). But all this does not suspend the human desire of integrative fullness, of some ultimate reconciliation among all tensions and moral dilemmas of our times.[12]

So what Taylor wants to suggest comes down to saying that all activities we consider as meaningful are part of a larger perspective on fullness, on what it means to lead a good life, integrating our awe and love for multiple constitutive goods and their mutual tensions. This brings us back to the issue of transcendence and immanence. It is clear that world views entailing some type of transcendence always articulate some view of ultimate human fullness, not only in the form of a supposedly transparent ideology, but foremost in tentative, suggestive, metaphorical language. It is also clear that in our immanent frame, this perspective on fullness could also come from some form of humanism, notwithstanding Taylor's criticism that humanism may in the end stifle human aspirations to transcend human categories altogether, as with the ultimate articulations of justice and peace. And as we have seen, Nietzschean anti- humanism also aspires to a richer and deeper humanity that fully embraces life and all its tragic dimensions, and in this sense provokes humanity to go beyond itself. So ultimately, what matters to Taylor is that an open spin on transcendence can be rephrased as openness for fullness, which is in its turn somewhat circularly understood as 'something going beyond human categories,' hence something transcendent. What we have here is a kind of Hegelian move towards an ultimate synthesis, where human aspirations and transcendence are no longer seen as opposites, but can be reconciled. But this integrative synthesis is in our days always fragile, which sets Taylor apart from Hegel. As we will see in the next chapter,

---

[12] Taylor delves into these dilemmas near the end *of A Secular Age* (2007), and further explores this theme in *Dilemmas and Connections* (2011).

Taylor is indeed very hesitant about the ontological commitment of his theory about morals and transcendence.

At the end of this chapter, I want to indicate two issues that will be further explored in the next chapters. We have seen that Taylor deems the ability to make qualitative discriminations to be part and parcel of our being strong evaluators. Strong evaluation involves the more or less articulated activity of weighing the power of various contrast experiences and their diverging constitutive goods. Contrast experiences of constitutive goods may also lay bare social imaginaries and constitutive goods that are religiously qualified. We are happy to refer to the chapter of Anbeek, Alma and Van Goelst Meijer for further exploration of this topic.

In the next chapter, Michiel Meijer and I will try to shed some light on the ontological nature of social imaginaries and their constitutive goods, an endeavour that bears no hope for arriving at full articulation or clarity, as we will shortly see.

Bibliography

Abbey, Ruth. 2000. *Charles Taylor.* Teddington, England: Acumen.
Anderson, Benedict. 1983. *Imagined Communities: Reflections on the Origin and Spread of Nationalism.* London: Verso.
Austin, John L. 1962. *How to do Things with Words: The William James Lectures delivered at Harvard University in 1955*, edited by J.O. Urmson and Marina Sbisà. Oxford: Clarendon Press.
Baumann, Zygmunt. 2000. *Liquid Modernity.* Cambridge: Polity.
Baumann, Zygmunt. 2007: *Consuming Life.* Cambridge: Polity.
Blumenberg Hans. 1983. *The Legitimacy of the Modern Age.* Cambridge, MA: MIT Press.
Castoriadis, Cornelius. 1987. *The Imaginary Institution of Society* (translation Kathleen Blamey). Cambridge, MA: MIT Press.
Cloots, André, Stijn Latré and Guido Vanheeswijck. 2013. "The Future of the Christian Past: Marcel Gauchet and Charles Taylor on the Essence of Religion and its Evolution." *The Heythrop Journal: A Quarterly Review of Philosophy and Theology* 56: 958–974.
Gaonkar, Dilip Parameshwar. 2002. "Toward New Imaginaries: An Introduction." *Public Culture* 14: 1–19.
Gauchet, Marcel. 1997. *The Disenchantment of the World: A Political History of Religion.* (translation Oscar Burge). Princeton, NJ: Princeton University Press.
Gauchet, Marcel. 2003. *La Condition Historique: Entretiens avec François Azouvi et Sylvain Piron.* Paris: Stock.
Gauchet, Marcel. 2007. *L'Avènement de la démocratie*, t. 1, *La Révolution moderne.* Paris: Gallimard.
Gauchet, Marcel. 2010, *L'Avènement de la démocratie*, t. 3, *A l'épreuve des totalitarismes, 1914–1974.* Paris: Gallimard.

Habermas, Jürgen. 1989. *The Structural Transformation of the Public Sphere* (translation T. Burger and F. Lawrence). Cambridge, MA: MIT Press.
Habermas, Jürgen. 2005. *Zwischen Naturalismus und Religion: Philosophische Aufsätze.* Frankfurt am Main: Suhrkamp.
Heidegger, Martin. 1926[1], 1993[17]. *Sein und Zeit.* Tübingen: Max Niemeyer Verlag.
Latré, Stijn, and Guido Vanheeswijck, eds. 2012. *Radicale secularisatie? Tien hedendaagse denkers over religie en moderniteit.* Kapellen/Kampen: Pelckmans/Klement.
Latré, Stijn, and Guido Vanheeswijck. 2014. "The Axial Age and the Dynamics of Transcendence" in *Radical Secularization?* edited by Stijn Latré, Walter Van Herck and Guido Vanheeswijck. New York: Bloomsbury, 190–206.
Löwith, Karl. 1949. *Meaning in History: The Theological Implications of the Philosophy of History.* Chicago, Ill: University of Chicago Press.
Taylor, Charles. 1976. "Responsibility for Self." In *The Identities of Persons*, edited by Amelie Oksenberg Rorty, 281–299. Berkeley: University of California Press.
Taylor, Charles. 1989. *Sources of the Self. The making of the Modern Identity.* Cambridge: Cambridge University Press.
Taylor, Charles. 1992. *Ethics of Authenticity.* Cambridge, MA: Harvard University Press.
Taylor, Charles. 1994. "The Politics of Recognition" in *Multiculturalism: Examining the Politics of Recognition*, edited by Amy Gutmann. Princeton, NJ: Princeton University Press.
Taylor, Charles. 1995. *Philosophical Arguments.* Cambridge, MA: Harvard University Press.
Taylor, Charles. 2002. *Varieties of Religion Today: William James Revisited.* Cambridge, MA: Harvard University Press.
Taylor, Charles. 2004. *Modern Social Imaginaries.* Durham/London: Duke University Press.
Taylor, Charles. 2007. *A Secular Age.* Cambridge, MA: Belknap Press of Harvard Universiy Press.
Taylor, Charles. 2011. *Dilemmas and Connections: Selected Essays.* Cambridge, MA: Belknap Press of Harvard University Press.

Stijn Latré and Michiel Meijer
Retrieving Realism in Social Imaginaries

1 Introduction

We have seen in the previous chapter that social imaginaries are, in Taylor's view, knit closely together with implicit moral and spiritual orientations. These implicit orientations are constitutive of our strong evaluations and come to the fore through articulation. But once, as strong evaluators, we get hold of the constitutive goods of these evaluations, difficulties arise concerning their (ontological) nature. Why is it so that we experience these constitutive goods as commanding our awe and respect? Is there any objective ground for our constitutive goods, or are they the result of our subjective projection of value on our actions and onto the world? As Taylor puts it:

> I want to speak of strong evaluation when the goods putatively identified are not seen as constituted as good by the fact that we desire them, but rather are seen as normative for desire. That is, they are seen as goods which we ought to desire, even if we do not, goods such that we show ourselves up as inferior or bad by our not desiring them. (Taylor 1985, 120)

This excerpt exhibits to a large degree the same structure as the argument from Plato's *Euthyphro*. In this dialogue between Socrates and Euthyphro, the argument goes around the central question: are customs and laws of piety good because the gods desire them, or do the gods desire them because they are good? Analogous to this question, Taylor raises the issue of the ontological nature of constitutive goods: are they good because we desire them, or do we desire them because they are intrinsically, that is, objectively good?

Plato's dialogue ends up in an *aporia*: the issue remains undecided, though the argument tends, of course, in the direction of an objective ground for piety, in line with Plato's realist position concerning the world of Ideas. The excerpt above seems to suggest that Taylor also tends towards a realistic solution of the objectivity-subjectivity dilemma. With regard to constitutive goods, our desire of them is secondary to the intrinsic goodness of these goods.

But to make things clear right away, Taylor does not advocate realism in the Platonic style. Instead he defends what he and Hubert Dreyfus have recently called "pluralistic robust realism" (Dreyfus and Taylor 2015, 131–168). Robust plural realism can be interpreted as holding the middle between a naive and supposedly natural form of realism, on the one hand, and different strands of relativism and projectivism, on the other. In order to elucidate this position, we need to take a closer look at how Taylor distinguishes scientific reality from moral reality. Instead of simply arguing about whether the distinction between 'objective' empirical facts and 'subjective' moral values is valid or not, he tries to draw attention to the fact that the actual opposition lies between the perspectives of science and ethics.

We elaborate on this in the next section (2), in which we analyze Taylor's remarks on the difference between scientific and moral objectivity. Since moral experience, according to Taylor, entails both subjectivity and objectivity, we then proceed with a section (3) on how this dichotomy showcases itself in the tension between ontology and phenomenology throughout Taylor's work. In the next section (4), we see how this tension is received in the secondary literature, and we confront Taylor with some methodological problems. Although the notion of *social imaginaries* is never far away in any of these sections, we make the connection between moral experience and social imaginaries more explicit in our last section (5).

2 Scientific and Moral Objectivity

A good starting point for analyzing Taylor's realism is his distinction between scientific and moral objectivity, as it comes to the fore in this quotation from *Sources of the Self*:

> It is widely thought that no constitutive good could have such a fragile ontological foundation as this, a niche simply in our best self-interpretation. Unless it is grounded in the nature of the universe itself, beyond the human sphere, or in the commands of God, how can it bind us? But there is no a priori truth here. Our belief in it is fed by the notion that there is nothing between an extra-human ontic foundation for the good, on the one hand, and the pure subjectivism of arbitrarily conferred significance, on the other. But there is a third possibility, the one I have just outlined, of a good which is inseparable from our best self-interpretation. (1989, 342)

The fragility Taylor speaks of in the first line refers to "ordinary fulfillments of human beings" (1989, 341), which have significance and even make "a universal demand such that, for instance, I may be called upon to work for a future world in which these fulfillments will be maximized" (1989, 341). Our constitutive goods are always fragile, because they figure in our "best self-interpretation." As a result of this, they are subjective: there is always the possibility that in the process of our self-interpretation as moral agents, we will discover moral sources that bind and commit us more deeply than the sources we were previously attached to, and unmask the latter as illusions. But in spite of their fragility, constitutive goods still have an *ontological* foundation, in that they appear *to us* as *objectively binding*. This is not just the case at the level of individuals: these constitutive goods also lie at the base of what scaffolds our social imaginaries, as we have seen in the previous chapter.

So for Taylor the hermeneutics of moral self-interpretation through strong evaluation lay bare constitutive goods that entail both a subjective and an objective dimension. The crux of the argument is how we should understand the relation between these two dimensions. We will dwell further on this in the next section. But before deepening the *relation* between 'subjectivity' and 'objectivity' with regard to morality, or 'phenomenology' and 'ontology' throughout Taylor's work, we must first explore what these terms mean for Taylor, in the context of human moral experience.

What is the nature of moral concepts? How do elements of subjectivity and objectivity play a part in our use of moral concepts? In *Ethics and the Limits of Philosophy* Bernard Williams (1985, 132–155) argues that we all use 'thick' moral concepts such as cowardliness, gratitude, generosity, and – why not – piety. These concepts are called thick because they say something substantial about the world we experience. The use of these concepts is informed by some form of perception of qualities in the world. We must perceive certain actions and a certain situation in the world as corresponding to, for example, cowardliness. In other words, some feature of reality justifies our use of that concept. We cannot arbitrarily project thick moral concepts on any situation in the world. This means that thick moral concepts are to some degree world-guided. But they are also action-guiding: when I call someone a coward, I distance myself from their actions, and will perhaps avoid contact with that person in the future, or else try to convince them to change their behavior. Thick moral concepts therefore involve both a descriptive and a prescriptive element. Moreover, these two dimensions cannot be torn apart. I cannot meaningfully say: "Cowardliness is bad. I regret that." Using certain thick moral concepts implies that one is familiar with both their descriptive and their evaluative components.

Now, Taylor follows Williams in his analysis of so-called thick moral concepts, but their ways seem to part when it comes to thin moral concepts. We now move to the more abstract level of meta-ethics. According to Williams, thin moral concepts such as good or just evidently cannot be linked to a situation in the world. They lose their world-guidedness or convergence with some state of affairs in the world. This makes meta-ethics different from science, and from scientific objectivity. In science, one can have recourse to meta-theories that can explain and justify why a certain scientific theory no longer holds. For example, perceptions about sunrise and sunset can be replaced by a Copernican theory of our planetary constellation. This new theory can also explain why former assumptions have now been proven to be false. According to Williams, there is no hope of ever achieving something similar for meta-ethics. Hence, meta-ethics rests on loose ontological foundations. Meta-ethics introduces a language game that has no direct sources in reality. As human beings, we determine by convention what we call good or just. We can learn what goodness or justice consists of only by entering the moral language game of a certain culture.

Taylor is not willing to make such a conclusion, however. With meta-ethics, we are at the level of what he calls 'constitutive goods' and 'moral sources.' These are not thin, abstract entities that we can define at our own will, subjectively or intersubjectively, in convention and deliberation with others. As we have seen, constitutive goods do not abandon some form of objectivity or ontological foundation, however fragile that foundation may be. Rather, our strong evaluations are 'strong' because they involve what we are most strongly committed to, because they appear to us as objectively binding. We admire certain constitutive goods for what they are, and do not value them because we desire them. Constitutive goods are seen by Taylor as 'normative for desire.'

As has become clear from the quotation above, Taylor wants to avoid two extreme positions of reductionism when it comes to the explanation and justification of morality: reductions to ontology in a naturalist guise on the one hand,[1] and reductions to different forms of projectivism on the other hand.[2] Naturalism has become increasingly popular in recent decades, a naturalist ontology reducing all human activity to biology. We use moral concepts, articulate strong desires and admire constitutive goods because we are biologically programmed to find the best strategy to cope with our surroundings.

Projectivism does not reduce moral experience to the objectivity of nature, but to the subjectivity of human language. We project moral categories onto the world, either voluntarily or involuntarily. "Involuntary" projectivism (1989, 54) is in fact some form of naturalist reduction: we cannot help projecting values onto the world, since it is in our human nature to do so; however, upon closer scrutiny we must recognize that our projections do not react to ontological features in the world, but are merely subjective projections. This line of argument has prompted some philosophers, such as Simon Blackburn, to articulate their projectivist position as quasi-realism: moral concepts remain so important

---

[1] In *Retrieving Realism* (2015, 160) Dreyfus and Taylor further distinguish between reductive and scientific realism. Reductive realism holds that the sciences can explain all modes of being, whereas scientific realism claims that all users of "natural kinds" terms must use these terms in correspondence with the scientific use of the terms.

[2] Here Dreyfus and Taylor (2015, 160) mention Rorty's "deflationary realism."

that, for their proper functioning, we should continue to believe in their objectivity, even though, upon theoretical reflection, we must admit that they rest only on subjective projections.

Taylor reacts to these arguments with his *ad hominem* argument. The sceptic and relativist arguments we see deployed in projectivism do not match human experience. According to Taylor, we are in need of a phenomenology of human moral experience. What is involved in this particular type of phenomenology is explained in the paper *Explanation and Practical Reason* (1995a). In this paper, Taylor seeks to undermine the naturalist conception of morality as a human projection on a neutral world by defending our commonsense moral reactions. In so doing, he refers to John McDowell, Alasdair MacIntyre, and Bernard Williams as his most important allies:

> The opposition to this naturalist reduction has come from a philosophical stance that might in a broad sense be called 'phenomenological.' By this I mean a focus on our actual practices of moral deliberation, debate, understanding. The attempt is to show, in one way or another, that the vocabularies we need to explain human thought, action, feeling, or to explicate, analyze, justify ourselves or each other, or to deliberate on what to do, all inescapably rely on strong evaluation. (...) It tries to show us that in all lucidity we cannot understand ourselves, or each other, cannot make sense of our lives or determine what to do, without accepting a richer ontology than naturalism allows, without thinking in terms of strong evaluation. (1995a, 38–39)[3]

He calls the appeal to our actual moral experience the "ad hominem mode of practical reasoning," a logic that in Taylor's view is "central to the whole enterprise of moral clarification" (1995a, 37). However, as he continues, it is precisely the inclination of "the naturalist temper, with its hostility to the very notion of strong evaluation (...) to make the ad hominem argument seem irrelevant to ethical dispute" (1995a, 59). Here we see Taylor expressing his most central concern from yet another angle: While most people remain quite unattracted by the naturalist attempt to invalidate basic moral responses – because on the contrary their moral reactions strike them as being right in a fundamental way – they can anxiously doubt whether, say, a strong sense of disgust at killing innocent people can really be justified. The naturalist, then, typically encourages the idea that this is a reasonable kind of doubt indeed; they do so by arguing that simply showing that we in fact experience a deep commitment to certain moral goals proves nothing about what we ought to do. To put it in classical philosophical terms, to invoke our moral experience when deciding issues of practi-

---

[3] The reference to McDowell, MacIntyre, and Williams is in note 7 of Taylor's text, after his assertion "that this case has been convincingly made out, in a host of places" (1995a, 39).

cal reason is to commit the notorious naturalistic fallacy, falsely deriving an 'ought' from an 'is.'

In Taylor's view, however, this charge is flawed, because it is based on a crucial misunderstanding of the nature of moral goals. This brings us to Taylor's Kantian image of morality, which states that something is not a moral goal simply by virtue of the fact that we are *de facto* committed to it, but because it lays claim to us and calls for our commitment. Obviously, the fact that I have a strong desire – for example, for vanilla ice cream – does nothing by itself to show that I ought to desire it. But in Taylor's view, this is-ought objection is simply beside the point, as it affects only our weakly evaluated goals, not those we recognize as moral. As we have seen in the previous chapter in the section about strong evaluation, the crucial point of Taylor's understanding of morality is the fact that we experience some of our desires and goals as more significant than other goals and desires. It is these goods that really matter to us as agents, that is, they determine the degree of fulfillment in our lives. Because of this, I identify myself by these strong commitments in such a fundamental way – and this is the main thrust of the argument – that I cannot really reject them in the full sense. If, for some strange reason, I suddenly stopped caring about people drowning (or being murdered, or tortured, or raped) I cannot simply shrug my shoulders and say that I do not 'feel like' drowning victims today. To do so would seem to us both awfully strange and terribly frightening.

In contrast, I do not think of my desire for vanilla ice cream in these terms. If, for example, I feel more like strawberry ice cream today, yesterday's preference for vanilla ice cream simply would no longer have a claim on me. In the case of strong evaluations, however, the fact that I identify with a diversity of strongly valued goods does nothing to reduce their respective claims. As Taylor puts it: "While some goals would have no more claim on us if we ceased desiring them, such as my present aim to have a strawberry ice cream cone after lunch, a strongly evaluated goal is one such that, were we to cease desiring it, *we* would be shown up as insensitive or brutish or morally perverse" (1995a, 37).

This gives us an anchor for practical reason without committing the naturalistic fallacy, Taylor believes, because "in the second case, we would have demonstrated that we can't be lucid about ourselves without acknowledging that we value this end" (1995a, 37). In other words, in the case of strongly valued goals my deep commitments indeed show that I ought to desire these goods, because without them, I would lose the very possibility of being an agent in the full sense. We would see this as pathological. It comes as no surprise, however, that all this cannot be made intelligible from a naturalist perspective that takes only our weaker, *de facto* desires as the ultimate in justification of our actions.

Taylor calls "the imagined agent of naturalist theory (...) a monster" (1989, 32). He therefore counters the objection of the naturalistic fallacy by convincing us that the charge can be made only on a highly distorted picture of a human being, one which insists that human agents cannot be motivated by anything stronger than mere impulse. In the light of Taylor's rivaling portrait of a strong evaluator, however, it is not a fallacious but an essential feature of humans that they are able to derive 'oughts' from their experience as moral agents. On this picture, a life that lacks the strong evaluations by which we give sense to and live our lives will be lacking in humanness. Analogous to personal life, social imaginaries without implicit or explicit strong evaluations could not bear any real significance for our lives. In this respect, social imaginaries need to be real in order to become meaningful, and not vice versa. What really matters and is to some degree objective or universal, determines what is meaningful to us as human beings.

But does this argument really escape a circular structure? Is the objectivity of morality for Taylor not located in human experience, and therefore in subjectivity? The question about the ontological nature of the objective foundation for morality remains open. Does the objectivity lie in some external reality that is independent of human subjectivity, or can the ontological objectivity of moral experience be located only within the (universal) structures of human subjectivity? Part of the answer lies in the following quotation:

> It seems to me that the various theories of moral judgements as projections, and the attempts to distinguish 'value' from 'fact,' fall afoul of this BA [best account] principle. In fact we find ourselves inescapably using terms whose logic cannot be understood in terms of this kind of radical distinction. If we live our lives like this, what other considerations can overrule this verdict?
>
> Of course, the terms of our best account will never figure in a physical theory of the universe. But that just means that our human reality cannot be understood in the terms appropriate for this physics. This is the complement to the anti-Aristotelian purge of natural science in the seventeenth century. Just as physical science is no longer anthropocentric, so human science can no longer be couched in the terms of physics. Our value terms purport to give us insight into what it is to live in the universe as a human being, and this is a quite different matter from that which physical science claims to reveal and explain. This reality is, of course, dependent on us, in the sense that a condition for its existence is our existence. But once granted that we exist, it is no more a subjective projection than what physics deals with. (Taylor 1989, 58–59)

In other words, since science and ethics are radically different approaches to reality, they must be looked at in their own right, as they analyze, clarify, and evaluate human life in their own separate ways. Furthermore, this means that although the distinction between facts and values is crucial to the scientific enterprise, it simply does not hold in the realm of ethics, because our moral concerns can neither be understood as neither 'crude' instinctive reactions nor as 'sophisticated' involuntary projections or mere historically contingent conventions. However, as we will see in the following sections, this conclusion has important implications for moral theory. In fact, what emerges from Taylor's rejection of externalist conceptions of morality and the fact-value dichotomy that underpins naturalist and projectivist approaches, is that we are in need of a wholly different approach to ethics, an approach that avoids 'naturalist' and 'subjectivist' reductions of ethics alike. After having analyzed a few excerpts from *Sources of the Self*, we now turn to the development of Taylor's thought in his entire oeuvre. The tension between ontology and phenomenology is present throughout his work. Our analysis of this tension will shed new light on the issue of the foundation of morality and social imaginaries.

3 Taylor Between Ontology and Phenomenology

3.1 Exploratory Remarks

Throughout his different writings, Taylor touches on the issue of what we are committed to ontologically by our ethical views and commitments, but there is always something tentative in his adherence. The problem of how ethics and ontology are related is evoked in all the key publications on strong evaluation and constitutive goods (*Philosophical Papers*, *Sources of the Self*, *Philosophical Arguments*) and are called to mind once more in *A Secular Age*; but it is not explored extensively in any of these works.

On the one hand, it therefore seems clear that Taylor views this question as a valuable one. On the other, he never fails to insist that it is not all that clear how we should go about answering it. Ironically, even at the very end of *Ethics and Ontology* (2003) – the paper in which he puts forward the connection between ethics and ontology as a central theme – Taylor is still becoming more aware of his own uncertainties, of how far he is from finding a proper formulation of the issue.[4] The same issue is raised in *A Secular Age*, in which Taylor asserts

---

4 "Here, on the brink of the really interesting question, I have to break off, partly through lack of time; and partly because the conceptual means at my disposal are still too crude to explore this in an illuminating fashion. I hope to return to this at another time." (2003, 320)

that one of the greatest challenges for ethics is "the issue of how to align our best phenomenology with an adequate ontology" (2007, 609).[5]

While the tension between subjectivist claims – of personal commitments, individual preferences, and the diversity of values – and claims of objectivity – of morality, impartiality, and the imperative nature of values – is really put to work only in these late,[6] highly tentative writings, it is implicit in Taylor's oeuvre as a whole. Most notably, the two components are already present in the very structure of *Sources of the Self*: the first part makes the case for the objective features of selfhood and morality, whereas the rest of the book addresses the historically specific connections between senses of the self and moral visions (cf. 1989, x). In other words, the nature of morality, as Taylor envisages it, requires a double approach: both subjective and objective. While his historical reconstruction of the modern moral identity maps the subjective or contingent commitments of modern moral life, the objective dimension of the good turns on something different, and therefore necessitates an ontological, non-anthropocentric approach.

Although Taylor's central aim is "to resolve the opposition itself by arguing that subjectivity and objectivity are essentially intertwined in the realm of value" (Anderson 1996, 17), there is a real tension from the outset with regard to his methodology. Taylor himself is fully aware of this. As he explains, "the really difficult thing is distinguishing the human universals from the historical constellations and not eliding the second into the first so that our particular way seems somehow inescapable for humans as such, as we are always tempted to do" (1989, 112). His critics have expressed similar concerns. Olafson, for example, finds it "extremely difficult to see what kind of balance Taylor thinks he has struck between a common and universal selfhood and the historically quite diverse versions of what selfhood involves" (Olafson 1994, 193), while Flanagan finds it "extremely puzzling that such a historicist as Taylor is tempted to make such essentialist claims at all" (Flanagan 1996, 154). In Taylor's defense, Abbey suggests that "a useful way of understanding Taylor's approach to selfhood is to distinguish (...) its historicist and its ontological dimensions" (Abbey 2000, 56). Smith draws a similar distinction between the "historical" and the "transcendental" levels of Taylor's project, while adding that "it is not

---

5 Note that this is a continuation of the same issue rather than a change of subject. Because Taylor's phenomenological approach to morality steers a course between phenomenology and ethical theory, the 'shift' from ethics to phenomenology in *A Secular Age* is in fact a continuation of the same concern.

6 The latest and most explicit of which is Dreyfus and Taylor 2015.

always clear where Taylor's philosophical anthropology ends and where his philosophical history starts" (Smith 2002, 7–8).

3.2 A Phenomenological Method with Ontological Implications

It would seem, therefore, that merely making a distinction between "things that change and those that stay the same" (Abbey 2000, 10) does not fully capture the *source* of the difficulty. However, the issue looks surprisingly different when we consider Taylor's two-dimensional approach from a different methodological perspective. In our view, the conflict does not reside in the distinction between a historical and a 'transcendental' or 'ontological' approach, but in Taylor's method of moral phenomenology, on the one hand, and his claims about ontology, on the other. The crucial point is this: Taylor wants to reject (what he sees as) narrow understandings of morality and to refute reductionist ontologies *at one stroke*.

We can illustrate this problem by looking at the beginning of *Sources of the Self*. In trying to understand our moral predicament, Taylor informs us, we must not let ourselves be influenced by "much contemporary moral philosophy" because it "has given such a narrow focus to morality" (1989, 3). In order to retrieve the moral and spiritual background of our ordinary reactions and responses we should rather put contemporary moral theorizing in brackets, or suspend its relevance, to put it in classic phenomenological terms.[7] For only if we succeed in doing so, Taylor maintains, will we be able to "uncover buried goods through rearticulation – and thereby to make these sources again empower" (1989, 520). Here, then, is the reason why Taylor incites his readers to go through a kind of moral phenomenological reduction with respect to their knowledge of what morality is, and to follow him in his disclosure of our 'original' moral and spiritual experience, without assuming the truth or validity of any moral theory. As a result, Taylor's alternative to the reductionist mindset in contemporary ethics is in fact another kind of 'reduction,' a methodological one:

---

[7] See Kerr (2004) for a complementary reading. Kerr argues that Taylor's account of morality is a continuation of the work of Elizabeth Anscombe, Philippa Foot, and Iris Murdoch. He notes that Taylor's strategy to suspend respect for recent philosophical theories sounds "very much in tune with Anscombe's own famous declaration (...) that moral philosophy should be laid aside 'at any rate until we have an adequate philosophy of psychology, in which we are conspicuously lacking'" (Kerr 2004, 91, 85).

More broadly, I want to explore the background picture of our spiritual nature and predicament which lies behind some of the moral and spiritual intuitions of our contemporaries. (...) Here is where an important element of retrieval comes in, because much contemporary philosophy has ignored this dimension of our moral consciousness and beliefs altogether and has even seemed to dismiss it as confused and irrelevant. I hope to show, contrary to this attitude, how crucial it is." (1989, 3–4)

What is essential to the paradigmatic phenomenological method in Husserl's sense, however, is that we consider any statement about the external world as void of ontological implications. But this is a step Taylor does not want to take.[8] Quite to the contrary, the question that evolves out of the later writings is precisely "how to align our best phenomenology with an adequate ontology" (2007, 609). It would seem, therefore, that unlike Husserl's phenomenology, Taylor's moral phenomenological investigations indeed have certain ontological implications.

3.3 Commenting on Taylor

The previous section ended with what may seem an oxymoron: an 'anthropocentric ontology' or a 'non-anthropocentric phenomenology.' But it has become quite clear by now that Taylor is quite ambivalent in his use of both 'ontology' and 'phenomenology.' Smith (2002, 31–32) and Laitinen (2008, 79–80) have emphasized Taylor's ambivalent relation to phenomenology. On the one hand, Taylor is clearly indebted to modern phenomenology for his critique of the subject-object ontology introduced by Descartes.[9] On the other hand, he has been skeptical from the outset of the very objective of a pure self-authenticating vocabulary of phenomenological description. He criticizes both Husserl and Merleau-Ponty in this regard, arguing that "the very attempt to describe the pre-predicative seems to destroy it. (...) We must always take some concepts for granted in examining others, accept some assumptions in order to call others into question" (1958, 113; 1959, 103). However, the late Taylor informs us, the fact that we are "always and inevitably thinking within such taken-as-there frameworks" does not mean that phenomenology's attempt to attain contact with reality is vain; but it does necessitate "a reembedding of thought and knowledge in the bodily and social-cultural contexts in which it takes place" (2013, 75, 73), and therefore

---

8 In this respect, Dreyfus characterizes Husserl's *Cartesian Meditations* as "the most recent and general version" of the inner/outer dichotomy Taylor opposes (Dreyfus 2004, 53).
9 See for example Taylor 1995a, 2013.

a re-embedding of phenomenology in social imaginaries. From here Taylor moves on to show that, *pace* the idea of 'pure,' presuppositionless description, the only contact with reality possible for human beings is "the contact of living, active beings, whose life form involves acting in and on a world which also acts on them" (2013, 73).[10] Therefore, unlike Husserl and Merleau-Ponty, who proposed that in practicing phenomenology we ought to bracket the question of the existence of the world around us, Taylor maintains that his moral phenomenology puts the question of "what [we] are committed to ontologically by our ethical views" (2003, 305), or "of what ontology can underpin our moral commitments" (2007, 607) right back on the agenda. In fact, he argues that his phenomenology of moral experience is allied to a realist ontology.[11]

Methodologically speaking, however, Taylor wants to have it both ways. His phenomenological critique of contemporary moral philosophy is based on – and therefore limited to – our own experience of being in the world; yet he also seeks to transcend human experience by raising the issue of what we are committed to ontologically by our moral intuitions. There is a real tension here: How to align Taylor's initial phenomenological turn 'inwards,' with the inner life of the subject, with his ontological claims about a world which also acts 'on us?'

The irony is that Taylor encounters this very problem right at the beginning of his academic career. As he says in the early paper on phenomenology: "Merleau-Ponty's descriptions like all descriptions *commit him to a certain ontology*. If so, what status should we give to his ontology?" (1958, 131, italics ours). This fundamental question can also be directed at Taylor's own account: What are we committed to ontologically by his moral phenomenology? As his thinking unfolds, Taylor touches on ethics and ontology all the time; but it is above all in the paper *Ethics and Ontology* (2003) that he deals with the issue of their relationship most centrally. As has been noted, Taylor's ontological investigations have been quite exploratory and tentative. The really astonishing thing is that, published 45 years later, this paper on the ontological implications of moral experience is hardly more explicit than the allusions of the early text on Merleau-Ponty. Note the open-endedness that characterizes both texts: He dismisses the

---

[10] Taylor's commitment to an embodied form of phenomenology is confirmed in Dreyfus and Taylor (2015, 133–39 and 164–66), where they praise Samuel Todes for his phenomenological account of *balance*. A human body can only find balance in finding a posture which is adapted to both objective features of reality (e.g. gravity) and subjective intentions.

[11] Taylor nowhere explicitly presents himself as an advocate of moral realism in his key publications. However, in reply to his critics he does admit to be "a moral realist" after all, arguing for "a kind of moral realism" (1991, 246, 243). For Taylor's recent point of view on realism, see Dreyfus and Taylor 2015.

issue of Merleau-Ponty's ontology as "too complex to be treated here," while the more recent paper breaks off with the comment that "the conceptual means at my disposal are still too crude to explore this in an illuminating fashion" (1958, 132; 2003, 320). In other words, Taylor is reaffirming a crucial uncertainty with which he has been struggling all along.

Many of Taylor's commentators praise him for his phenomenological account of moral experience,[12] but seem to lose track of what he is trying to do along the second, ontological dimension. As Bernard Williams brilliantly puts it: "From a strong base in experience, Taylor very rapidly moves uphill, metaphysically speaking" (Williams 1990, 9). Johnston sees more than an argumentative sleight-of-hand in this two-stage approach, writing that Taylor's conceptualizations "both point towards subjectivism as much as objectivism" in such an ambiguous way that "the nature of his own position becomes fundamentally unclear" (Johnston 1999, 105). The central concern, it would seem, is not that (part of) Taylor's thought necessarily turns to the subject and its interiority, but rather that he also makes a move outwards, raising the issue of the ontological underpinnings of morality. Both this outer ontological turn and his analysis of human subjectivity are constitutive of Taylor's rich philosophical framework. But nowhere is it clarified – either by Taylor or by his interpreters – how these different investigations actually solve the tension between the subjective and the objective character of his claims. Put differently, what is this intersecting zone between ethics and ontology; between our experience as moral agents, on the one hand, and the ontology to which we want to subscribe, on the other?

There is more. As we have seen in the previous sections, Taylor's project primarily presents itself as a critique of the reductionist attitude he believes to be commonplace in our culture. He therefore also raises the issue of ontology to criticize a reductionist ontology, arguing that there is a "lack of fit" between our experience as moral agents, on the one hand, and "the ontology we allow ourselves as post-Galilean naturalists," on the other (2003, 320). At one stroke, Taylor thus wants both to diagnose our moral predicament in phenomenological and ontological terms and to refute naturalism. He then seems to overplay his hand when he seeks to establish the critique of naturalism through transcendental argumentation. As Taylor himself emphasizes, the reach of this phenomenological type of argument is necessarily limited, as we have also seen in the previous chapter: "Transcendental arguments (...) prove something quite strong about the subject of experience and the subject's place in the world; and yet

---

[12] See for example Kymlicka 1991, 159; Rorty 1994, 199; Weinstock 1994, 174; Williams 1990, 9.

since they are grounded in the nature of experience, *there remains an ultimate, ontological question they can't foreclose*" (1995b, 33, italics ours).

Since transcendental arguments are anchored in human experience, it must also be clear that ontological questions lie beyond their scope. This implies that, in his critique of naturalism, Taylor himself cannot get away from the qualitative discontinuity between morality and ontology. But he does not stop here. Given the initial polemical thrust of his thought, Taylor surely does not want his account to have merely diagnostic validity. The question that arises out of all this is whether his moral phenomenological strategy does not cut him off from the issue of ontology that he is trying to delineate at the same time. Is Taylor overplaying his hand here? Or is his predicament rather symptomatic of the problem initially brought forward by his own diagnosis? How does one explore this issue – that the cross-pressures between ethical and ontological commitments are manifest even in Taylor's own critical efforts – in an illuminating fashion? To what extent is transcendental argumentation a proper mode of dealing with the problem?

Of course, in separating Taylor's ontological investigations from his philosophical anthropology and moral phenomenology, we are "trying to sever themes that resist separation" (Abbey 2000, 3–4), because he not only combines ontology with philosophical anthropology, but also has a way of entwining ontological reflections with his account of morality.[13] Yet we think that making these distinctions will add some clarity, or at least uncover fundamental difficulties. In so doing, however, we are resisting a common trend in recent studies of Taylor's work. In reply to Taylor's inclination to make connections where the more familiar categories used by philosophers aim at separation, most commentators simply follow his language and employ a broad or relaxed notion of ontology, using, for example, the terms 'philosophical anthropology' and 'ontology' interchangeably. It is clear that Taylor does not see a contradiction in synchronizing philosophical anthropology and ontology. As he writes in a paper on Stephen White's book on ontology in political theory: "My term 'philosophical anthropology' is meant to cover much the same matters as White does with 'ontology': it tries to define certain fundamental features about human beings, their place in nature, their defining capacities (…) and their most powerful or basic motivations, goals, needs, and aspirations" (2005, 35).

White makes the same point when he assures that his own notion of "weak ontology" is "largely appropriate for the kind and level of philosophical reflection he [Taylor] has in mind," because "he [Taylor] speaks, for example, of the 'ontology of human life: what kinds of things can you invoke in talking about

---

[13] See his concept of moral ontology.

human beings in the different ways we do: describing, deliberating, judging, etc.?'" (White 2000, 43; Taylor 1990, 261). There are many other commentators who uphold Taylor's broad notion of ontology. Abbey, for example, speaks of the "ontological features of the self" (Abbey 2000, 56). Saurette sketches strong evaluation as "an inescapable ontological element constitutive of human agency," whereas Smith, Kerr, and Laitinen literally follow Taylor in depicting his philosophical anthropology as "an ontology of the human," a "moral ontology of the human," or an "ontology of human persons."[14]

It would seem, therefore, that his commentators, like Taylor himself, do not take a great interest in differentiating these topics from one another. At the same time, however, most of Taylor's interpreters do recognize a kind of tension implicit in his terminology. Abbey notes that "not all of Taylor's interpreters have appreciated his two-dimensional approach to the self" (Abbey 2000, 56) referring to the critiques of Olafson (1994, 192–193), Rosa (1995, 25) and Flanagan (1996, 154). Saurette ensures that Taylor's "definition of human agency is not guaranteed by the authority of an ontology" (Saurette 2005, 208). Analogously, Smith observes that "Taylor runs the risk of 'anthropologizing' or 'ontologizing' historically contingent features of subjectivity" (Smith 2002, 8), while Kerr insists that we "might want to hear much more about the ambiguities inherent in this version of a 'moral ontology of the human,'" stressing the uncertain and tentative nature of Taylor's ontological view (Kerr 2004, 101). Surprisingly, though, despite their observations, none of these authors takes the opportunity to challenge Taylor's terminology at this point.

Against the background of these discussions one might conclude that, since neither Taylor himself nor his commentators see the need to question his vocabulary, the burden of proof is with those who claim that this kind of terminology is distorting. This is our claim indeed, for the crucial point is that an overly broad or relaxed notion of ontology conceals the fundamental tension between the subjective and the objective we mentioned earlier, between Taylor's methods of philosophical anthropology and moral phenomenology, on the one hand, and his defense of moral realism, on the other. Rather than rate these on a par, we want to push beyond this and criticize Taylor at this point.

In our view, it is a source of great confusion that Taylor does not clearly separate his anthropological and phenomenological claims about human subjectivity from his objectivist account of the ontological underpinnings of our subjective commitments. Essentially, our point is that you can account for a large part of Taylor's work without invoking the word 'ontology' at all. There is some-

---

14 See Saurette 2005, 208; Taylor 1989, 5; Smith 2002, 237; Kerr 2004, 96; Laitinen 2008, 15.

thing puzzling about the very expression *ontology of the human* as a designation of certain features of human experience. However, the fact that the transcendental argument that is supposed to secure Taylor's most fundamental claims, has, as he says, both a "phenomenological moment" and establishes a kind of "realism" (1994, 209), suggests at least that there is more at stake than merely some conceptual confusion. As we noted above, simply charging Taylor with idiosyncrasy or conceptual mistreatment is beside the point. It's not as if you could simply solve the issue by having recourse to a more conventional vocabulary.[15] And yet, at the level of transcendental justification, Taylor is open to the charge that philosophical anthropology and moral phenomenology are not the correct methods to use in defense of ontological claims. To conclude this point, what gets lost from view in a relaxed notion of ontology is how Taylor's realist claims are backed up by his arguments, since these can be supported neither by philosophical anthropology nor by moral phenomenology. The really puzzling thing is that Taylor himself insists on this point.[16]

4 The Ontology of Social Imaginaries

In the previous sections, we have analyzed Taylor's clarification of the difference between the scientific explanation of reality and the explanation of moral experience. We have seen that Taylor, in his elaboration of this distinction, refutes narrow understandings of both ethics and ontology. We have also seen how Taylor himself cannot overcome certain methodological problems: the ontological backing of moral experience is argued for with transcendental arguments that do not escape human experience. The interplay between phenomenology and ontology therefore seems to exhibit the same circular structure as the Euthyphro dilemma. Moral phenomenology points to an objectivity that raises ontological questions, but in Taylor's understanding of the concept, ontology can never be completely disentangled from human experience. Can we now draw a parallel between moral experience and social imaginaries?

---

15 White has certainly understood Taylor on this score, writing that it was not until he encountered the problem that at this level of interpretation "many familiar analytical categories and operations become blurred or exhibit torsional effects" that he came to realize "the full significance of Charles Taylor's *Sources of the Self*." "For example," White explains, "the more I pondered the relation between ethics and ontology, the more they seemed mutually constitutive at this level and the less possible it seemed to accord one or the other clear primacy" (White 2005, 14).

16 See the quotation above on transcendental arguments (1995b, 33).

Our claim is that we can, because Taylor's notion of social imaginaries is, as we have seen in the previous chapter, closely linked to notions such as strong evaluation and constitutive goods. Social imaginaries flourish within an expressivist culture. Having exposed Taylor's conceptual apparatus of social imaginaries in chapter 2 and Taylor's tentative remarks about ontology in this chapter, we are now ready to compare Taylor's use of social imaginaries with the original use by Castoriadis.

In the previous paragraphs, we observed that Taylor, in a way, fights fire with fire when it comes to his criticism of a naturalistic ontology. Reducing moral experience to biology indeed testifies to a rigid ontology of materialism. But in order to save the phenomena of moral experience, Taylor also has recourse to an ontology of the human, or a kind of ontologized philosophical anthropology. It seems, therefore, that Taylor proposes a homeopathic therapy for reductionist ontology, albeit that the remedy for a naturalistic ontology is to be found in a hermeneutic ontology – which is, after all, of a different nature. With his homeopathic treatment, he seems to run with the hare and hunt with the hounds: he substitutes (hermeneutic) ontology for (naturalist) ontology. He wants to do justice to the experience of objectivity in human moral experience, starting with a moral phenomenology, which is to a very large degree historical, a historicity to which the second part of *Sources of the Self* testifies. But then the issue of ontology is never far away, and Taylor is always eager to develop arguments that point to transcendental structures of human experience.

As we have indicated, Taylor has never fully articulated his thoughts on this fundamental tension,[17] and seems to avoid the issue systematically whenever it turns up in his writings. But there may be very good reasons for Taylor not to choose between either phenomenology or ontology. We will make this clear by comparing Taylor's use of social imaginaries to Castoriadis's conception.

As we have seen in the previous chapter, Castoriadis developed his notion of social imaginaries to redefine the political and the social. According to Castoriadis, the social was always approached in an essentialist fashion, from ancient Greek philosophy to Marxism. Castoriadis's purpose was to launch a notion of the social that was more dynamic, more historical, and without the articulation of an essentialist purpose of history. So we could argue that Castoriadis chose the side of radical historicity and therefore, rephrased in the vocabulary we have employed in this chapter, of moral phenomenology.

---

17 As already indicated, Dreyfus and Taylor (2015) may seem to offer their 'final' words on this issue in *Retrieving Realism*. However, the tension between subjectivity and objectivity is not resolved here either – and for very good reasons, as we shall see below.

But Taylor warns us to be vigilant for two types of reductionism. On the one hand, reducing social (and moral) experience to historicism denies certain transcendental structures that shape the way we can live our times at the level of experience and think about our social organization at the level of social and political theory, though admittedly always in a certain historical context. So historical reductionism tends to lose sight of its own ontological foundations. That history would be 'all there is' is a metaphysical assumption that cannot be justified in purely historical terms.

On the other hand, an increasingly popular material reductionism nowadays holds sway which reduces the richness of (moral and social) human experience to biology. This is a new and powerful deterministic ontology, which in fact denies historicity altogether, by reducing it to material, biological conditions.

To sum up our comparison of Taylor and Castoriadis, we could state boldly that Castoriadis seeks to escape ontology in the guise of essentialism in favor of historicity, whereas Taylor wants to retrieve Castoriadis's view by pointing to inescapable transcendental and thus ontological features of human experience, however problematic this retrieval of realism may be.

The reason for Taylor to keep subjectivity and objectivity together in analyzing moral experience cannot be separated from his conceptions of expressivism, art and religion. 'Objective' sources for morality, art and religion can still resonate within human experience, but they come to being only through subjective expression and appropriation. In this way, with regard to moral experience, Taylor makes objectivity and subjectivity ultimately interdependent. The same accounts for his approach to social imaginaries. We also need *subtle languages* to articulate the social imaginaries we live in and by: their historical features as well as the 'ontological,' transcendental level that shapes these imaginaries. To give just two examples: in the Western world, we all share the social imaginary of the free market. Even if we oppose it at an ideological level, we take part in it by our inevitably acting in it as consumers. Or to take freedom of speech as another example: even if we discuss the limits to freedom of speech in the wake of terrorist attacks in France, no one participating in the Western social imaginary is serious about discarding freedom of speech altogether. Freedom of speech shapes our social imaginary at a transcendental level to the same extent as certain radical interpretations of the Koran or sharia law shape the imaginary of certain radical Muslim groups, although the latter 'ontologize' their social imaginary in an essentialist way, in what Taylor has called a 'closed world structure.'

The previous chapter has already indicated the struggle needed to come to terms with our social imaginaries. Plural as they are, the danger of violence and conflicting social imaginaries is always lurking. But we have also seen that Taylor is rather optimistic about the chances of a pluralistic dialogue between social imaginaries. After all, he is a romantic thinker, trying to reconcile the subjective and objective dimensions of moral experience, and the historical and transcendental features of social imaginaries. Hence it may be wise to retain the Euthyphro-dilemma between the subjective and objective foundations of morality open. For all the differences between Platonic realism and Taylor's hermeneutic approach of objectivity, Taylor, like Plato, seems to arrive at a fundamental *aporia*. And, as we have seen, Taylor has very good reasons to call the tension, for now at least, irresolvable.

Yet Taylor remains a romantic who continues to believe in some kind of reconciliation. He fully admits this in the text *Apologia pro libro suo*, his afterword to the book *Varieties of Secularism in A Secular Age*: "(…) I plead guilty as charged: I'm a hopeless German romantic of the 1790s. I resonate with Herder's idea of humanity as the orchestra, in which all the differences between human beings could ultimately sound together in harmony." (Warner et al. 2010, 320)

Bibliography

Abbey, Ruth. 2000. *Charles Taylor*. Teddington/Princeton: Acumen Press/Princeton University Press.
Anderson, Joel. 1996. "The Personal Lives of Strong Evaluators: Identity, Pluralism, and Ontology in Charles Taylor's Value Theory." *Constellations: An International Journal of Critical and Democratic Theory* 3 (1):17–38.
Dreyfus, Hubert. 2004. "Taylor's (Anti-) Epistemology." In *Contemporary Philosophy in Focus: Charles Taylor*, edited by Ruth Abbey, 52–83. Cambridge: Cambridge University Press.
Dreyfus, Hubert, and Charles Taylor. 2015. *Retrieving Realism*. Cambidge, MA: Harvard University Press.
Flanagan, Owen. 1996. *Self Expressions: Mind, Morals, and the Meaning of Life*. New York, Oxford: Oxford University Press.
Johnston, Paul. 1999. *The Contradictions of Modern Moral Philosophy: Ethics after Wittgenstein*. London/New York: Routledge.
Kerr, Fergus. 2004. "The Self and the Good: Taylor's Moral Ontology." In *Contemporary Philosophy in Focus: Charles Taylor* edited by Ruth Abbey, 84–104. Cambridge: Cambridge University Press.
Kymlicka, Will. 1991. "The Ethics of Inarticulacy." *Inquiry* 34:155–182.
Laitinen, Arto, and Nicholas Smith, eds. 2002. *Perspectives on the Philosophy of Charles Taylor*. Helsinki: Societas Philosophia Fennica.
Laitinen, Arto. 2008. *Strong Evaluation without Moral Sources*. Berlin: Walter de Gruyter.
Olafson, Frederick. 1994. "Comments on *Sources of the Self* by Charles Taylor." *Philosophy and Phenomenological Research* 54 (1):191–196.
Rorty, Richard. 1994. "Taylor on Self-Celebration and Gratitude: Review of *Sources of the Self*." *Philosophy and Phenomenological Research* 54 (1):197–201.

Rosa, Hartmut. 1995. "Goods and Life-Forms: Relativism in Charles Taylor's Political Philosophy." *Radical Philosophy* 71:20–26.
Saurette, Paul. 2005. *The Kantian Imperative: Humiliation, Common Sense, Politics*. Toronto: University of Toronto Press.
Smith, Nicholas. 2002. *Charles Taylor: Meaning, Morals and Modernity*. Cambridge: Polity.
Taylor, Charles. 1985. *Philosophical Papers II: Philosophy and the Human Sciences*. Cambridge: Cambridge University Press.
Taylor, Charles. 1989. *Sources of the Self: The Making of the Modern Identity*. Cambridge: Cambridge University Press.
Taylor, Charles. 1990. "Rorty in the Epistemological Tradition." In *Reading Rorty: Critical Responses to Philosophy and the Mirror of Nature (and Beyond)*, edited by Alan R. Malachowski, 257–275. Cambridge: Blackwell.
Taylor, Charles. 1991. "Comments and Replies." *Inquiry* 34:237–254.
Taylor, Charles. 1994. "Reply to Commentators." *Philosophy and Phenomenological Research* 54 (1):203–213.
Taylor, Charles. 1995a. "Overcoming Epistemology." In *Philosophical Arguments*, 1–19. Cambridge, MA: Harvard University Press.
Taylor, Charles. 1995b. "The Validity of Transcendental Arguments." In *Philosophical Arguments*, 20–33. Cambridge, MA: Harvard University Press.
Taylor, Charles. 2003. "Ethics and Ontology." *The Journal of Philosophy* 100 (6):305–320.
Taylor, Charles. 2005. "The Weak Ontology Thesis." *The Hedgehog Review: Critical Reflections on Contemporary Culture* 7 (2):35–42.
Taylor, Charles. 2007. *A Secular Age*. Cambridge/London: Belknap Press of Harvard University Press.
Taylor, Charles. 2013. "Retrieving Realism." In *Mind, Reason, and Being-in-the-World. The McDowell-Dreyfus Debate*, edited by Joseph Schear, 61–90. London: Routledge.
Taylor, Charles, and A.J. Ayer. 1959. "Phenomenology and Linguistic Analysis." *Proceedings of the Aristotelian Society, supplementary volume* 33:93–124.
Taylor, Charles, and Michael Kullman. 1958. "The Pre-Objective World." *The Review of Metaphysics* 12 (1):108–132.
Warner, Michael, Jonathan VanAntwerpen and Craig Calhoun, eds. 2010. *Varieties of Secularism in A Secular Age*. Cambridge, MA: Harvard University Press.
Weinstock, Daniel. 1994. "The Political Theory of Strong Evaluation." In *Philosophy in an Age of Pluralism: the Philosophy of Charles Taylor in Question*, edited by James Tully and Daniel Weinstock, 171–193. Cambridge: Cambridge University Press.
Weinstock, Daniel. 2000. *Sustaining Affirmation: the Strengths of Weak Ontology in Political Theory*. Princeton: Princeton University Press.
Weinstock, Daniel. 2005. "Weak Ontology: Genealogy and Critical Issues." *The Hedgehog Review: Critical Reflections on Contemporary Culture* 7 (2):11–25.
Williams, Bernard. 1985. *Ethics and the Limits of Philosophy*, Chapter 8: *Knowledge, Science, Convergence*. Cambridge: Fontana Press.
Williams, Bernard. 1990. "Republican and Galilean: Review of *Sources of the Self*." *The New York Review of Books* 37:1–11.

Section 2: **Social Imaginaries as Meaningful Spaces**

Christa Anbeek, Hans Alma, Saskia van Goelst Meijer
Contrast Experiences and Social Imaginaries as Spaces for Truth-Seeking

1 Introduction

As Zygmunt Bauman (2000) argues, we live in *liquid modernity*. People, information, ideas, weapons etc. are on the move and the meaning of boundaries changes. This is not only the case for boundaries between nation states, but also for boundaries between worldviews and religions. People have to find new ways for their moral and existential orientation. We witness an age of uncertainty and Bauman warns for a loss of sensitivity or moral blindness (Bauman and Donskis 2013). To understand the new situation this creates for worldview and religion, we need a conceptual framework that does justice to the characteristic fluidity with which many people relate to existential issues. Of course, we can still study institutional (religious) worldviews as separate phenomena with strong boundaries. However, especially in Western, so called secular societies, these boundaries lose significance as people enter an eclectic search for meaning in life. Alma and Anbeek (2013) speak of *worldviewing* in this regard and explore whether a new existential, ethical and spiritual language arises out of the reflection on concrete, particular experiences people have. The central question of this chapter is whether social imaginaries can be helpful in understanding contemporary processes of worldviewing.

As will be discussed in chapter 7 by Vandevoordt, Clycq and Verschraegen, the concept of social imaginaries has particular heuristic value because it places emphasis on the creative, interpretative capacities of individuals and groups in a context of cultural complexity. We will argue that these interpretative capacities are especially needed when people are confronted with *contrast experiences:* positive or negative experiences that question everyday interpretations of existence. We relate the concept of contrast experiences and the quest for the articulation of meaning that arises from them to basic human insights or configurations of truth as they are offered by (religious) worldviews. However, against the background of the *immanent frame* (Taylor 2007) these configurations of truth have lost their self-evidence and convincing power. This is where Taylor's concept of social imaginaries shows its heuristic value: it can be understood in terms of dynamics of truth-seeking. We clarify this notion with the help of Eastern philosophy (especially the Jain doctrine of *anekantavada*) that does more justice than Western thinking to "the many sidedness of all phenomena" (Steger

2006, 342). Yet, it does leave room for strong evaluation and isn't a relativistic approach.

With the help of a casus we will explore how our theoretical endeavor relates to an interpersonal process of truth-seeking, following on an extreme contrast experience: the sudden loss of husband and children by a Dutch woman. We will witness the search for a new existential language (that need not be verbal) where insights from different worldviews are explored critically in their value for understanding and enduring lived experience. We hope to show that contrast experiences can offer a 'site' where social imaginaries are expressed and can be studied empirically. This would not only help us in understanding contemporary processes of worldviewing, but would also have important implications for the professional guidance of people in their search for meaning.

2 Contrast Experiences

Many philosophers of religion and also anthropologists point to basic human experiences as the most important source for religious interpretations of (human) existence. According to Taylor (2007) several kinds of deep experiences can play a role in people's existence: they give insight into what it's like to live as a believer or as a non-believer. These experiences make life fuller, richer and more worthwhile. Sometimes we catch a glimpse of something special, sometimes we are touched deeply by something. An experience like that can take place in different ways, but always lifts us beyond ourselves. "There may just be moments when the deep divisions, distractions, worries, sadnesses that seem to drag us down are somehow dissolved, or brought into alignment, so that we feel united, moving forward, suddenly capable and full of energy. Our highest aspirations and our life energies are somehow lined up, reinforcing each other, instead of producing psychic gridlock." (Taylor 2007, 6)

These experiences help us to situate a 'place of fullness' for our moral or spiritual orientation. In current times several sources that give meaning to these experiences have become available to us besides religion. The experience of fullness can be explained in a Humanistic or Buddhist fashion, from the perspective of the Philosophy of Nature and from many other points of view. This makes the interpretation of the experience truly ambivalent, because people realize that our view is but one in an array of possible points of view.[1] Everyone looks for meaning within the boundaries of his/her own existence and daily con-

---

[1] Cf. the discussion of 'cross pressures' by Latré in the second chapter of this volume.

cerns. Happiness, fulfillment and joy are important for finding meaning. But *"Alle Lust will Ewigkeit"* is Nietzsche's famous line. All pleasure wants forever, not because you would like to continue indefinitely, but because happiness loses a large part of its meaning if it is not sustainable. The big spoilsport here is death. The here and now – this moment – is not enough, because it is over before you realize it. According to Taylor the longing for the eternal is not superficial and childish, but belongs to the human condition. In these times death is even more dreaded. This has everything to do with the role that love relationships play. Never before were they of such importance in our existence. We surround ourselves with loved ones who give our lives colour, scent, flavor and grip. Hell has disappeared, but has been replaced by the great pain of *"la mort de toi"* (Taylor 2007, 721). We search for meaning and according to Taylor, we are not nearly ready for disbelieving. The brokenness and fragility, but also the wonder of existence, makes us look for more.

> All this is true, and yet the sense that there is something more presses in. Great numbers of people feel it: in moments of reflection about their life; in moments of relaxation in nature; in moments of bereavement and loss; and quite wild and unpredictably. Our age is far from settling into a comfortable unbelief. Although many individuals do so, and more still seem to on the outside, the unrest continues to surface. Could it ever be otherwise?" (Taylor 2007, 727)

So, according to Taylor, two sorts of deep experiences drive people to search for meaning: on the one side fleeting experiences of wholeness and wonder, on the other side the fundamental experiences of brokenness and fragility. In this article we use for both experiences the term contrast experiences – they shatter the everyday interpretation of existence and an unknown area appears.

3 Vulnerability, Fragile Life and the Need for Re-orientation

In those moments when the self-evident is no longer self-evident in life, and one experiences the vulnerability of existence, we speak of contrast experiences. Because of such a contrast experience people start searching for new meaning that fits their experience. A part of humanity turns to religion. According to the philosopher of religion Henk Vroom religious traditions are made up of a configuration of truths, or basic insights. Basic insights are fundamental to a religious tradition and they hark back to human experiences. These experiences are not so much 'religious experiences,' but experiences that are connected to genuine characteristics of human existence, called by Vroom 'existentials.' It is about experiences of being finite, of responsibility and failure, of insight, goodness, evil and suffering. Religious traditions explain these human experiences from the perspective of the transcendent – that which transcends the experience itself and places it in a larger perspective.[2] The teachings of a religious tradition (*dharma, veritates*) must be viewed as an interpretive, explanatory description of existence (Vroom 1989). "Serious religion gives guidance and shelter. It should help to face life and make choices, and give shelter and comfort in difficult times, and challenge us to care for others." (Vroom 2013, 54)

Here, Vroom presents an anthropologically based view of religion with the human perspective as a starting point. Also, according to anthropologist Jan van Baal, at crucial moments religion points people the way in the world. It enables people to feel at home in this existence with feelings of happiness, peace and warmth, but also of insecurity, restlessness and disharmony (Van Baal 1981). Religion, or world viewing, is a way to keep at bay the chaos, which threatens to take over when someone can no longer understand the events he/she experiences, can no longer endure them or can no longer give meaning to them in a moral sense (Geertz 1993).

The Belgian theologian Edward Schillebeeckx emphasized the *negative contrast experience* as the fundamental human experience from which theological reflections arise. Human language about God has no other ground than the experience of precariousness, contingency, uncertainty and limitation. This is a pre-religious experience which is accessible to everyone and which evokes a 'no' to the world as it is experienced. The human experience of suffering, evil, suppression, violence and unhappiness is the source of human's veto to the world. This experience is more evident and certain than philosophy or science can learn us about falsifiable and verifiable knowledge.[3] Indignation is a basic experience of our being in the world. Without doubt there is also goodness and beauty and much enjoyable in our world, but these fragments are contra-

---

[2] Usually the term transcendence is used to indicate a reality that is situated above the everyday reality, but this is not a must. Ter Borg (2010) and Kunneman (2005) speak about 'horizontal transcendence,' which occurs when the boundaries of the here and now are crossed. As an example Ter Borg mentions making plans for the future or developing new ways of living together. According to Kunneman horizontal transcendence indicates on the one hand the relationships with other people, and on the other hand the horizon of values that have a guiding role in life. This horizon of values cannot have an absolute base, but begets form from the dialogue with others (2005, 72).

[3] See Latré and Meijer, chapter 3 of this volume, for a discussion of the distinction between scientific and moral objectivity, and Taylor's plea for a phenomenology of human moral experience.

dicted and pulverized by evil and hatefulness, by suffering, power-abuse and terror. A positive element in the negative contrast experience is the never ending human indignation – this includes openness to another situation, which has a right to our affirmative 'yes.' It is a consensus to a better, other world, which is still unknown and not yet given (Schillebeeckx, 1989). In his article *Disenchantment-Reenchantment* Taylor elaborates on the experience of wonder as a source in which 'strong evaluations' disclose themselves.

> Do we not now experience wonder at the vast yet intricate universe and the manifold forms of life, at the very spectacle of the evolution of higher forms out of lower ones? Do we not find beauty in all this? In this case, a part of the very change which is held to have disenchanted the world, here that bit of modern science which we call the theory of evolution, has in fact given us further, deeper cause to wonder at the universe. As Levine puts it, the world hasn't lost meaning; 'it is stunning, beautiful, scary, fascinating, dangerous, seductive, real.' The first four of these epithets might be thought to be rather aesthetic than ethical. But one can argue that this sense of greatness and beauty fosters a love for the world which is one of the wellsprings of generosity. (Taylor 2011, 295)

Butler (2003, 2010), Pulcini (2013) and Anbeek (2013) plead to take experiences of fragile and vulnerable life as the source for an existential and moral re-orientation. Anbeek emphasizes that in real life the so-called positive contrast experiences and the negative contrast experiences cannot be distinguished from each other so easily. Although a positive experience of wonder, beauty, love, harmony, unity, feels very different from the experience of brokenness, loss, injustice, violence, fragmentation – that what becomes visible in both sorts of contrast experiences is the same. Life manifests itself as fragile, fleeting, transient, beautiful and chaotic, tragic and full of wonder at the same time. In contrast experiences the self-evident and well-known world is radically called into question. Life reveals itself as beyond ratio and beyond control. We are not able to create enduring love, beauty and happiness. In spite of all our efforts our life is not makeable, we are not in control and less autonomous than we would like to imagine. In contrast experiences the otherness of 'beyond myself' breaks in, sometimes in the shape of wonder and beauty, sometimes in the shape of fragmentation and loss, many times these two forms go hand in hand in creating an openness to the unknown. In this openness something of deep importance reveals itself, a person feels it bodily, and intuits that something of strong value is at stake. This intuition is clear and evident and at the same time elusive and obscure.

Taylor, Schillebeeckx, Anbeek and Butler point to the need of articulation to make the contrast experience a meaningful experience that can guide us to a moral re-orientation.

4 The Articulation of Contrast Experiences

Many philosophers emphasize that in order to become meaningful contrast experiences need to be articulated. This is a central issue in Taylor's book *The Language Animal* (2016): "Prior to the articulation, the as yet unnamed import may be felt in a diffuse, unfocused way, a pressure that we can't yet respond to. After articulation, it becomes part of the explicit shape of meaning for us. As a result it is felt differently; our experience is changed; it has a more direct bearing on our lives." (Taylor 2016, 189)

Following Taylor we could say that the contrast experience brings with it an unstructured sense that something important needs to be brought to light (Taylor 2016, 187). Latré (this volume, chapter 2) argues that in contrast experiences constitutive goods are at stake. This evokes strong evaluation of diverging constitutive goods. Latré points out that strong evaluation is a necessary condition of articulation; one becomes (more) articulate about one's moral choices by acquiring a strongly evaluative language. This is by necessity a *subtle language* that allows one to clarify the goods that come to the fore in a contrast experience. The implicit understandings need to become explicit in order to be able to function as a moral orientation in life (Taylor 2011, 2007; Schillebeeckx 1998; Arendt 1998; Butler 2010; Jackson 2002; Anbeek 2013). As contrast experiences and their moral values escape full theoretical articulation, a subtle language means looking for other dimensions of expression. Besides expressing ourselves verbally, people can use images, actions, practices, rituals, and arts to demonstrate what is of value to them. Like social imaginaries, to which we will relate contrast experiences in the next section, moral re-orientation is carried in images, stories, narratives and legends (Taylor 2004, 23).

Taylor, and also other philosophers, point to another difficulty by trying to articulate the constitutive goods that become manifest in contrast experiences. The practice of language itself is constitutive of meanings and new realities.[4] The articulations are not simply derivative and secondary; expression has a creative dimension, making possible its own content (Taylor 2016, 38). Language

---

[4] This is one of Taylor's central arguments in *The Language Animal* (2016). Acknowledging this is a crucial condition for reflectivity. "Once we lose sight of the language-constituted background which enables these activities, once we just take it as given, it is easy to slide into seeing our emotions, footings, normative understandings as well as simply given, as it were, in the nature of things." (2016, 35)

can bring about existential innovations.[5] Each way of giving expression to what appears as a similar reaction modifies it, develops it, gives it a different thrust. The background of different persons resonates in their articulations of strong values.

> Thus we see how today in the sphere of humanitarian work, people of all convictions, religious and nonreligious, work side by side. They are in a sense actuated by the same impulse, but some very different ethics lie behind the common dedication in each case: different views of human life, of the possibilities of transformation, of the modes of spiritual or mental discipline that are to be engaged in, and so on. (Taylor 2011, 299)

The expressions of strong evaluations will always be plural, there is no single truth. No single articulation can ever be complete, we are captured in an endless striving to increase articulacy (Taylor 2016, 177). Articulation always leaves a gap where the mystery intrudes, where the claims to truth are not fully grounded, where seeming refutation or contradictions lie half visible (Taylor 2011, 299). Uncertainty remains a characteristic of all our efforts to ground ourselves in a beyond ourselves. We cannot escape this human condition of precariousness,[6] although we can make error-reducing moves (Taylor 2016, 301). Another significant issue in the search for giving an account of deep and impressive experiences of vulnerable life, is that this is not about thinking and thought, but anchored in corporal experience and bonds with other people. As Taylor argues, language evolves in the interspace of joint attention or communion (2016, 50). This means that articulation is not an activity of an isolated philosopher or theologian, but it is an *inter-human activity*. This inter-human activity is based on dialogue, it means appearing to others and exposing yourself to others. Hannah Arendt speaks here of the miracle of life, a second birth. We must tell the story of our life, then, before we can ascribe meaning to it. "With word and deed we insert ourselves into the human world and this insertion is like a second birth, in which we confirm and take upon ourselves the naked fact of our original physical appearance." (Arendt 1998, 176)

---

5 Again, language should be read in a broad sense. "The linguistic capacity is essentially more than an intellectual one; it is embodied: in enacted meanings, in artistic portrayals, in metaphors which draw on embodied experience, and also in the iconic gestural portrayal which accompanies everyday speech, not to mention the ubiquity of 'body language' – tone of voice, emphasis, expressive gesture, stances of intimacy, of aloofness – which surround ordinary discourse." (Taylor 2016, 333)
6 See Latré and Meijer, chapter 3 of this volume, for a thorough analysis of how Taylor tries to keep subjectivity and objectivity together in analyzing moral experience.

Especially when these dialogues concern deep personal experiences about the fragility of bodily existence, goodness, happiness and the disruptive moments that take these all away, we have to realize that exposing ourselves to others makes us extra vulnerable. This is why *acknowledging* is crucial. People need to be respected and recognized – otherwise the search for the values (strong evaluations) that manifest themselves in these experiences will collapse and harm will be done. Arendt underscores the equal worth of each human being.

> This revelatory quality of speech and action comes to the fore where people are with others and neither for nor against them – that is, in sheer human togetherness. (...) Because of its inherent tendency to disclose the agent together with the act, action needs for its full appearance the shining brightness we once called glory, and which is possible only in the public realm. (Arendt 1998, 180)

Butler observes that this equal worth is quite problematic. Not everyone counts in the same way as a human being, some people are not seen as human beings, but as enemies, living shields of weapons, untouchables, illegals. "There are 'subjects' who are not quite recognizable as subjects, and there are 'lives' that are not quite – or, indeed, are never recognized as lives." (Butler 2011, 4) She argues that there ought to be a more inclusive and egalitarian way of recognizing precariousness and that this should take the form of concrete social policy regarding such issues as shelter, work, food, medical care and legal status (Butler 2011, 13).

For our project, giving an account of impressive experiences of the fragility and vulnerability in order to be able to articulate strong values in them, this acknowledging and recognizing of each other as a unique and treasured person is of ultimate importance. So, before we could start writing and talking about a re-orientation of social imaginaries that results from contrast experiences one strong evaluation is already there – it is not a neutral, but a value laden enterprise.

5 Contrast Experiences and Social Imaginaries

As we have seen, contrast experiences, articulation and re-orientation stand in a dynamic relationship to one another. Contrast experiences don't emerge in an existential and moral vacuum but in a background of meanings shared with others, creating an openness in which something of great value is at stake. Contrast experiences evoke strong evaluations that question self-evident meanings and inspire an existential and moral re-orientation. We now want to relate the dynamics described more explicitly to Taylor's notion of social imaginaries.

Taylor defines a social imaginary as "the way our contemporaries imagine the societies they inhabit and sustain" (2004, 6). Social imaginary is about "the ways people imagine their social existence, how they fit together with others, how things go on between them and their fellows, the expectations that are normally met, and the deeper normative notions and images that underlie these expectations" (Taylor 2004, 23).

Taylor stresses that the notion of social imaginary is closely related to the notion of moral or spiritual order. The understanding that a social imaginary incorporates is both factual and normative: our sense of how things usually are, is interwoven with an idea of how they ought to be and with our ability to recognize ideal cases. "And beyond the ideal stands some notion of a moral or metaphysical order, in the context of which the norms and ideals make sense" (Taylor 2007, 172). Taylor emphasizes that the background which is used to make sense of any given act is "wide and deep" and involves "our sense of our whole predicament in time and space, among others and in history" (Taylor 2007, 174). Social imaginaries always imply an orientation towards what we consider to be good, towards "the values we hold most precious" (Goodman 2014, 2). According to Latré (this volume, p. 60) this gives them erotic power, as we love and admire this constitutive good and want to move ever closer to it. In terms of Thomas M. Alexander, social imaginaries manifest the Human Eros: the urge of the human psyche toward the full, embodied experience of meaning and value in the world (2013, 5).[7]

This brings us to a circularity similar to the one described by Latré with regard to social imaginaries and social practices: on the one hand social practices are enabled by the background understandings offered by social imaginaries, but they also constitute or carry these imaginaries. The same seems to hold for contrast experiences: they both depend on, and constitute and carry social imaginaries. Social imaginaries are the spaces in which the values we hold most precious are embedded and guide our daily practices and the stories we tell about them. This space is punctured by contrast experiences that break through the self-evidence of our practices and stories and that make it necessary to clarify our strong evaluations. Articulation is not just bringing out in the open what was hidden inside the contrast experience; as was clarified before, expression always means modification and re-orientation and transformation, thus opening up new possibilities for experience.

---

[7] Alexander's view on Human Eros seems to be in agreement with Taylor's view that human beings do not seek for meaning as such, but aspire to *fullness* as it is embodied in specific meaningful traditions, narratives, persons etc. See Latré, chapter 2 of this volume.

We suggest that social imaginaries manifest or are even driven by the Human Eros understood as the search for a concrete, embodied experience of meaning and value in the world (Alexander 2013, 6). We see a connection here to what we said earlier about existentials as a notion coined by the philosopher of religion Henk Vroom: experiences that are connected to genuine characteristics of human existence. According to Vroom, religious traditions offer interpretations and explanations of these experiences and are made up of a configuration of truths, or basic insights. As Taylor argues, however, in the immanent frame these religious explanations have lost their self-evidence and much of their convincing power. Taylor's concept of social imaginaries that imply a notion of moral and metaphysical order, are not so much configurations of truths, but should rather be understood in terms of dynamics of truth-seeking. We think this understanding is in line with Taylor's discussion of strong evaluations as related to the experience of wonder.

6 Social Imaginaries and the Dynamics of Truth-Seeking

According to Alexander, the feeling that one's life is meaningful and has value, is an urgent human need. "This is a biological claim insofar as if this need is denied, we either die or become filled with destructive rage." (Alexander 2013, 6) How is this need related to truth-seeking? Alexander doesn't relate the Human Eros to the identification of truth understood in terms of substance, essence, unity. He stresses the importance of relation, process, transformation, interbeing and polymodality. From Alexander we can learn that truth can only be approached through "the cultivation of polyphonic listening as well as speaking" (Alexander 2013, 21). He argues that this approach finds little support from Western philosophical thinking: "One of the persistent troublesome legacies from the Western tradition has been its obsession with identity as the mark of 'Being'" (Alexander 2013, 18). This challenges us to study the notion of truth-seeking from the perspective of Eastern philosophy in the next section. But first we will elaborate on the relationship between social imaginaries and the dynamics of truth-seeking.

One basic question when it comes to the concept of social imaginaries has to do with Taylor's choice of a concept that refers to people's imaginative capacity. Doesn't this choice point in quite another direction than truth-seeking? What kind of phenomenon or process is the imagination that feeds social imaginaries? Alexander holds that imagination plays an important role in the Human Eros.

Based on the thinking of the pragmatist philosopher John Dewey, he describes imagination as "the ability to see the actual in light of the possible" (2013, 9).[8] Imagination is not to be understood as free-floating phantasy, but as firmly rooted in past and present that hold – when being closely attended to – possibilities for experience and action. Dewey distinguishes between two closely related types of imagination: a) taking the perspective of others (empathy) and b) creatively tapping a situation's possibilities (cf. Fesmire 2003). Imagination is based on an attentive perception of what is going on in the actual situation, helped by an understanding that is rooted in past experiences and knowledge acquired through cultural transmission. This allows for mental experimenting with the perspectives that are thus brought to the perceived situation, resulting in the anticipation of new possibilities for action. For Dewey, imagination is not complete without action that brings about change, a change that should be critically reflected upon and corrected if necessary through a new cycle of the imaginative process. In fact, the imaginative process is our pivotal way of truth-seeking, a truth that is not 'out there' to be found by rational, logical reasoning, but that can only be related to – partially, tentatively – through the imagination that engages our whole being: sensuously, bodily, emotionally, cognitively and socially. From this point of view, *learning* – that has of necessity an imaginative quality[9] – is more important to truth-seeking than *knowing*. Alexander stresses the importance of the social dimension: "Through this mutual imaginative ability, symbolic action and symbols themselves become possible, as does the establishment of a world of shared experience, in which 'you' and 'I' become a 'we'" (Alexander 2013, 10). This description brings us as close as we can get to what Taylor tries to capture with his notion of social imaginaries.[10] So we can add to our earlier formulation that we understand social imaginaries as *shared* spaces for the dynamics of truth-seeking.

---

8 Elsewhere, Alexander conceives of imagination as "the ability to employ and play with alternative interpretive schemata" (2013, 83).
9 Cf. Alexander (2013, 52): "It is, after all, learning in which imagination, not merely reason, transforms our past into a meaningful future."
10 Alexander speaks of the community of social imagination. Perhaps more than Taylor's social imaginaries, this conception points to expression, self-reflectivity and creativity as part of an imaginative community life: "The idea of the community that emerges is one which through its imaginative, dynamic intelligence actively seeks for conditions that fulfil the deep aesthetic needs of human beings to experience the world with meaning and value in an expressive, reflective, and self-critical way." (2013, 147) This cannot be taken for granted: "Communities need a pluralistic orientation to maintain their imaginative creativity and self-interpretation" (2013, 155). A community that realizes this, would be called a *democracy* by Dewey. It places high demands on the education of vision and imagination.

7 Truth-Seeking in the Perspective of Eastern Philosophy

According to Alexander, "philosophy must seek a broad, global literacy of human cultures. It must become aesthetically and spiritually attuned to the 'shapes of wisdom' expressed in diverse cultures" (2013, 76). This holds especially with regard to the dynamics of truth-seeking, for which the epistemological concerns of Western philosophy might be insufficient. For this reason, we will explore truth-seeking from the perspective of Eastern philosophy in this section. In this way, we hope to contribute a new perspective to the question of retrieving realism in social imaginaries, as it was addressed by Latré and Meijer in chapter 3 of this volume.

In Eastern thinking, truth-seeking efforts, especially within a deeply pluralistic context (cultural, religious, linguistic) have led to questions on how to understand and deal with vastly differing understandings of truth and reality. Jain philosophy is one branch of Indic thinking which has such questions at its core. Although questions on truth and reality and our human abilities to understand it appear in different ways throughout Jain thinking, they can be found most emphatically in the central Jain doctrine of *anekantavada* (Polk 2012), literally: non-onesidedness (Long 2009; Mardia and Rankin 2013), but better understood as "the many sidedness of all phenomena" (Steger 2006, 342). Briefly stated *anekantavada* points to the understanding that there can be no single point of view that is the complete truth both because humans are conditioned beings and limited in their capacity for understanding reality, and because the reality itself is plural (Dundas 2002; Mardia and Rankin 2013). This position is often explained through the parable of the Blind Men and the Elephant. Wanting to know what an elephant is like, the blind men gather round the animal and each examines the elephant by touching it. Every man comes to a completely different conclusion as to what an elephant is like, based on the part he was able to touch (the tail, leg, trunk, ear and so on). None of the men are really wrong, since each has felt something that is indeed part of the elephant. But the actual elephant is all these parts put together, and more. More formally we could say that from the point of view of *anekantavada* everything that exists has infinite qualities and modes of being, and finite human perception can never grasp all aspects at once (Polk 2012). This doctrine of *anekantavada* implies that its adherents consider the beliefs, views and truth-claims of others, even those truths that run counter to their own, as being equally true in their own right, certainly for those that hold them, which John Koller describes as "epistemological respect for the views of others" (Koller 2004, 88).

Though from an outsider-perspective *anekantavada* is quite easily confused with moral relativism (Long 2013) or linked to the post-modern understanding that 'real' (objective) truth does not exist (Mardia and Rankin 2013), the Jain position is actually quite different (Polk 2012). *Anekantavada* states that objective reality or truth does exist, but it is complex and pluralistic. To be able to understand it, many different viewpoints are necessary, and each is true in some sense, and in some sense also not. Putting them together might lead us to a fuller, more complex understanding of reality, but even if the viewpoints seem irreconcilable, *anekantavada* allows for the possibility of each of them to be acknowledged as truth in itself or as equally representing an aspect of truth. When one encounters a religious or philosophical claim, therefore, that is contrary to one's own view, the proper attitude to take is to adhere to one's own view, but also to be open to the possibility that a kernel of truth – a genuine insight into an aspect of reality that one has not yet considered – must rest at the core of the worldview of the other (Long 2013, 14). *Anekantavada* has radical implications for the ways in which we live together and deal with pluralism and diversity, something that was understood for instance by Mohandas Gandhi whose search for nonviolent ways to change the social reality of colonized India was bound up with these Jain insights. For Gandhi the search for truth formed the essence of his life and work. He gave his socio-political struggles the name *satyagraha*, meaning 'truth-force,' and his life was to become a string of 'experiments with truth' (Gandhi 1927). Profoundly influenced by Jain philosophy (though a devout Hindu himself), Gandhi is convinced that there is such a thing as universal truth, but also that people can only understand it in a relative sense. Moreover, they can only find it in experience (Bilgrami 2011). Because people have very different experiences in life, their views on truth will also differ vastly. However, each particular understanding of truth represents something of the human experience.

For Gandhi, truth-seeking is intertwined with one of the other fundamental principles in nonviolence[11]: *ahimsa*, or "the absence of the intention to do harm" (Nagler 2004). Harm here does not only point to the effects of physical, emotional or verbal violence, but is also the consequence of ill will, of negative attitudes and criticisms against others. When we create universal principles from our own experiences it follows that others, who do not follow the same principle, are wrong and deserve our criticism and contempt. It is this attitude that to Gandhi lies at the basis of violence. This understanding encompasses the insight that other beings are not 'other' to themselves; that they are themselves just as

---

[11] For an analysis of the five different elements on which nonviolence rests, two of which are truth-seeking (*satya*) and *ahimsa* see: Goelst Meijer, 2015.

much as we are ourselves. "It is this insight that enables us to see the 'other' on its own terms, from its own side, rather than as merely the 'other' that is opposed to us. And this ability to see the other person as not merely the 'other,' but as identical to our own self (...) operationalizes ahimsa" (Koller 2004, 86–87).

Ahimsa implies the active attempt to create a situation in which each can fully live. In Gandhi's work *ahimsa* and *satya* are the core concepts, and his truth-seeking becomes over the course of his life an active method for creating social change. To Gandhi, truth-seeking is also about putting his own truth at the service of others, so that everyone has the opportunity to develop a deeper level of *satya*. Our experience of truth cannot lead to a rule for everyone to follow, but it does lead to a rule for oneself to follow: "the very idea of principles (or doctrines) is replaced by the idea of exemplarity" (Bilgrami 2011, 118). Thus, Gandhi's truth-seeking implies that "we are dedicated to the truth we perceive, to the truth we understand" (Thakar 2005, 20). If we live from our own truth as we understand it, setting an example, we can share our truth with others and other truths become available to us. Since these truths are all representations of reality, the confrontation with other views leads to a new experience, making a deeper understanding of truth possible. When confronted with a view that is in direct opposition to our own, or which is perceived as wrong, the only option is that of persuasion, not coercion. By completely and honestly acting upon the truth we perceive, thus presenting a different reality, we might persuade the other to change their view, or we might change our own.

Thus Gandhi's nonviolent opposition to the British colonization consisted of openly declaring and acting upon his views of how Indians should live, leading to his defying of what he perceived as unjust laws (civil disobedience), and many other forms of open protests, while accepting the consequences that those actions would bring. The option that his mind would be changed instead of that of the colonizers thus remained open. The other option is to search for a "mutually satisfactory and agreed-upon solution" (Bondurant 1965, 195), which in Gandhi's case finally happened when the British regime decided to grant independence. But such a solution can only come about if we take the experience and the truth of others as seriously as those of ourselves. Conflicts can then be an opportunity to come to a higher, more complex understanding of truth, provided they are dealt with nonviolently. In other words, to Gandhi, real truth emerges in the 'in-between,' in the spaces between different experiences that are related.

8 Contrast Experiences, Social Imaginaries and Truth-Seeking: Where do we Stand?

We started our reflections on social imaginaries and worldviewing with the discussion of contrast experiences that shatter the everyday interpretation of existence and evoke feelings of vulnerability. They call for moral re-orientation that may be guided by a worldview, understood as a 'configuration of truths' (Vroom 2013). In our age of super-diversity (Vertovec 2007) however, the interpretation of a contrast experience remains truly ambivalent, because people realize that their view is but one in an array of possible points of view. Yet, the contrast experience creates an openness to the unknown in which something of deep importance reveals itself that is felt bodily. The intuition that something of strong value is at stake is clear and evident and at the same time elusive and obscure. It calls for an articulation of constitutive goods, made possible by what Taylor calls strong evaluation. This articulation or expression will always be plural, but is nonetheless a claim or aspiration to truth. Articulation is an inter-human activity in which we appear and expose ourselves to others and need their acknowledgement. Arendt (1998, 180) speaks of the revelatory quality of speech and action, thus relating articulation to truth in the sense of truth-speaking. We took the normative standpoint that truth-seeking and truth-speaking take place where impressive experiences of fragility and vulnerability and the articulation of strong values in them meet with acknowledgement and recognition of each other as unique and treasured persons.

From this perspective, truth can only be thought of in terms of relation, process, inter-being. We have defined social imaginaries as the shared spaces in which the values we hold true are embedded; where these spaces are 'punctured' by contrast experiences it becomes necessary to clarify our strong evaluations in a process of truth-seeking. This process is driven by human eros: the urge toward full, embodied experience of meaning and value. It is helped by the human imaginative ability to see the actual in light of the possible. Alexander (2013) holds that truth can only be approached by 'polyphonic listening and speaking' and by the cultivation of our imagination. Alexander warns that Western traditions that focus on identity as the mark of 'Being,' are not very helpful in our endeavors to understand truth-seeking. To broaden our view, we turned to Eastern thinking, especially the Jain doctrine of *anekantavada* understood as "the many sidedness of all phenomena" (Steger 2006, 342). Truth is always complex and pluralistic; many different, even contradicting viewpoints are necessary in the process of truth-seeking. Gandhi relates truth-seeking to nonviolence with the absence of the intention to do harm (Nagler 2004) as one of its fundamental principles. In this perspective, truth-seeking becomes an active method for creating social change. We have given the example of Gandhi's nonviolent opposition to British colonization. In the following section, we turn to a case-study that can show us how our conceptual analysis may inform (and may be informed by) an interpersonal practice of truth-seeking instigated by a very disruptive contrast experience and leading to an open ended change process.

9 Contrast Experiences, Social Imaginaries and Truth-Seeking: a Case-Study

In this part of our article we will study how contrast experiences can be the 'locus' where implicit social imaginaries find a way of expression. However, through their disruptive potential, many times contrast experiences also create a vacuum of meaning. Then a re-orientation, which consists of a search for the meaning and values hidden in this concrete contrast experience is needed. To be able to illustrate how this re-orientation could work, we will take as our starting point an extraordinary contrast experience, which is the core of the book *De Berg van de Ziel* (*The Mountain of the Soul*; Anbeek and De Jong 2013). This book is written by two Dutch women. One of the authors writes how she, her husband and three adolescent children used to spend their holidays in the Alps in Switzerland or Italy. They trained for a couple of weeks and then decided to climb a mountaintop. In the summer of 2008 the Mount Dolent in the Alps of Italy was chosen. One hour before they reached the top, the mother, who was not in perfect form, decided to give up and let the others go. She found a nice place to rest where she could wait for the others. Step for step they walked out of her view moving towards the top. On the top they telephoned their mother to tell her quite euphorically that she had missed something beautiful and magnificent. On their way back, already in sight of the mother, one of them stumbled and fell. The others who were connected by a climbing cord also fell down. Later a helicopter found them. No one had survived the accident.

The co-author of *The Mountain of the Soul* is a philosopher of religion who published several books about death and bereavement and the search for meaning that can result from impressive experiences of loss. The guiding question of the book the authors wrote together is: What could be of help in finding a way to new meaning if everything meaningful to you has gone? What resources are of help and which hindrances do you meet on your way? The approach in this quest for meaning is explicitly open in a religious or 'worldviewing' sense. Starting from their own experiences, it includes wisdoms, insights and practices from

Humanism, Buddhism, Christianity, but also wider, from literature, philosophy, film and art. The search is guided by a hunger for meaning, but it is also critical: if something does not fit in with own experiences, it is rejected. Stated in the terms of this article, the project is about confronting implicit understandings involved in social imaginaries with explicit articulations of constitutive goods in worldview traditions, whereas the value or truth intuited in the contrast experience is guiding the process.

The whole book can be read as the expression of the process of truth-seeking the two authors enter together. It is a dialogical process in which the many-sidedness of phenomena is explored from different perspectives. The authors expose themselves in their vulnerability to each other and to the readers. They seem to have built a relationship in which they can respect each other's experiences and acknowledge one another as unique persons. They do not search for a final truth; the reader witnesses an example of what Alexander calls polyphonic speaking and listening, to which he or she can relate with own intuitions of what is valuable or true. The book punctures one's own social imaginary, thus evoking strong evaluation that allows for the articulation of constitutive goods. Reading the book is truth-seeking in full progress and without the possibility of coming to a final conclusion.

Although the search for truth of the two authors is explicitly related to religion or worldview in a traditional sense – the book is organized around central themes of Christian dogmatics – no religious language is used for the interpretation of the experiences described. Glimpses of the social imaginaries in which the strong values of the authors are embedded come to the fore in small narratives of coping with pain and loss in daily life. Sometimes, the people that play a role in these narratives, seem to find their own 'worldviewing language' to articulate what they value deeply in the present situation. An example is the story that the friends of the twenty years old son told during the funeral ceremony. On the coffin they painted mountains encircled by many bees. It is a picture that belongs to a tale that they told as instructors to children during sailing camps – her son used to be one of those instructors. For this special day they modified the story. By articulating this story they try to relate themselves to a new, unknown reality, in which their friend is not among them anymore but in which his death becomes meaningful by creating light and warmth for the bereaved.

> In the beginning of the earth everything was in harmony and light was everywhere. One day, a hyena was killed by another animal. The gods were so angry that they covered the earth with a thick cloth, which took away the light. Darkness was everywhere. First the animals liked the darkness, but after sometime they started longing for light. They

tried to remove the cloth, but failed. Then the bees got an idea. They flew to the cloth and pricked little holes in it. But the job took much energy and almost no progress was made. Then four brilliant bees made an excellent plan. They climbed upon the highest mountain and from there they flew with all the power they had right across the cloth. Four big holes were created through which the light and warmth comes through. Look above and see it yourself and be grateful to those four special bees. (Anbeek and De Jong 2013, 34, translation HA)

What we see at work here, is the imaginative process as a way of truth-seeking: rooted in an experience they shared during sailing camps, the friends manifest "the ability to see the actual in light of the possible" (Alexander 2013, 9). They integrate the story of what happened in the mountains with the children's story to find some meaning in the otherwise unbearable experience of vulnerability and loss.

We can learn from the book that the process of truth-seeking is fully embodied. It is in the body that we sense how the contrast experience breaks through our self-evident and well-known world. The mother writes:

Some nights I am desperate, I am wailing. From deep inside a noise rises and comes out. A grievous shriek turns into a screaming crying. The first time that I heard this sound was in the second night after the accident. Before this time I did not know myself as someone making uncontrolled, loud shouts. Not during orgasms and not during giving birth. I even never really cried. Sometimes there were silent tears by fear, pain of sorrow. This scream comes with a primordial strength from deep within and cannot be stopped. (Anbeek and De Jong 2013, 39, translation HA)

Later she writes that the imagination of being a surfer gives comfort.

When despair comes, I imagine to be a surfer. I stand on my surfboard in a strong wind. Waves become higher and higher. Finally, I fall and it seems that I am drowning. After a while the wind and the waves calm down and I climb on my surfboard again. (Anbeek and De Jong 2013, 163, translation HA)

Although Taylor mentions ritual as a form of practice that is both enabled by and constitutive of social imaginaries and argues that ritual serves to reconnect us to the whole (2016, p.343), we have paid little attention to ritual in our conceptual analysis. Our case-study makes very clear however, that daily life is full of ritual elements in which fundamental values are both celebrated and strengthened. About the family life before the accident the mother writes:

If it is someone's birthday we come together in the bedroom to bring our presents and to have a feast-breakfast: warm bread, fresh orange juice and softly boiled eggs. The person whose birthday it is may say what we will have for dinner. For a long time French fries with applesauce were popular. Later it was pizza, peanuts-soup and stew meat. (Anbeek and De Jong 2013, 206, translation HA)

These simple rituals do not seem to be very important. She writes that her own birthday was not very significant for her. Due to the contrast experience, however, she discovers how much value was embedded in the birthday rituals her family had developed. She writes:

> For the first time I do not want to leave my bed. I cannot face this day. At this moment, the singing of my children should wake me up. They should be sitting at my bedside and proudly give their carefully chosen presents to me. A friend comes by and I get up. We have a coffee and go to the beach. There we walk and I cry. Totally unexpected, nine months after the accident, my own birthday is the most difficult day of the year. It feels strange, because my birthday was never very important to me. You celebrate that you are alive. This day I realize I wish that I did not live anymore. It would have been better if I had fallen from that mountain too. (Anbeek and De Jong 2013, 209, translation HA)

In many parts of *The Mountain of the Soul* a very important philosophical and also practical insight of the family (before the accident) becomes clear: life is more worthwhile if you share important moments with others. Many friends and family surrounded them, holidays were spent together with others and neighbours were taken care of. Although the situation changed dramatically, the importance of 'being connected' did not change.

> Through the dark I bike to the yacht harbour. I have an appointment with two friends of my son. It is still dark when we try as silent as possible to climb into the boat. It is not easy to sail out of the haven unnoticed. The friend pushes off against the other boats along the bank. People are still sleeping. Especially on Eastern morning it is not nice to be roughly woken up. After a while of sailing in the dark, we see the first orange stripes. Sometime later the sun rises beautifully. This sunrise is their precious gift to me. (Anbeek and De Jong 2013, 80, translation HA)

With examples like these, the book gives witness to the relational dimension of the process of reorientation or truth-seeking. It shows that articulation of strong values is an inter-human activity based on dialogue, experiences of being together and mutual recognition. Acknowledging this gives a new impetus to the discussion Latré and Meijer opened in chapter 3 about subjectivity and objectivity in Taylor's analysis of moral experience: how does this relate to the importance of intersubjectivity when it comes to strong evaluation and the search for truth? We are reminded here of the view of Gandhi, that from a certain perspective, truth emerges in the 'in-between,' in the spaces between different experiences that are related.

In the case-study we find concrete examples of the dynamics of truth-seeking as they take place in everyday life as a consequence of an extraordinary contrast experience. Inarticulate though they may be, social imaginaries find a tentative articulation in the subtle language of loss and refound or newly found meaning. The case study points to important aspects of truth-seeking that can be further explored not only theoretically, but also with regard to professional practices: imagination, embodiment, ritualizing and intersubjectivity. The importance of these aspects with regard to (religious) worldviewing are recognized more and more in religious studies (Meyer 2010, 2014). We think our exploration of social imaginaries and related notions in Eastern and Western thinking offers conceptual tools that add to these new developments in the study of 'religion and its others.'

10 Conclusion

In this chapter, we have tried to answer the question whether social imaginaries can be helpful in understanding contemporary processes of worldviewing. The starting point for our research was the clarification of contrast experiences that question everything that is taken for granted in life. By doing so, they inspire the articulation of what we value most deeply in life, thus bringing to the surface what is usually implicit in the way we (inter)act. They truly offer a 'site' where social imaginaries can come to expression. Social imaginaries themselves can be understood in spatial terms as well: they are spaces in which the creative, imaginative potential of individuals and groups can be realized in relation to the search for existential meaning. We understand social imaginaries not as configurations of truth, but as shared spaces for the dynamics of truth-seeking and we have related this notion to conceptions of truth that can be found in Jain philosophy and the work of Gandhi. We come to the conclusion that social imaginaries do indeed offer an important heuristic tool for understanding worldviewing, by doing justice both to shared implicit meanings and values that inform people's search for truth, and to imaginative processes involved that allow people to enter the perspectives of others and see the actual in light of the possible.

In our case-study, we characterized *The Mountain of the Soul* as an expression of the process of truth-seeking shared by the two authors. 'Expression' is not meant as the bringing into the open of some hidden, ready-made meaning. We have seen that according to Taylor, expression itself is constitutive of meanings and new realities. In line with Eastern thinking, we can understand articulation as an exploration of the infinite qualities and modes of being of what exists, bringing about changes in the way we understand existence. As we have seen, this articulation or expression will always be plural, but is nonetheless a claim or aspiration to truth. The authors of *The Mountain of the Soul* manifest that it is possible to enter a shared space – a social imaginary – that is hospitable to the process of truth-seeking. This makes our conceptual analysis relevant for the development of professional practices of guiding people in their search for meaning in life. We hope to have contributed to an interest in social imaginaries that leads both to empirical studies and to an understanding of contemporary (religious) worldviewing that does justice to the lived experiences of people in a globalizing world.

Bibliography

Arendt, Hannah. 1998. *The Human Condition*. Chicago: The University of Chicago Press.
Alexander, Thomas M. 2013. *The Human Eros: Eco-ontology and the Aesthetics of Existence*. New York: Fordham University Press.
Alma, Hans, and Christa Anbeek. 2013. "Worldviewing Competence for Narrative Interreligious Dialogue: A Humanist Contribution to Spiritual Care." In *Multifaith Voices in Spiritual Care*, edited by Daniel S. Schipani, 149–169. Ontario: Pandora Press.
Anbeek, Christa. 2013. *Aan de Heidenen overgeleverd: Hoe Theologie de 21ste Eeuw kan overleven*. Utrecht: Uitgeverij Ten Have.
Anbeek, Christa and Ada de Jong, eds. 2013. *De Berg van de Ziel: Een Persoonlijk Essay over Kwetsbaar Leven*. Utrecht: Ten Have.
Baal, Jan van. 1981. *Man's Quest for Partnership: The Anthropological Foundations of Ethics and Religion*. Assen: Van Gorcum.
Bauman, Zygmunt 2000. *Liquid Modernity*. Cambridge: Polity Press.
Bauman, Zygmunt and Leonidas Donskis. 2013. *Moral Blindness: The Loss of Sensitivity in Liquid Modernity*. Cambridge: Polity Press.
Bilgrami, Akeel. 2011. "Gandhi's Religion and Its Relation to His Politics." In *The Cambridge Companion to Gandhi*, edited by Judith M. Brown and Anthony Parel, 93–116. Cambridge: Cambridge University Press.
Bondurant, Joan V. 1965. *Conquest of Violence: the Gandhian Philosophy of Conflict*. Berkeley: University of California Press.
Borg, Meerten B. ter. 2010. *Vrijzinnigen hebben de Toekomst: Een Essay*. Zoetermeer: Meinema.
Butler, Judith. 2003. *Giving an Account of Oneself: A Critique of Ethical Violence*. Assen: Van Gorcum.
Butler, Judith. *Precarious Life: The Powers of Mourning and Violence*. London/New York: Verso.
Butler, Judith. 2010. *Frames of War: When is Life Grievable?*. London/New York: Verso.
Dundas, Paul. 2002. *The Jains*. London/New York: Routledge.
Fesmire, Steven. 2003. *John Dewey and Moral Imagination: Pragmatism in Ethics*. Bloomington: Indiana University Press.

Gandhi, Mohandas K. 1927. *An Autobiography: The Story of My Experiments With Truth* (translation by M. Desai). Ahmdabad: Navajivan Publishing House.

Geertz, Clifford. 1993. "Religion as a Cultural System." In *The Interpretation of Cultures: Selected Essays*, 87–125. London: Fontana Press.

Goelst Meijer, Saskia. L.E. van. 2015. *Profound Revolution: Towards an Integrated Understanding of Contemporary Nonviolence*. Utrecht: University of Humanistic Studies.

Jackson, Michael. 2002. *Politics of Storytelling: Violence, Transgression and Intersubjectivity*. Copenhagen: Museum Tusculanum Press.

Koller, John M. 2004. "Why is Anekantavada Important?" In *Ahimsā, Anekānta and Jainism*, edited by Tara Sethia, 85–98. Delhi: Motilal Banarsidass Publishers.

Kunneman, Harry. 2005. *Voorbij het Dikke-Ik: Bouwstenen voor een Kritisch Humanisme*. Amsterdam: Humanistics University Press.

Latré, Stijn. 2018. "Social Imaginaries: A Conceptual Analysis." In *Social Imaginaries in a Globalizing World*, edited by Hans Alma and Guido Vanheeswijck. Berlin: De Gruyter.

Latré, Stijn and Michiel Meijer, M. 2018. "Retrieving Realism in Social Imaginaries." In *Social Imaginaries in a Globalizing World*, edited by Hans Alma and Guido Vanheeswijck. Berlin: De Gruyter.

Long, Jeffery D. 2009. *Jainism: An Introduction*. London: I.B. Tauris.

Long, Jeffery D. 2013. *Anekānta and Ahimsā: A Jain Philosophy of Universal Acceptance*. Virchand Gandhi Lecture, Claremont School of Theology.

Mardia, Kanti V. and Aidan D. Rankin. (2013). *Living Jainism: An Ethical Science*. Winchester, UK: Mantra Books.

Meyer, Birgit. 2006. *Religious Sensations: Why Media, Aesthetics and Power matter in the Study of Contemporary Religion*. Amsterdam: Vrije Universiteit.

Meyer, Birgit. 2012. *Mediation and the Genesis of Presence: Towards a Material Approach to Religion*. Utrecht: Universiteit Utrecht.

Nagler, Michael N. 2004. *The Search for a Nonviolent Future: A Promise of Peace for Ourselves, Our Families, and Our World*. Novato, CA: New World Library.

Polk, Steffanie. 2012. *All about Jainism*. Delhi: University Publications.

Pulcini, Elena. 2013. *Care of the World: Fear, Responsibility and Justice in the Global Age*. New York: Springer.

Schillebeeckx, Edward. 1989. *Mensen als Verhaal van God*. Baarn: Nelissen.

Steger, Manfred B. 2006. "Searching for Satya through Ahimsa: Gandhi's Challenge to Western Discourses of Power." *Constellations* 13 (3):332–353.

Taylor, Charles. 2004. *Modern Social Imaginaries*. Durham: Duke University Press.

Taylor, Charles. 2007. *A Secular Age*. Cambridge, MA: Belknap Press of Harvard University Press.

Taylor, Charles. 2011. *Dilemmas and Connections: Selected Essays*. Cambridge, MA: Belknap Press of Harvard University Press.

Taylor, Charles. 2016. *The Language Animal: The Full Shape of the Human Linguistic Capacity*. Cambridge, MA: Belknap Press of Harvard University Press.

Thakar, Vimala. 2005. *Glimpses of Raja Yoga: an Introduction to Patanjali's Yoga Sutras*. Berkeley, CA: Rodmell Press.

Vandevoordt, Robin, Noel Clycq and Gert Verschraegen. 2018. "Studying culture through social imaginaries." In *Social Imaginaries in a Globalizing World*, edited by Hans Alma and Guido Vanheeswijck. Berlin: De Gruyter.

Vertovec, Steven. 2007. "Super-diversity and its Implications." *Ethnic and Racial Studies* 30 (6):1024–1054.
Vroom, Henk M. 1989. *Religions and the Truth: Philosophical Reflections and Perspectives*. Amsterdam: Rodopi.
Vroom, Henk M. 2013. *Walking in a Widening World: Understanding Religious Diversity*. Amsterdam: VU University Press.

Laurens ten Kate
The Play of the World

Social Imaginaries as Transcending Spaces: From Taylor to Nietzsche

1 Introduction

1.1 Super-Diversity

This world's 'super-diversity,' as analyzed by Steven Vertovec (2007), is one of the most compelling features of the social and cultural reality in an era of globalization. The many encounters and confrontations between groups and individuals that result from this diversity refer us to what has recently been coined by Charles Taylor as *social imaginaries* (Taylor 2004; 2007, chapter 4). In the present volume, the concept of social imaginaries serves as a tool to describe, analyze and understand super-diversity.

What is super-diversity? The working definition I will take as a take-off to my analyzes is the following. Super-diversity is the fundamental condition of global *pluralism* on an existential level: a plurality of traditions, world-views, cultural habits, religious practices and rituals, and, most of all, of new mixes of these time and again.

1.2 Sense and Super-Diversity

It is easy to diagnose this condition of pluralism as one that excludes the experience of *sense*; for sense and meaning would only be possible if they rest in a single, more or less determined value system. However, in my view that is too easy a conclusion.

In a super-diverse world the 'sense of life' should be thought in a different way. The French philosopher Jean-Luc Nancy even equates the new mixes of world-views, traditions etcetera, *with* sense (Nancy 1997).[1] This concept of sense is in itself first of all a condition: something in which we are and from

---

[1] In fact, almost Nancy's entire oeuvre is focused on a rethinking of sense against the backdrop of a secularizing and globalizing world.

which we live our existences. But it is a condition that *occurs* time and again and is never the same. Sense as a name for the super-diverse mix of world-views is, in Nancy's view, an *event*. It offers itself to us so that we can shape it to a concrete story, image, practice. In this way, the sense we receive from the condition of super-diversity we are embedded in, can be turned into 'our' sense: the sense we appropriate and attribute to life, to the world. In other words, only because the world *is* sense, it can *have* sense and *make* sense to us. And as soon as the world of super-diversity makes sense to us, we create sense. Such creations, however finite and fragile they are, make it possible to claim sense: "This is what I'm going for, this is the sense of my life." 'Going for...': in the end, sense is not an entity or substance, let alone a foundation. It is a direction, a perspective and an aspiration.[2] People need these in order to endure pluralism and its complexity on the one hand, while on the other playing with it, creating and recreating it, thereby affirming that it can never have any *duration*. Living in a super-diverse world means to endure what cannot last: to take on the non-lasting status this world is in.

This plurality of sense is active on an intimate, private level and on a social level. It is at work *in* individual humans and *between* them. Social imaginaries are the *spaces* where this plurality – in always new forms – is constituted and actually 'takes place' as a temporarily shared mix of sense. If the present volume devotes itself to the study of this pluralism of social imaginaries, in this chapter I will contribute to that by investigating to what extent Friedrich Nietzsche's concepts of *play* and *world-play* are relevant to our understanding of social imaginaries.

Before we turn our attention to Nietzsche (3), we will have to take a closer look at the theory of social imaginaries, develop our own definition and create a framework that will enable us to connect the concept of social imaginaries with world theory and play theory (2).

2 Social Imaginaries: Towards a Spatial Analysis

Let me again begin with a possible working definition. Social imaginaries are often implicitly shared sets of assumptions of a certain socio-cultural group, involving moral or religious claims about the society they are part of: claims about the basic values of society and how it should be organized. This is the way Taylor would approach the definition of social imaginaries. He therefore defines them

---

[2] In French, the word *sens* has the doubling meaning of sense and direction.

as incorporating "the kind of common understanding which enables us to carry out the collective practices which make up our social life. This incorporates some sense of how we all fit together in carrying out the common practice" (Taylor 2007, 172).

2.1 Shared Imaginaries

A preliminary but important remark is necessary here. 'Social' should not be read as 'societal,' but rather in a broader sense, as 'shared.' Imaginaries are shared claims at work on many levels of human relations: society as a whole, but also smaller communities, like a town or village, a sport club or a family.

Moreover, underlining the shared character of imaginaries implies that they are versatile, even chaotic in their functioning. The terms 'common' and 'collective' in Taylor's definition do not entirely do justice to the fact that many imaginaries are less dependent on a particular group, or are at work in very loose and intangible pluralities. Think of national ("We Dutch") or international imaginaries ("We Europeans"), of imaginaries related to a profession ("That's a typical doctor's perspective"; "Only a philosopher could reason like that") or to a hobby ("We motorbikers"). Think also of digital communities, that are usually highly flexible and elusive, like a Facebook-group. Particularly in the last two decades, the reality of imaginaries mingles material or physical with virtual or digital modes of being. And we should add an important note here: we can also share imaginaries with and within ourselves, for we never simply belong and adhere to just one common understanding or common practice. People combining an intercultural or cross-cultural mix of backgrounds form an obvious example here. With the increase of global migration their numbers are growing fast.

Consequently, we should treat the adjective 'social' in social imaginaries with a lot of nuance, even reserve. Imaginaries are shared on many existential levels, and do not only express claims about society.

2.2 Imagination against Foundation

As the term suggests, social imaginaries refer to the way communities *imagine* their background assumptions and ideals, rather than to their explicit intellectual doctrines or beliefs. Social imaginaries have always been part of the way humans relate to the world – for instance, a medieval tryptich, the interior of a gothic cathedral, or the goal of a long pilgrimage (think of the sacred *locus* of

Santiago in Spain) are all strong and wide-spread imaginaries, that have given sense to many lives. Nevertheless, in late-modern super-diverse societies these implicit imaginaries become more and more central in the human sense-giving process. When the so-called grand narratives of humanism, nationalism, socialism, fascism, or of the religious traditions still present in modern, secular life – Christianity as their most dominant example, all over the globe – have to recline gradually in our time, social imaginaries respond to the need to at least *imagine* sense: our imaginaries compensate for the loss of doctrines, beliefs, and ideologies. Humans are left to their own devices when it comes to visualizing why the world is a worthful place and what its destination could be: a logic of imagination slowly interrupts, absorbs and replaces the logic of foundation.

The notion of a foundation, Nancy explains in his *The Sense of the World*, always presupposes a Founder from outside our existence. If sense is understood as a founding value or principle, instead of as an event stemming from the condition of super-diversity, if sense is thought to have as its prime attribute stability instead of instability, then it is always someone else, outside humanity and the human world, that should be believed to bestow sense on us. However, the sense of the modern world lies exactly in its lack of such an outside Founder. But this implies that modern culture is, in a radical way, without foundation. It has to found itself on itself – impossible gesture – and this can only be achieved in imagination.

2.3 'Secularity 3' and the Importance of Social Imaginaries

Needless to say, in placing the analysis of social imaginaries at the heart of his exploration of the secular age, Taylor criticizes the idea that the process of secularization would primarily be an intellectual story, belonging to the history of ideas. The great theorists of secularization have fallen into this trap, Taylor states, although their approach "explicates some very important truths, and draws on crucial connections" (Taylor 2007, 774).

Indeed, Karl Löwith and Hans Blumenberg, for example, have touched upon a crucial discovery that complexifies our entire perspective on the secular age: its secularity does consist of new connections between... religion and the secular way of life, that is, between transcendence and immanence (Blumenberg 1983; Löwith 1969). The *Neuzeit*, Löwith claims, is a continuation of the Christian era with different means, and to him these new means – belief in progress, rationalism, the end of history etcetera – are a degeneration with regard to a certain balance between the other world and the here and now that would have constituted the Christian era. Blumenberg goes the other way, claiming that the *Neuzeit* is a radical displacement *(Umbesetzung)* of Christian doctrine, metaphors and experiences, that possesses its own complex legitimacy. Although these thinkers disagree on how to assess the secular age, they both start from the insight that secularity can only be understood as a new interaction between religion (and especially Christianity and its massive heritage in modern culture) and secular life. In this interaction both transform one another. This is what Taylor calls "secularity 3" (Taylor 2007, 15).[3]

But Taylor is not satisfied with the way these thinkers address secularity 3 and its new entanglements of transcendence and immanence. They remain stuck in a view on history as a development of ideas, with its ruptures and revolutions. The entanglements of secularity 3 – the way in which religion does not disappear in the secular age, but transforms itself *and* secularity – are investigated and analyzed much more productively at the level of concrete, lived practices. Meanwhile we know that these practices are first of all practices of imagination, and that they can be conceptualized as social imaginaries. Social imaginaries are new touching points between transcendence and immanence. I will briefly return to this in the final section of this chapter.[4]

---

[3] Secularity 1 and 2 refer to the more common definition of a retreat of religion from the public realm (1), and of the disappearance of the human need to believe in a God (2). Secularity 3 complements these definitions, but problematizes them as well, as I demonstrate here, since it opens the private and public space to new interactions and mutual transformations between religion and secular life. In this context, Taylor speaks of 'new conditions of belief' (2007, part IV).
[4] Taylor calls the history of these touching points the "story" of Reform (see in particular Taylor, 2007, Part I: "The Work of Reform"), and he presents his work as a counter-narrative against (1) those who think the secular as an exclusion of religion and (2) those who treat secularization as a new relation to religion, but on the level of idea's, like Löwith and Blumenberg in his view. This counter-narrative he calls "Reform Master Narrative" (Taylor 2007, 773–776).

Reform refers to the historical situation that religion *and* secularity transform themselves *and* one another. This leads Taylor to a new understanding of the secular age as an era in which religion (esp. Christianity in the later Middle Ages and in early Modernity) secularizes itself to a certain extent, and in which secular life retains within itself multiple religious features. This surely is Taylor's first theoretical mission in his book; the second is that this situation of Reform can only be explored successfully by focusing on practices in which new imaginaries are at work. One of his countless examples is that of the New Devotion movements toward the end of the Middle Ages, proclaiming a more secular, that is personal, individual and self-achieved relation to Christ and his suffering, a relation that declares any mediation through the clerical hierarchy obsolete, while at the same time installing a new, disciplined life style (Taylor 2007, 70). "Reform not only disenchants, but disciplines and re-orders life and society. Along with civility, this makes for a notion of moral order which gives a new sense to Christianity, and to the demands of faith. (…) It induces an anthropocentric shift, and hence a break-out of the monopoly of Christian faith." (Taylor 2007, 774)

2.4 The Essential Instability of Social Imaginaries

Let us resume: social imaginaries are rarely explicit, almost always implicit background understandings, in the form of imaginations. This means that one should always understand social imaginaries as *practices*. This is probably why Taylor immediately introduces the term 'practice' in the aforementioned definition of social imaginaries. A social imaginary is more than a set of ideas one can hold or reject, adapt or replace. They are not even something we have, but something we do. They only become *real* in and through lived practices that exceed the level of cognitive frameworks, like a grand ideological narrative.

The shared practices that social imaginaries entail, are less dependent on traditional sources, offering a stable framework of meaning, value and truth, as these were often brought about by religion: a transcendent God who, from outside the world, gives meaning to that world, to nature and to humanity. In such a context of an external God as Giver-of-sense, the sinner, for example, can receive meaning to his life by stating: only God can judge me; the prosperous calvinist can experience his wealth as a gift of God; the French soldiers can consider their war against the Germans as God's war. But these stable frameworks have been eclipsed or even dispelled from contemporary views on man and nature. And social imaginaries are by no means their successors. In the super-diversity that characterizes the global condition, the new, immanent social imaginaries do not offer new systems of belief.

Consequently, social imaginaries are characterized by a high degree of *instability*, a term that serves me as an umbrella for various other features. We have already considered the *shared* and the *practical* character of social imaginaries above. Being unstable also implies that social imaginaries are finite, ephemeral, *temporary* creations by which we live and act from moment to moment, from time to time, from phase to phase in our lives. Next to being fundamentally unstable because of their temporariness, they function only in the *plural*. There is never one imaginary that can inform and determine a complete social or cultural environment. This instability and this plurality engender their *inarticulacy:* social imaginaries escape full scientific definition, and necessitate a broader theoretical and empirical analysis that has no clear limits.[5]

---

[5] This is one of the central statements of Braidotti and others 2014.

2.5 Imaginaries as Spaces and Worlds

Having stressed the shared, practical and unstable character of social imaginaries, and having refined that instability in their temporary, plural and inarticulate way of functioning, we arrive at a crucial feature in which all previously discussed characteristics merge and converge: their *spatial* mode. This brings me to the key question of this chapter that will guide me in the following pages: how can social imaginaries be understood as spaces? This question starts from the idea formulated by Benedict Anderson and Cornelius Castoriadis: social imaginaries are 'lived' spaces in which people share as well as contest the meaning of their existence, often in an unconscious way.[6]

Social imaginaries do not remain external to us, as our objects. We do not *have* social imaginaries as tools to make and share claims about our existence. We *do* social imaginaries and in this creative dynamics something remarkable happens. We start to live in what we create: imaginaries become spaces for us to dwell in. In this sense, every imaginary *transcends* us to a certain extent. I will give just a preliminary example. We use our smartphones: we design them as our personal digital environment, downloading our preferred apps on it, embellishing it with our symbols, pictures, sounds etcetera. But in this 'doing' the smartphone becomes active too – it 'does us,' shapes us in becoming a 'world' we live in.

Hence I aim to explore the possibility to think these spaces as *worlds*. These worlds-to-think are not of the order of the 'globe' that forms the substance of most globalization theories: they do not point towards an increasingly unified and liberal world, and to a humanity at last in an intensely intimate state of contact with itself. On the contrary, they consist in plurality and complexity, according to the features of social imaginaries described and analyzed in this section.

2.6 Playful Worlds

In attempting to analyze social imaginaries as worlds, I will develop the argument that, in order to understand *who we are* in these worlds, and *what we do* in them, we have to think these worlds as fundamentally playful. They are the spaces that we create playfully, and *in which* we actually play at the same

---

6 Anderson (1983) applies this conceptualization of social imaginaries specifically to an analysis of nationalism, and Castoriadis (1987) thinks imaginaries as 'spaces of contestation' in a more existential sense.

time. In a social imaginary, our actions take the form of playful practices, and such a imaginary is the outcome of that play at the same time. They are of the order of a condition *and* of a result. In other words, it appears that we make imaginary spaces and that they make us simultaneously.

As mentioned above, I will analyze this paradoxical structure starting from Nietzsche's notions of *world-play* (*Welt-Spiel*) and *world-creation*. I will read the first hymn of his *Thus Spoke Zarathustra* as well as the first of the 'songs' Nietzsche has added as an appendix to his *The Gay Science*. In order to articulate how Nietzsche's idea of play has traversed and influenced twentieth-century thought, I will occasionally refer to thinkers who in my view explicitly (Maurice Blanchot, Eugen Fink) or implicitly (Hannah Arendt, Nancy, Peter Sloterdijk) take up the challenges formulated by Nietzsche for a theory of play.

3 The World as Play: Nietzsche's View

In 1974, Lawrence Hinman has argued that "the category of play is fundamental to Nietzsche's interpretation of man and the world" (Hinman 1974, 107). Throughout his oeuvre, so full of complexity, contradictions and lived dilemmas, Nietzsche criticizes modern humanism and its claim that humans are rational, autonomous subjects who make the world as their object:

> The whole attitude of man '*against* the world,' of man as a 'world-negating' principle, of man as the measure of the value of things, as judge of the world who finally places existence itself on his scales and finds it too light – the monstrous stupidity of this attitude has finally dawned on us and we are sick of it; we laugh as soon as we encounter the juxtaposition of 'man *and* world,' separated by the sublime presumptuousness of the little word '*and!*' (Nietzsche 2001, 204, fragment 346)

But it is in play that another humanism announces itself, according to Hinman. A few years before Hinman, Maurice Blanchot has suggested this too: in Nietzsche's concept of world-play another view on human existence is experimented with, he states, that leaves behind all humanist belief in progress and in a future for man to realize and assert himself in. For Blanchot, even the notions of man and humanity stand in the way of "an inquiry into the play of the world, that orients us toward an entirely different question..." (Blanchot 1993, 247). A new humanism should *cry out* this question – the question of man, the question man *is* — as the madman does in an earlier famous fragment of *The Gay Science* (1882/1887), when he announces the death of God (Nietzsche 2001, 119–120, fragment 125).

In the same passage, Blanchot admits he is wary of Nietzsche's concept of the overman (*Übermensch*), since it seems a continuation of the old notion of man, in the form of a future fulfilment of man as the subject of the world and of the history of that world. Nietzsche's dictum: "All gods are dead: now we want the overman to live" (Nietzsche 1969, 104, Part I: XXII–3)[7] is in the end, Blanchot thinks, only a rephrasing of traditional humanism, that has always been a 'theological myth.' It replaces the old subject of the world, God, by a new one, man.

Hinman, on the other hand, develops the view that it is exactly in this new vision of human life as playful existence that lies the meaning of Nietzsche's concept of the overman (Hinman 1974, 116–119). The overman is "the player *par excellence*" (Hinman 1974, 118), who achieves "the highest ranks of human activity" not by being superior to other, lower beings, but by "creating as fully as possible its own world" (Hinman 1974, 107). Parallel to this interpretation of the overman, Hinman also connects Nietzsche's theory of the will to power with a will to play, that is, the will to create a world.

But why and how are Nietzsche's theory of play and of the world connected? And on what basis does he think that a concentration on the play of the world necessarily leads to a critique of humanism involving a radical decentering of the subject? In order to answer these questions, we first have to understand why Nietzsche sees play as an essential feature of humans.

3.1 The Camel, the Lion, The Child

Thus Spoke Zarathustra (1885) consists of a long series of hymn-like 'discourses' (*Reden*): sermons or reflections, mostly in prose, sometimes in poetic form. Every hymn finishes with the solemn words "Thus Spoke Zarathustra." In the famous opening hymn, entitled "Of the Three Metamorphoses," Nietzsche introduces three shapes of the human "spirit," that would follow each other in developing metamorphoses (*Verwandlungen*) (Nietzsche 1969, 54–56).

The first stage is that of the "camel." The camel is the stage of morality in human existence. It longs for "the heaviest things," for it is a "weight-bearing spirit" (Nietzsche 1969, 54). It is devoted to the logic of achievement through submission to tasks: it "(…) wants to be laden well" (Nietzsche 1969, 54). It finds its strength in obeying the 'I should' and 'I must.' The world of the camel-spirit is a world one has to endure through hard work; the world, seen this way, imposes

---

7 Translation modified.

itself on us as our 'other.' The world is what is *given*. Humans can only carry it, but in this act they "rejoice in their strength" (Nietzsche 1969, 54): "The weight-bearing spirit takes upon itself all these heaviest things: like a camel hurrying laden into the desert, thus it hurries into the desert" (Nietzsche 1969, 54).

Without referring to Nietzsche, Hannah Arendt distinguishes in her *The Human Condition* three modes of human activity too: three conditions of how humans appear in and relate to the world. She analyzes what Nietzsche calls the spirit of the camel as *labor:* survival by taking on the world as it is as a burden and a law. Both Arendt and Nietzsche call this the basic dynamic of the life process (Arendt 1958, Part III, 79–135).

The second stage in the three metamorphoses is that of the "lion." The lion is close to the camel, for both are caught up in a struggle with the world. Where the camel submits to its weight, the lion, however, "creates freedom for itself" by saying a "sacred No" to all moral duties (Nietzsche 1969, 55). The lion posits *itself* as the other of or to the world, liberating itself from its givenness. The perspective changes: no longer the world is our other imposing itself on us, but man himself becomes the other of the world. Instead of the logic of the "Thou shalt" the lion adopts the logic of the "I will" (Nietzsche 1969, 55). "But in the loneliest desert the second metamorphosis occurs: the spirit here becomes a lion; it wants to capture freedom and be lord in its own desert" (Nietzsche 1969, 54).

This stage of the lion metaphorically reflects what Karl Jaspers, and later on many contemporary scholars have called the *axial process* that would determine the cultural history of mankind: a break away from the world dominated by the gods and by fate, towards a world in which humans acquire autonomy and the possibility self-assertion (Jaspers 1953, Part I, chapters I & V).[8] The axial process, that Jaspers still treated as a specific period (first millennium B.C.) but that the majority of scholars now consider to be a continuous process still at work in (late) modernity, is also the time in which man becomes *technical* and *rational:* by means of technique and reason he frees himself from the world and starts to work on and in it. Traditionally this shift has been addressed as the turn from *mythos* to *logos*. Humans surmount the burden of the word by gradually controlling and mastering it – turning it into their object, or in Nietzsche's metaphorical language, their 'prey.' Arendt names this second phase of the lion the condition of *work* (Arendt 1958, Part IV, 136–174).

---

8 See for a good survey of the present debate on axial theory Johann P. Arnason and others (2005). Jörn Rüsen (2012) proposes to think the 21st century as a new axial age. Key protagonists in this debate are Charles Taylor, Marcel Gauchet, Robert Bellah, Hans Joas, Karen Armstrong and others, as studied in Ten Kate 2014.

The lion-spirit has created for itself the conditions to transform the world, and to transform itself in relation with the world. It corresponds with man as "measure of the value of things, as judge of the world," quoted above, a view on humanity and the world fiercely criticized by Nietzsche. But here In Thus Spoke Zarathustra Nietzsche does not conceal a certain admiration for the camel and the lion as stages of the human spirit: they are necessary in the history of metamorphoses.

The third stage forms a rupture with the camel-lion relation to the world. It is the last metamorphosis, that of the "child." Instead of a "sacred No" to the world, the child is a "sacred Yes" to it (Nietzsche 1969, 55).

> But tell me, my brothers, what can the child do that even the lion cannot? Why must the preying lion still become a child?
> The child is innocence and forgetfulness, a new beginning, a game (Spiel), a self-propelling wheel, a first motion, a sacred Yes. (Nietzsche 1969, 55)[9]

Here the relation to the world is not one of surmounting and conquering, but one of *creating:* 'a new beginning' in which, at the same time, one is absorbed by that creation with 'innocence and forgetfulness,' like a child that can be enveloped in its game. Needless to say, at this point in the line of thought Nietzsche sets out in this hymn, we are touching upon the paradox of the spaces social imaginaries are, as we have demonstrated in the previous section. The creative relation to the world obliterates the division of man *and* the world: it is rather an opening toward the world and into the world. Creating a world, that remarkable capacity of children, simultaneously means that one lives in that world. In his trilogy *Spheres*, Peter Sloterdijk opens the first volume with a beautiful miniature, painting with words a little boy who is blowing bubbles with a small pipe and a bowl of soap and water. The boy follows a big bubble he has just blown, floating through the air for the few seconds it is meant to last. The child follows the bubble so intensely that the attentive gaze of its eyes mingles with the fragile 'sphere' dancing in the air. For a moment, it is absorbed by this microspace, it actually lives in the bubble. Bubble and child become a "breathed commune" (Sloterdijk 2011, 16–20).[10]

The strange coincidence of acting and 'being acted' we are coming across here, is the anthropological *structure of play* Nietzsche is looking for. The remarkable consequence of this is that humanity, in the end and at the apogee of its possibilities, should become like a child: a central theme that runs through

---

9 Translation modified.
10 Sloterdijk bases his miniature on a painting by G.H. Everett Millais, dating from 1886.

the veins of almost all of Nietzsche's works. "Yes, a sacred Yes is needed, my brothers, for the play (*Spiel*) of creation: the spirit now wills *its own* will, the spirit sundered from the world now wins *its own* world." (Nietzsche 1969, 55)

We can observe that the child brings aspects of the camel and the lion together. For the child as for the lion, the world is no longer given as a burden; but neither is it an external object to be appropriated, as the camel shows. We create worlds beyond any givenness, as a new beginning that never stops beginning, and in the same movement these worlds create us by the space we live from and thus are dependent on. It is important to realize that Nietzsche shifts from a discussion of *the* world to a discussion of *a* world, that is, of a plurality of worlds created by man. Every human spirit 'wins its own world,' at every time and place, always anew. Nietzsche's notion of play concurs with a theory of imaginaries so it appears.

The stage of the human spirit as the playing child resonates in the vocabulary of Arendt's *The Human Condition* as *action*. For her, action is the essence of the political as a particular feature of the human condition, as opposed to labor and work. Political action and speech always form a new beginning, and they open up the space of plurality: the space of appearance that the public realm is. Not surprisingly, Arendt baptizes this space of action as *natality* and *plurality*. In a reciprocal event of creation, both man and the world are formed and transformed, are born and reborn *(natus)* here (Arendt 1958, 175–247, especially chapters 28–29).

3.2 A Song on World-Play

Two years later, Nietzsche adds a series of songs to the second edition (1887) of his book *The Gay Science*, entitled "Songs of Prince Vogelfrei." The first song, "To Goethe," is a parody of the "Chorus Mysticus" concluding *Faust* (Nietzsche 2001, 249). Nietzsche's critique of romantic historicism, as already laid out in his "On the Use and Abuse of History for Life"[11] is expressed in his ironical rephrasings of Goethe's idealization of human divinity and eternity, as this is exemplified in the sublime womanhood of Gretchen. This idealization would only be a "parable" (*Gleichnis*) of the poet himself, who celebrates his power to imagine and fictionalize the "ever-enduring," the stable goal and fulfilment of divinized history. The "God" of that history is "all-blurring" (*Verfänglich*) because he is nothing but man in disguise, that is, the poet himself who cheats us about his true nature

---

[11] This is one of the essays in *Untimely Meditations* (1874).

and elevates himself fictitiously. But this fiction of a metaphysics of humanity is "unbearable..." The poet's *Gleichnis* turns out to be *Dichter-Erschleichnis*.[12]

> *To Goethe*
>
> The ever-enduring
> is merely your parable
> God the all-blurring
> your fiction unbearable...

Then, in the second stanza, Nietzsche, the poet who problematizes his fellow poet Goethe, introduces a different figure, or in Zarathustra's language, a different human spirit: the "fool" (*Narr*). Here, a different power of imagination is presented: not the one that masters the world in an ever-enduring fiction, as does the lion in Zarathustra's hymn, but one that "plays."

> World-wheel, the turning one
> spawns goals each day:
> Fate — sighs the yearning one,
> the fool calls it — play.

Now, the world is compared with a wheel that is turning independently from man's control, from his "yearning" to be the world's subject. In other worlds, the world is a space that is too complex and super-diverse for the lion-spirit not to lose himself in it. This loss is called play. The fool, in whom we may recognize Zarathustra's child, plays with *and* in the world without appropriating it, without winning it in the form of an enduring image or worldview. It only wins its own temporary world.

In the last stanza this dynamic of playing with and in, of imagining and being imagined, is resumed in the notion of "world-play."

> World-play, the ruling one [*das herrische*],
> blends truth and tricks [*Mischt Schein und Sein*]: —
> The eternally fooling one [*Das ewig-Närrische*]
> blends *us* — in the mix!... [*Mischt* uns — *hinein!...*]

In playing we imagine and in this way create worlds, whereby the strict division between "truth and tricks," reality and fiction, is no longer valid. The fictions be-

---

[12] See on the parodical character of the song also the editor's note on the same page, which draws on the elaborate annotations by Colli and Montinari in the German *Gesamtausgabe*.

come instances, forces of the real; this is why in our time social imaginaries can be material and virtual, physical and digital at the same time, as we remarked in the previous section.

In his major study *Spiel als Weltsymbol* (Play as Symbol of the World; 1960) Eugen Fink stresses in a similar way that the "worldliness" (*Weltlichkeit*) of play consists in its capacity to blur the distinction between appearance and being *(Schein und Sein)*. Fink conceptualizes this ambiguity of play in a definition: play is the "ecstacy of man towards the world." The player has to leave and lose himself, but in this ecstacy he does not create a false world, but rather a different mode or dimension *of* the real world. The "*being* and *sense*" (*Seins-Sinn*) of "the imaginary scene of play" has therefore to be taken very seriously. This mode of being of play Fink calls a "world-symbol," but, treading in Nietzsche's steps, he deliberately leaves the question open whether this symbol is not just as "real" as the "real world" (Fink 2010, 216, all citations).

Hence, play is not a different world from reality: neither a higher world, that of the gods, as the epoch of *mythos* advocates, nor a lower world, that of appearance as opposed to the truth of the ideas, as the epoch of *logos* (Fink uses the example of Plato's metaphysical thought) holds. Play is *this* human world, seen in a different mode.

> The world of play is neither 'less' nor 'more' compared to the other things (…) The world of play is, in its medium of appearance, symbol of the world. The imaginary does not mark its rank out of a distance to the world of things, of ideas or of the gods; it proves its rank and meaning out of the human relation to the world. (Fink 2010, 217)

Returning to Nietzsche, we can conclude that precisely *because* in the spaces that imaginary worlds are, a solid distinction between real and unreal is undermined, we cannot remain external to them. As children, as fools we are always already caught up in the play of the world. We lose ourselves in the world-spaces we have created, and this loss is essential for play – it is essential for the imaginaries to succeed.

In the end, Nietzsche presents "world-play" as a personified figure: "the ruling one," "the fooling one", who "blends *us* in" our imaginaries, in our play. In the theory of human action and creation Nietzsche seeks to formulate in his hymns and songs, every action we start immediately acts "back" on us: we are always part of our actions. This is the dynamic of the play of the world. In other words: humanity has to lose itself in order to find itself.

3.3 Acting/Being Acted

We have thought social imaginaries as lived spaces in which humans in a globalizing era creatively imagine the sense of the world as an event, as Nancy analyzes this: shared imaginaries, without foundation, without stability, temporary, plural and inarticulate. We have also seen, reading two evocative texts by Nietzsche, that this is how the late-modern world 'works': *as* a complexity of imaginary worlds that form our finite homes. This should be understood as dynamically as possible, as if one could change the grammatical status of the words world and worldview from noun to verb. We 'world' the world and the world 'worlds on us,' time and again, in ever new imaginaries. And we do not hold worldviews, but are are constantly 'worldviewing' (Alma and Anbeek 2013).

Nietzsche's theory of the world coincides with a theory of play. In the play of the child and the fool the dynamics of the process of world-imaginaries can be addressed in a radical and productive way. It is not only a new theory of the world and of how we view the world that is at stake here; a new theory of action is involved as well. This comes down to the following: we start an action, and immediately we are part of that action – our action is no longer simply our act, controlled by us as subjects external to that act, on the contrary, our action takes over and 'acts on us.' This double bind in our actions makes them playful. Play is: to act/to live in your act. We are 'blended' in world-play. In other words: we always play *with* the world (that is, with *a* world: with the many worlds the world consists of) and simultaneously we play *in* the world.

It is this remarkable structure of playful action that continues to influence twentieth-century and contemporary philosophy to a large extent. I can only hint at a few examples here. We have already related this structure of play to Arendt's theory of action in *The Human Condition*. The political dimension of human speech and action consists of humans appearing in the world, sharing that world over and again, in a new beginning that never stops beginning. According to this action theory, that is close to Nietzsche's account of play, "action discloses the agent together with the act (...), which is possible only in the public realm" (Arendt 1958, 180). In this specific sense, action is always a leap and a venture: one does not know where one will end when one imaginatively creates a world. The creator cannot remain external to his creation, we have to *enter* the world we have just started, and 'appear' in its realm, as Arendt stresses. Hence, the principle of *natality*, as stated above, is crucial to an understanding of the playful spaces we are investigating.

> To act, in its most general sense, means to take an initiative, to begin (as the Greek word *archein*, 'to begin,' 'to lead,' and eventually 'to rule' indicates), to set something into mo-

tion (which is the original meaning of the Latin *agere*). Because they are *initium*, newcomers and beginners by virtue of birth, men take initiative, are prompted into action. [*Initium*] *ergo ut esset, creatus est homo, ante quem nullus fuit* ('That there be a beginning, man was created before whom there was nobody'), said Augustine in his political philosophy.[13] This beginning is not the same as the beginning of the world; it is not the beginning of something, but of somebody, who is a beginner himself. With the creation of man, the principle of beginning came into the world itself (...) (Arendt 1958, 177)

In Nietzschean terms one could vary on Arendt's words: with the creation of man, the principle of play and of imagination came into the world. Or rather: with the creation of man, the world stops being a stable foundation (the "beginning of the world" rejected by Arendt as the doctrine of creationism: a unique event out of which the universe would have emerged thanks to the deed of a timeless, almighty God). Instead, with the creation of man, the world itself becomes the principle of beginning.

Nancy re-reads the Judeo-Christian doctrine of the *creatio ex nihilo* along these lines. The *ex nihilo* does not mean, as Christian theism has it, that a pre-existing creator would suddenly create man and the world out of nothing. The 'beginning' that the creation is (Genesis 1:1) is a radical beginning: the creator only becomes someone *in* the act of creating and in the encounter with his creature, humanity, who is imagined to be his partner, his fellow creator. "So God created man in his own image, in the image of God he created him..." (Genesis 1:27). The creator was no one before this beginning, he was *nihil*. This strange God only becomes a god when he enters into the relation with the world, with man. And the creative beginning will begin again and again; this is why the Hebrew text speaks of "In *a* beginning," without definite article. The creator coincides with his act of creating, outside this act "God is nothing," and only in this way, between God and man, something new can happen: a world can be created. Nancy even considers this counter-interpretation of the *ex nihilo* the starting point for his project of a 'deconstruction of monotheism,' and in particular of the Christian heritage in the modern world.[14] This deconstruction is not only one of Nancy's research projects of the last twenty years, it is a historical break line in the axial process we briefly discussed above – Nietzsche's stage of the lion. The *ex nihilo* pinpoints the disappearance of the gods into the distant, invisible, transcendent God of monotheism... the disappearance of God in his act of creation: "(...) the creator necessarily disappears in the very midst of its act, and with this disappearance a decisive episode of the entire movement that I

---

13 Arendt cites from *De Civitate Dei* xii, 20.
14 See on this also Alexandrova, Devisch, Ten Kate and Van Rooden 2012.

have sometimes named the 'deconstruction of Christianity' occurs, a movement that is nothing but the most intrinsic and proper movement of monotheism as the integral absenting of God (...)" (Nancy 2007, 68)

Sloterdijk has emphasized the same point in his *Spheres*. In a long excursion in the Introduction to the first volume he interprets the well-known scene in the second chapter of Genesis in which the creator creates humanity by breathing into Adam's mouth; only in this intimate act God and man *become* someone, their beginning relation lets them *be* for the first time (Sloterdijk 2011, 31–45).[15] In a very different context Sloterdijk again uses this theory of action. In his *You Must Change Your Life* he develops a theory of exercise in which man works on himself ('antropotechnics' or 'autoplasticity' he names this) by losing himself in his act: the actions "return to affect the actor." "Being human means existing in a (...) space in which actions return to affect the actor, works the worker, communications the communicator, thoughts the thinker, and feelings the feeler." (Sloterdijk 2013, 110)

4 Conclusions, Perspectives

With the rise of digital culture, the imaginary worlds of social imaginaries, are getting a strongly increasing impact on our existences. I will conclude this spatial analysis of imaginaries with three remarks, as an invitation to further research.

4.1 The game of the world

Needless to say, the digitalization of the world has introduced new possibilities for people to create playful worlds and temporarily live in these worlds. First computer games and then X-boxes and Play Stations have led to what scholars call a ludification of culture. These games are fascinating examples of radically interactive social imaginaries. The more obvious ones, like FIFA 16, involve you into a soccer match in which you are simultaneously a player – preferably the star player – a coach – you can build your own team – and a controller from outside, sitting before your screen. Others are often filled with an array of images that you can play with and that play with you. These games are real spaces of hybrid worldviewing. They work with symbols, rituals, practices borrowed

---

[15] See also Ten Kate forthcoming.

from all possible worldview traditions, mixing them, exaggerating them, intensifying them, filling them with old and new meanings: the complex event of sense in a super-diverse world, as we explored this in the first section. And, most importantly, these spaces of mutual imagination between play and player recreate our identities in part: on the limit between material and virtual reality, we are someone else in either world (De Mul and others 2015).

4.2 Social Media as Spaces of Transcendence

Moreover, social imaginaries are in many cases spaces where religion and secularity, transcendence and immanence meet. We already touched upon this remarkable entanglement in section 1. This is the fundamental structure of secularity 3, which is at the heart of Taylor's program. Insofar as social imaginaries let us share sense on a temporary basis, the images that inspire us to experience ourselves as member of a communal space, necessarily refer to the realm of spirituality: to what lies beyond our limits. Hence, secular life and religious experience often become intermingled in social imaginaries.[16]

A striking example of this are the popular confession apps used on smartphones. In these apps the user can confess his or her sins, mistakes, uncertainties, disappointment, grief or anger in the digital environment of an app. The app – the software – takes your confession and gives you back to yourself, absolved, relieved. All apps, more traditional versions condoned by the Roman Catholic Church, and experimental ones, connect secular ideals of self-expression and an individualistic view on life as my own project, with the old religious ritual of confession. But the imaginary space, the smartphone, has taken the place of the priest. Some versions also operate online: here one confesses before a large community of co-users who can electronically vote: either forgiveness or punishment. Most of these apps live a short life; they are immensely popular for a few years, and then retire from the web.[17]

---

[16] See on this also the work of the international consortium *Simagine: Social Imaginaries between Secularity and Religion in a Globalizing World (2017–2020)*, hosted by the University of Humanistic Studies in Utrecht, the Netherlands.
[17] See also Pauline Hope Cheong and Charles Ess 2012 1,2.

4.3 The Transcendence of Social Imaginaries

However, the main conclusion I want to draw from the analyses in this chapter relates social imaginaries and transcendence in an even more essential way. Indeed, social imaginaries are spaces where secularity 3 is at work: it mingles in new, often unexpected ways secularity and religion. The games and apps of our time are just an example of this. But the play of the world that I have presented and examined as the kernel of imaginaries also involves a transcending movement on a fundamental level.

This transcendent feature of social imaginaries has to do with the theory of playful action I have developed in the previous section, in dialogue with Nietzsche. It is a concept of transcendence that does not refer to a God, nor to an Other World or an Afterlife. It is a transcendence that happens in the here and now, in a recurring event; it gives sense to life and the world, but always just for a moment, and always in the twilight zone between stability and instability, truth and doubt, hope and despair. It is a transcendence that refers to disappearance, loss and abandonment: in entering social imaginaries we enter the creative *nihil* that is articulated by Nancy. Disappearance of God, disappearance of man. And still, in this vanishing act both reappear playfully.

Maybe such a strange interaction between absence and presence is the hallmark of transcendence in the secular age.[18] And maybe it is the spirit of the child and of the fool that hints at this new transcendence, while incorporating it at the same time. Then, maybe, we will have to go back from Nietzsche's hymn and song to Hölderlin's poetry. For the human spirit playing in, with and *as* the world – that spirit Nietzsche looks for in the metamorphoses of life – is evoked by the poet in the "bold spirit" who plays with what is and what is not. He imagines creatively what is still absent in what is fully present, and announces who will come in who are already there, behind him: "his own Gods."

> In seed grains he can measure the full-grown plant;
> And flies, bold spirit, flies as the eagles do
> Ahead of thunder-storms, preceding
> Gods, his own Gods, to announce their coming. (Hölderlin 2004, 181)

---

[18] See also Ten Kate 2016.

Bibliography

Alexandrova, Alena, Ignaas Devisch, Laurens ten Kate and Aukje van Rooden, eds. 2012. *Re-treating Religion: Deconstructing Christianity with Jean-Luc Nancy*. New York: Fordham University Press.

Alma, Hans, and Christa Anbeek. 2013. "Worldviewing Competence for Narrative Interreligious Dialogue: A Humanist Contribution to Spiritual Care." In *Multifaith Views in Spiritual Care*, edited by Daniel S. Schipani, 149–169. Ontario: Pandora Press.

Anderson, Benedict. 1983. *Imagined Communities: Reflections on the Origin and Spread of Nationalism*. London: Verso.

Arendt, Hannah. 1958. *The Human Condition*. Chicago: University of Chicago Press.

Arnason, Johann P., S.N. Eisenstadt and Björn Wittrock, eds. 2005. *Axial Civilizations and World History*. Leiden/Boston: Brill.

Blanchot, Maurice. 1993. "Atheism and Writing, Humanism and the Cry." In *The Infinite Conversation*. Minneapolis: University of Minnesota Press, 1993.

Blumenberg, Hans. 1983. *The Legitimacy of the Modern Age*. Cambridge MA: MIT Press.

Braidotti, Rosi, Bolette Blaagaard, Tobijn de Graauw and Eva Midden, eds. 2014. *Transformations of the Public Sphere: Post-Secular Publics*. London: Palgrave MacMillan.

Castoriadis, Cornelius. 1987. *The Imaginary Institution of Society*. Cambridge, MA: MIT Press.

Fink, Eugen. *Spiel als Weltsymbol*, edited by Cathrin Nielsen and Hans Reiner Sepp. München/Freiburg: Karl Alber, 2010.

Hinman, Lawrence M. 1974. "Nietzsche's Philosophy of Play." *Philosophy Today* 18 (2/4):106–124.

Hölderlin, Friedrich. 2004. "Rousseau," from the "Later Odes" (1798–1803), in *Poems and Fragments*, edited by Michael Hamburger. London: Anvil Press.

Hope Cheong, Pauline, and Charles Ess. 2012. "Introduction: Religion 2.0? Relational and Hybridizing Pathways in Religion, Social Media, and Culture." In *Digital Religion, Social Media, and Culture*, edited by Hope Cheong, Pauline, Peter Fischer-Nielsen, Stefan Gelgren and Charles Ess, 1–21. New York: Peter Lang.

Hope Cheong, Pauline, Peter Fischer-Nielsen, Stefan Gelgren and Charles Ess, eds. 2012. *Digital Religion, Social Media, and Culture*. New York: Peter Lang.

Jaspers, Karl. 1953. *The Origin and Goal of History*. London: Routledge & Kegan Paul.

Kate, Laurens, ten. 2014. "To World or not to World: An Axial Genealogy of Secular Life." In *Radical Secularization: An Inquiry into the Religious Roots of Secular Culture*, edited by Stijn Latré, Walter Van Herck and Guido Vanheeswijck, 207–230. New York: Bloomsbury Academic.

Kate, Laurens ten. 2016. "Humanism's Cry: On Infinity in Religion, and Absence in Atheism – A Dialogue with Blanchot and Nancy. In A. Szafraniec & E. van den Hemel (Eds.), *The Future of the Religious Past – II: Words* (pp. 181–198). New York: Fordham University Press/NWO.

Kate, Laurens, ten. forthcoming. "Something is in the Air: Deconstructions of the Creation, starting from Peter Sloterdijk's 'Breathed Commune'". In *Of Dawns that Have not yet Been Broken: Essays in Honour of Peter Sloterdijk's 70th Anniversary*, edited by Peter Weibel. Frankfurt a.M: Suhrkamp.

Löwith, Karl. 1969. *Permanence and Change: Lectures on the Philosophy of History*. Cape Town SA: Haum.

Mul, Joost de, Michiel de Lange, Joost Raessens, Valerie Frissen, and Sybille Lammes, eds. 2015. *Playful Identities: The Ludification of Digital Media Cultures.* Amsterdam: Amsterdam University Press.
Nancy, Jean-Luc. 1997. *The Sense of the World.* Minneapolis: University of Minnesota Press.
Nancy, Jean-Luc. 2007. *The Creation of the World, or Globalization.* New York: SUNY Press.
Nietzsche, Friedrich. 1969. *Thus Spoke Zarathustra: A Book for Everyone and No One.* London: Penguin Books.
Nietzsche, Friedrich. 2001 *The Gay Science, with a Prelude in German Rhymes and an Appendix of Songs.* Cambridge etc.: Cambridge University Press.
Nancy, Jean-Luc. 2001. *The Gay Science, with a Prelude in German Rhymes and an Appendix of Songs.* Cambridge: Cambridge University Press.
Rüsen, Jörn. 2012. "Anthropology – Axial Ages – Modernities." In *Shaping a Humane World: Civilizations – Axial Times – Modernities – Humanisms,* edited by Oliver Kozlarek, Jörn Rüsen and Ernst Wolff, 55–79. New Brunswick/London: Transaction Publishers.
Sloterdijk, Peter. 2011. *Spheres,* Vol. I: "Bubbles: Microspherology." Los Angeles: Semiotext (e).
Sloterdijk, Peter. 2013. *You Must Change Your Life: On Antropotechnics.* Cambridge: Polity Press.
Taylor, Charles. 2004. *Modern Social Imaginaries.* Durham: Duke University Press.
Taylor, Charles. 2007. *A Secular Age.* Cambridge, MA: Harvard University Press.
Vertovec, Steven. 2007. "Super-diversity and its Implications." *Ethnic and Racial Studies* 30 (6): 1024–1054.
Wolde, Ellen, van. 2009. *Terug naar het begin* (Back to the beginning). Nijmegen: Valckhoff Pers.

Joeri Schrijvers
'Plus de Biens': Jacques Derrida and Charles Taylor

1 Introduction

It may surprise the readers that the citation in my title is not Derrida's but Charles Taylor's. It is in effect Taylor who writes that "if we try to examine it further secularism involves in fact a complex requirement. There is *more than one good* sought here" (Taylor 2011, 34). One might even call this question and this formula, namely the question of a conflict between more than one good – to the point of having no more Good/One at all – the best summary available for the practice of deconstruction (cf. Derrida 2002, 100).[1] Let us listen, though, to which 'goods' Taylor has in mind here, since he continues: "We can single out three [:] liberty, equality, fraternity" (Taylor 2011, 34).

Yet a dialogue between Taylor and Derrida on this question of the good and how to imagine the relation between these revolutionary goods never really happened. On the contrary, Taylor has often been rather dismissive of Derridean deconstruction. This has come to the attention of most commentators, who question Taylor's stubborn deafness toward 'postmodern philosophy.' Few of the 'postmodernists' and of the 'post-Nietzschean position' Taylor mentions, as Iain Thomson rightly argues, actually "believe that the border of any knowledge domain can be secured in a way that will rigorously exclude the covert appeal to something transcending this domain" (Thomson 2011, 156n.12). This chapter will therefore endeavor to examine the convergences between Derrida and Taylor in more than one respect. For, even if the connection between postmodern philosophy and Taylor's thinking has not been researched extensively, it is clear that many questions today circle around just this connection: granted that we, believers and unbelievers living in a secular age, are 'cross-pressured,' receiving impulses from secular, postsecular, immanent and transcendent worldviews alike, it remains to be asked: *who* is cross-pressured, and *by what* or *by whom*?

In this regard, Iain Thomson argues that there is something of a contradiction in Taylor's thought when on the one hand granting a political and ontolog-

---

[1] A similar (anything but) playful wording in (Derrida 2000, 74): on the French use of *pas de hospitalité*, meaning *simultaneously* there is no one hospitality (there is always more than one) and stepping toward, being open toward hospitality, as if being the first one (...).

ical pluralism and opting for a theological monism on the other (Thomson 2011, 143–44). In a similar manner, Alexander Karolis has recently defended the view that the various ways of being open to the world or 'the openness of the world' from out of various social imaginaries and the very fact of being cross-pressured does not necessarily "involve the religious call that Taylor assumes" (Karolis 2013, 678). On the contrary perhaps, the very fact of being cross-pressured might not solely call for a sociological and somewhat biased ideological account but rather calls for a thorough ontological exploration, especially if its aim is to spell out the contemporary conditions for belief in God – the professed aim of Taylor's *A Secular Age*.[2]

Taylor's conflation and dismissal of the entire philosophical tradition, Nietzsche, Camus, Foucault, Bataille, and Derrida "among others" (Taylor 2007, 612) has therefore raised quite some debate. Most of the commentators have been critical of Taylor's rather theological take on modernity and what comes after. Our aim here, however, is not polemical but rather seeks to show that what Taylor so dismisses, Derrida 'among others,' is actually much more worthy of our attention than Taylor seems to think, especially when it comes to matters of transcendence.

For the sake of scholarship and science, though, it must be noted already that all points that Taylor advances *against* Derrida will be falsified here one by one: it is, first, not true that Derrida is an anti-humanist thinker that rejects life; it is, secondly, not correct to state that there is no transcendent hope beyond history in Derrida at all; thirdly, it is even less the case that the universality of rights is defended by Derrida without being grounded in the nature of things. Lastly, it is simply false to state that because there is no leap of faith in Derrida, the latter would lack all access to a "more powerful and effective healing action in history" (e.g. Taylor 2007, 373, 599, 695, 703).

On the contrary perhaps! But, again, our aim here is not polemical, it is rather to see to just where these cross-pressures of us seculars extend. For this, we will begin with the convergences of Derrida and Taylor on what we call here 'the European exception.'

---

[2] We are here summarizing Jean Grondin (2012, 245–62). Grondin is particularly critical of Taylor's use of sociological and ethical examples as 'evidence' for or 'testimony' to religious faith. Yet, even on this account, Taylor is much closer to Derrida than one would expect, for Derrida too turn to Mandela as an 'exemplar' of the deconstructive account of the incarnation of meaning into matter, of words into flesh. The question should rather be: an incarnation *of what exactly*? See Derrida (2003b, 69–88).

2 The European Exception: 'Freedom or the Grave'

If Taylor then dismisses an entire strand of contemporary philosophy, it is all the more awkward that this tradition was aiming toward similar goals: if Taylor seeks that which comes 'after' secularization, just how different would this be from Derrida, who writes:

> As for secularism (...) I believe that at present it is calling for its own transformation, and I believe this is occurring in France today. I believe that the democracy to come (...) assumes secularism, that is, both the detachment of the political from the theocratic and the theological (...) while at the same time encompassing freedom of worship (...) and absolute freedom guaranteed by the State. [I believe] that today we need a concept of the secular that no longer has that sort of aggressive compulsion that it once had in France. (Chérif 2008, 50)

All that we will call the European exception is present in this citation: something that is conditioned by and happened within a certain history in France is now happening in a certain sense 'without' this very history and context in the entire globalized world. This is why Derrida will defend both a certain form of secularization *and* a certain form of faith. The secularization of the political will have made us aware of a sort of "universal faith" conditioning the social bond onto which the concrete and more traditional religions could graft themselves (Chérif 2008, 58). Yet this secularization and the concomitant globalization has also brought about "a universal Europeanization through science and technology" (Chérif 2008, 61). Derrida importantly adds: "even those who (...) claim to oppose this violent Europeanization (...) do so most often using a certain technical, techno-scientific (...) Europeanization" (Chérif 2008, 61). In *Faith and Knowledge* Derrida will in effect elaborate on the example of 9/11, where jet planes were used for the destruction of the West as if the spokespersons of a certain antimodernity necessarily need to use modern means (Derrida 2002, 61–2).

Yet, as for the future fate of this violent globalization and religion in a globalized world, Derrida looked at, as we will see Taylor do, Europe rather than the US:

> I believe that today we must abandon the idea that there is a Europeanization, a violent hegemony of the West that includes the United States and Europe against the rest of the world (...) There is a specificity of a Europe in formation, which I hope (...) will transform the world configuration in which we live, and this in the spirit of [the] democracy to come. (Chérif 2008, 65)

It is to such 'a new international' or new universalism that Derrida is pointing when he invests his hope in Europe. Derrida explains this European exception, a Europeanization "without Eurocentrism" (Chérif 2008, 62),[3] in its distinction from the United States in the following way. Such a distinction between "a certain American power, a certain American politics – the division between a certain American politics and a virtuality of European politics is increasingly possible" (Chérif 2008, 62).

Why? First of all – and again Taylor will agree – because of a certain history; a history that is different in the United States and in Europe. Yet one must be acutely aware of Derrida's phrasing here, which will set him apart from Taylor. Derrida speaks about a virtuality and a *possibility* of and for Europe that is happening now, although it is not yet here. It is increasingly possible, although it remains only virtual and is therefore as of yet haunted with a certain impossibility just as well. It 'signals;' there are symptoms and "signs of a new alliance (…) in all movements of antiglobalization today, all the movements that bring together so many men and women, against economic violence, against terrorist violence, against State violence, against all the imperial and imperialist violence" (Chérif 2008, 74). This signal or this symptom, for Derrida, resembles a certain messianism and a certain Kingdom as something 'already' here although 'not yet' fully present. A virtual kingdom to come.

But, again, why this distinction between the United States and Europe, especially if the science and the technology present in these regions would be more or less the same? Because "there is something common to all the European States which is a certain principle of separation between the State and religion, without scorn for religion. By contrast, in the United States [there is] very often merging or an alliance between politics and the theocratic which, today, we must (…) question and transform." (Chérif 2008, 65)

Thus the hope for a messianic turnaround, so to say, for Derrida comes from those states who have abandoned the merging of religion and politics: it is 'without religion' that the messianic is possible (virtually), yet it is 'through' religion that we will have an idea of a messianic democracy to come. Furthermore, both secularism 'in its European aggressive form' and this merging of politics with religion, attributed to the United States, are calling for transformation and need to be questioned.

It is hard to see just where Taylor would disagree with Derrida's assessment of the European exception. He might denounce Derrida's somewhat optimistic *soixante huitard*-like belief in the Enlightenment as one of those moments

---

[3] See also Derrida (1994, 85).

where the birth of modernity would also give rise to 'the great disembedding', resulting in an 'age of authenticity' where all are wolves for all. But then Taylor's account would forget Derrida's critiques of such an Enlightenment and its all too "inadequate, sometimes hypocritical, and in any case formalistic and inconsistent (...) discourse on human rights as long as the law of the market (...) maintain[s] an effective inequality" (Derrida 1994, 85). And, after all, "what would the Enlightenment be without the market?" (Derrida 1994, 152)

Taylor's uncalled for dismissal of Derrida and the likes is even more questionable once we realize that concerning the difference between the American and the French revolution – *plus d'un* revolution equals multiple modernities – Taylor and Derrida are in complete agreement. Let us listen to Taylor: "we have moved in many Western countries from an original phase in which secularism was a hard-won achievement warding off some form of religious domination, to a phase of (...) widespread diversity of basic beliefs, religious and areligious" (Taylor 2011, 48). Taylor is clear that these Western countries are European, for "the young American republic" conceived and imagined itself as "adopting a form that was clearly part of God's providential plan" (Taylor 2011, 47).[4]

In fact, Taylor points out how the American revolution did not need a distinction between a 'secular' state and a 'religious' viewpoint, simply because the state then could be identified completely with the Christian protestant religion – there simply was no other religion than the Protestant religion at the time (if we are allowed to exempt the 'otherness' of the native Americans' religion). It was, so to say, 'held as self-evident' that this was a Protestant nation. Taylor, moreover, argues that it is because of Catholicism's growing sense of being excluded from the laws and the practices of the young country that the call for a secular state, a state guaranteeing the freedom of all observances, was introduced in the United States around 1870. Yet it took a long time before the native Americans were given a voice (Taylor 2011, 38–39). It is precisely over such an otherness and such a voice that Derrida, as we will, see worries.

Given these similarities in Taylor and Derrida's assessment of the American and European heritage, it is all the more surprising that both thinkers draw quite different conclusions from this situation: whereas for Derrida, it is a matter of 'internationalizing' Europe, so to say, Taylor argues for a 'provincializing' of Eu-

---

[4] It is this 'self-evident' right that makes Taylor wary of the contemporary religious Right and more generally of the "underlying absolutism" of the United States. See for this Taylor (2007b, 38). On such a remnant of theological sovereignty in the United States, see however also Derrida (2003, 148), commenting on Litwak's phrase 'a rogue state is whoever the United States says it is.'

rope – a phrase borrowed from Dipesh Chakrabarty. For Taylor, instead of aiming for an *extension* of the European exception, what is needed is a sort of limitation of the European moral order: "[we need] to get over seeing modernity as a single process of which Europe is the paradigm, and that we understand the European model as the first, certainly, as the object of some creative imitation, naturally, but as (…) one among many" (Taylor 2004, 196).

The *'plus d'un'* of our title, be it the 'more than one good' or 'more than one modernity', leads Derrida and Taylor in entirely different directions: whereas Taylor would state that the events in Europe would be *but one* form modernity can take, Derrida argues that *more than one* Europe can (and should) be imagined. Derrida argues for a possibility that is dormant in Europe but that is not yet actualized, Taylor is discontent with the form that Europe has actually taken and settles for a different form of modernity that has been actualized elsewhere, namely in the United States where modernity need not be accompanied with a violent secularism. If for Derrida one needs to move 'beyond' Europe and Eurocentrism from 'within' Europe – *plus est en vous, Europe* – for Taylor it is important to look 'beyond' Europe to see that Europe, and its concomitant secularism and Enlightenment, was *but one* form that modernity can take and that its hostility against religion seems to be no issue at all elsewhere.

2 *Plus de droits?* Taylor on Human Rights and the Break-Away from Christendom

"Modern liberal political culture is characterized by an affirmation of universal human rights", which, Taylor argues, are universally valid but not dependent on Christianity and religion: these rights are "an undeniable prolongation of the gospel" and yet are accompanied by a "denial of transcendence" (Taylor 1999, 16, 25, respectively). Christianity, Taylor might argue, is a necessary but not a sufficient condition for the affirmation of human rights: without Christianity, there would not have been such an affirmation, but one does not need Christianity to affirm these rights. With such statements Taylor is on a par, however, not only with Derrida but also with Jean-Luc Nancy who writes that "the democratic ethic of the rights of man (…) constitutes (…) the durable sediment of Christianity" (Nancy 2008, 37). Nancy's deconstruction of Christianity, insofar as it wants to think without Christianity, recognizes Christianity's lasting influence on today's globalized world. Nancy (and Derrida), would therefore concur with Taylor's keen analysis: "as long as we were living within the terms of Christendom (…) we could never have attained to [the] unconditionality [of these rights]. It is difficult for a 'Christian' society to accept full equality of rights for atheists" (Taylor 1999, 17).

We should wonder, with Derrida and Nancy, what exactly these scare quotes around 'Christian' can mean. Our argument can be summarized by saying that Taylor does not wonder enough about his use of scare quotes here: on the one hand, he seems to be implying that a real and genuine *Christian* society should give rights to all, whether that society be Greek or Jewish or whether one is atheist or homosexual (and thus perhaps not in line with religious doctrine), since it is not exactly Christian to deny rights to the other. On the other hand, Taylor seems to be granting the fact that the extant Christian *societies* have difficulty recognizing that others (with their otherness) have rights too – the gates to the Kingdom are not exactly opened unconditionally. The Christian should take the atheist seriously because he or she has rights (but perhaps also on the terms of 'Christianity' itself); yet similarly the Christian cannot take the atheist seriously because he or she is not 'in the Christian truth.'

Taylor is therefore, not unlike Derrida, imagining a Christianity with and without Christendom. It seems as if a 'Christianity without Christendom' would take the rights of the non-Christian other seriously, even on Christian grounds, whereas a 'Christianity with Christendom' obviously cannot. We will argue that Taylor does not take such a split in the Christian identity seriously enough. Yet Derrida will point precisely to such disconcert in the 'essence' of Christianity and see in this 'ghostly' possibility within Europe and within Christianity the resources needed for a resourcement of contemporary culture.

Contemporary culture's "breakaway from Christendom" (Taylor 1999, 37) is, for Derrida, Nancy and an entire philosophical tradition that conceives of a deconstruction of Christianity today "what we are really dealing with, [namely] the demise of Christendom [as] an ideal of civilization and society. This is an extremely difficult and painful process for many. If there is a certain greatness in this gesture, there is also a risk" (Taylor 2007b, 38). One needs to wonder whether the 'despisers' of religion would disagree with such a statement. The end of metaphysics, a theme raging through contemporary philosophy ever since Martin Heidegger and Derrida, is concerned with precisely the demise of such a civilization. Taylor's description of the culture of 'mutual benefit,' where "each acts (...) to benefit others mutually" (Taylor 2007, 447), as long as the freedom of one does not limit the freedom of the other, could be complemented with Nancy's haunting question whether the capitalism that issues from such mutuality – where you benefit from me *as long as* I can benefit from you – might in the long run be destructive, for "it matters to respond to a question: do [we] still want a civilization? One worthy of the name?" (Nancy 2012, 62n.) The breakaway from Christendom in this sense concerns deconstructionists and Christians alike. Taylor again shows himself oblivious to an entire tradition of questioning. For on the end of metaphysics *and* what comes after, should we not consult precisely Nietzsche (and not only his heirs), when he likens the rat-race accompanying the 'civilization' of mutual benefit and its concomitant rush and stress – there is always something or someone to benefit from – to a new barbarism (Nietzsche 1976, 620)?

Somewhat rushed Taylor then advances the claim that one must avoid the choice between Christianity and modernity – rushed since this is exactly what Derrida, Nancy and perhaps Nietzsche as well would argue. Taylor opts for a *tertium datur* of sorts.

> From the Christian point of view, the (…) error is to fall into one of two untenable positions: *either* we pick certain fruits of modernity, like human rights, and take them on board but then condemn the whole movement of thought and practice that underlies them, in particular the breakout from Christendom, *or* in reaction to this first position, we feel we have to go all the way with the boosters of modernity and become fellow travellers of exclusive humanism. Better, I would argue, after initial (and, let's face it, still continuing) bewilderment, we would gradually find our voice from within the achievements of modernity, measure the humbling degree to which some of the most impressive extensions of a gospel ethic depended on a breakaway from Christendom, and from within these gains try to make clearer to ourselves and others the tremendous dangers that arise in them. (Taylor 1999, 36–7)

The first option picks from modernity whatever it wants – a very modern gesture in its own right – and declares all other modern accomplishments to be but an *errorum* – Taylor is one of the few Christian thinkers who still dares to mention the infamous *Syllabus Errorum*. This option, of which the *Syllabus* is an extreme figure, in any case agrees that a modernity without Christianity is not desirable. The second option states that once modernity has reached the thinking of universal rights it can do without Christendom entirely and settle for autonomous man —'*Freedom or the Grave*' as the first bill of rights have it.

The question therefore is what the third option, Taylor's, would entail exactly, as it is neither a Christianity without modernism (first option) nor a modernity without Christianism (second option). Rather, it concerns a gain that builds on a loss: without a *certain kind* of Christianity, something essential to Christianity is gained – the 'breakaway from Christendom' delivered us into an 'impressive extension of the gospel.' This leaves Taylor in the somewhat curious position that although one is better off without *certain kinds* of Christianity one surely is not better off *without Christianity* entirely, although it is at the same time the case that from a 'breakaway' from Christendom the most impressive account of a gospel ethics arose. The latter would indeed imply that it is indeed *without Christendom* that a certain essential kind of Christianity emerged.

This allows us to better understand Taylor's position on the European exception and the concomitant human rights. If Taylor wants to move 'beyond' Europe 'without' Europe, then this has a twofold meaning. 'Without Europe', the provincialization of its history, means neither a 'Christianity minus modernity' (first option above) nor 'modernity minus Christianity' – the second option. The New Europe, if there is any, would be neither *entirely* modern nor *entirely* Christian. Taylor moves in mysterious ways here: just as there seems to be a 'Christianity without Christendom' – there is something utterly unchristian in extant Christianity – there also is a European modernity without the (secular, enlightened) modernity – something remains Christian even in its anti-Christian guise. We need to doubt later on with Derrida whether it is this 'cross pressure,' where the Christian can turn unchristian (and vice versa,) that Taylor has in mind.

Elsewhere Taylor terms his ambivalent stance towards a Christian modernity a "loyal opposition" (Taylor 2007, 745). For Taylor, whether Christian or modern, "we are all partisan of human rights" (Taylor 2007, 419). In fact, "a crucial feature of the modern moral order [is] its endorsing of universal human rights [as] one of our goals. I want to understand this as our stepping into a wider, qualitatively different sense of inter-human solidarity, involving a break and a partial replacement of earlier narrower ties." (Taylor 2007, 608) This 'break' is already familiar to us: it is the break from Christendom. A rather peculiar feature of this citation is, however, that Taylor considers this break 'qualitatively' different from the earlier ways of construing the social bond: the 'universal human rights' are to be regarded as *better* than the guilds and the hierarchies of Christian Europe.

Yet all accounts are not settled with this jump toward a universalization of the democratic ethic. It is here that Taylor approaches Derrida again. On the one hand, Taylor states, "we now *live with*, and partly *by*, notions of human rights" (Taylor 2007, 658). On the other hand, however, Taylor questions whether the demands coming from this break with Christendom are actually met, and whether "[we have found] the moral resources which can enable us *to live up to* our very strong universal commitments to human rights and well-being" (Taylor 2007, 726). Another peculiar feature of cross pressures here: on the one hand, we are *already* 'living by' human rights, while we, on the other are *not yet* living up to these rights. It is here, as well, that Taylor shows himself theologically biased – it is a certain theology that causes the bias, it is not biased because it is theological – for it is obvious that these 'moral resources' will have to come from a certain Christianity. Taylor, however, never really specifies *which* (or rather *whose*) Christianity nor how much modernity this Christianity requires precisely.

Yet theologically, too, there is a problem here. Taylor seems to indicate that *as long as* we have not found the appropriate moral resources, namely those of a certain Christianity, we will not be able *to live up to* the demands of the universal commitments to human rights. Here Taylor shows himself at his most complacent (and one should remember that this might be one of the reasons why we left Christendom in the first place: its supposed clear and distinct grasp of the truth and the concomitant judgement of those 'in the untruth'). In the wake of Rousseau, Taylor argues, "democracy and human rights are conceived as inseparable from a view of humans as innocent or fundamentally good by nature (...) Religion, particularly the Christian doctrine of original sin, cannot but undermine it, sap its foundations. The free society must (...) build a social imaginary, which is grounded in exclusive humanism" (Taylor 2007, 412).

One might debate which side Taylor would take here – humanism *or* Christianity – considering that 'original sin' is in the Christian tradition a highly debated topic. In the wake of the Protestant tradition, one could argue that the Fall not only contaminated reason (and the power to know the divine) but also contaminated the very essence of the human being as bearing the likeness of God; in the Catholic tradition, however, there is a consensus, generally speaking, that however much damage original sin has brought about, this will never eradicate all possibility of salvation precisely because the 'image of God' indelibly remains – in *Genesis*, God's pronouncement of the 'likeness' of man is prior to man's sin (cf. Gen 1:27). When Taylor speaks of 'human rights without an account of sin,' he seems to have in mind a version of modernity that could dispense with Christianity. Whenever he speaks of human rights on the basis of an account of sin, suddenly his preferences change: it is not Rousseau's affirmation of life and of goodness, but the full-fledged balance between being created in the image of God and the limitations of original sin of the Catholic church. Taylor needs sin, but apparently a delimited form of sin to fit his purposes: neither entirely without sin (Rousseau) nor entirely with sin (Protestantism).

When reading Taylor, therefore, one is never sure whether his account of the secular age is due to his Catholicism or whether it is due to his particular reading of the history of Christianity that delivers us into a secular age. In all this, one can sense some sort of secret identification with *one* moral order as *the* moral order par excellence: this is Taylor's complacent certainty we noted earlier.

4 *Le droit de l'autre:* Derrida on Human Rights

If Taylor has a tendency to identify one moral order with the moral order – not coincidentally his own order – then Derrida's 'cross pressuredness,' if any, is such that it desires to welcome the moral order of the other. Such a cross pressure, we will see, is closer to the Protestantism we have just detected Taylor dismissing, but such a cross-pressure equally seems to avoid simultaneously the pride of inventing a democratic right that would be entirely autonomous or the pretence pertaining to the ethic of the authentic self-made man. Yet Derrida's account of such pressures (between the self and the other) can also do without the complacency of identifying one's own moral resource as the only moral resource available or preferable. Let us listen to Derrida on the topic of human rights and how (not) to live up to the demands they pose: "More than ever, one must take sides for human rights. One must have [*il faut*] human rights. We need them and they fulfil a need, because there always is a lack, a shortage, a falling short, an insufficiency: human rights are never enough, never sufficient. This alone should remind us why they are not natural." (Derrida 2013, 132)

In Taylor's terms, Derrida would thus argue that we never can live up to the demands posed on us by the very idea of human rights. Why? Because at the very moment the idea – that is, as we will see, the transcendence – of human rights intimates itself in human history, the 'limits of this discourse' become plain as well: "never have violence, inequality, exclusion, famine and thus economic oppression affected as many human beings in the history of the earth and of humanity" (Derrida 1994, 85). Why? Because at the very moment of putting these rights into practice, which is the moment of an incarnation, an (unjust) identification takes place. Here is another important convergence between Derrida and Taylor: whereas Taylor decries "the identification of civilization and the modern order [of liberal democracy]" (Taylor 2004, 181), Derrida states, "it must be cried out [that] at a time when some have the audacity to neo-evangelize in the name of the ideal of a liberal democracy [that] has realized itself as the ideal of human history" (Derrida 1994, 85) there has never been so much injustice. Derrida's reference to a Christian realized eschatology – normally reserved for the Eucharist and the Kingdom to come – is no doubt a coincidence, but provides something worthy of thought nonetheless.

Derrida seems more attentive to the exclusion present in all identification: recall that one must move 'beyond' Europe from 'within' Europe. Derrida is arguing here for an ethical transcendence conceived from within the politics that is immanence. If indeed our social imaginary, within Europe and within the framework of human rights, is an 'immanent frame,' Derrida would argue that this immanence is opened up from within – never entirely immanent – whereas Taylor, it seems, wants to open it from without – from a 'transcendence' uncontaminated by immanence. Yet, for Derrida, it is *within* the 'sheer' politics of a liberal Europe that there lies the moment of a transcendence, of an infinite waiting and wanting to be realized, even if the moment of such realization will always border on injustice because such a realization borders on a limitation. Derrida is borrowing here from Levinas' thought of hospitality toward the Other: the call of this other here – be it the orphan, the widow or the *sans-papiers* at Lampedusa – is such that I must respond immediately and act responsibly by giving my time to the other. The appeal for human rights, for instance, is such that it calls *for action:* a theoretical discourse on the rights of the other is nothing if it does not realize itself in policies and in a polity. Yet there are others besides this Other here: no matter how just we would act and how responsibly we think we are towards this Other here, it would simultaneously be an injustice toward the others of this other who 'remains in the cold' or in the waters of the Mediterranean Sea. This is why the political 'incarnational' moment – the call *for action* – remains an ethical and transcendent *call:* as long as I am not hospitable *for all* I cannot rightly consider myself hospitable *at all*. This movement of *infinition* – the harbouring of an infinite call within finitude and immanence —is, for Derrida and Levinas, what can rightly be called 'transcendent' and is also why Derrida states that this movement, in the case of human rights, is not natural: it cannot be deduced from the nature of things, as Taylor has rightly noted, even while it happens nowhere else than in the order of immanence and politics (and therefore, as we will see, precisely *because* of the nature of things).[5] What Taylor misses in Derrida's account of transcendence, however, is that this incarnation of the infinite is not entirely 'cultural' or a matter of 'nurture' either. For Derrida, the point is precisely that even though this transcendence of the Other *must* incarnate in our practices, in a moment of giving to the other, it may never be reduced to just such *an* incarnation. For Derrida, on this topic at least, there are *plus d'incarnations*. It is to this that our discussion of the relation between Derrida and Taylor will now turn.

For if Taylor needs and desires one or the other *moral resource* for the (sufficient?) upholding of human rights, be it Christian in Taylor's case or Buddhist in another,[6] then the discussion between Derrida and Taylor would quickly end: Derrida would insist on the limitations that the particulars of this or that world-

---

[5] One has underestimated Derrida's complete agreement with Levinas here, see Derrida (1999, 116–117): "It marks a *heterogeneity*, a *discontinuity* between two orders, even if this be on the *inside* of the earthly Jerusalem (…) This discontinuity, moreover, allows us to subscribe to everything Levinas says about peace or messianic hospitality, about the beyond [*au-delà*] of the political in [*dans*] the political." Compare Derrida (1997, 201).

[6] See for this Taylor (2002, 101–119) where he investigates whether there is a necessary link between Western democracy and human rights and whether the Western idea of 'human rights' should not be replaced by a concept of human 'dignity' or a Buddhist and Confucian stress on 'well-being'.

view would bring to the demands of universal rights, just as a 'Catholic would have difficulties indeed to preserve the rights of atheists' at the era of 'Christendom.' Derrida would argue, in Taylor's terms, that every 'take' on the 'immanent frame' at one point or another will turn into a 'spin' on this frame (Smith 2014, 92). More precisely, the problem Derrida would have with Taylor's position would not be Taylor's catholic 'take' on things – after all, everyone has the right to be catholic – but rather that this take too cannot avoid turning into a 'closed' spin at a given moment. For Derrida, this 'moment' when an ethical transcendence is swallowed by the politics of an immanent frame or in which the 'open' take turns into a 'closed' spin is structurally present in every (moral) discourse: prior to every take and every spin, there lies the ever-present possibility that no matter what 'take' one has on reality it turns into a 'spin' nonetheless.

Hence Derrida's somewhat awkward certainty that the universal demand of human rights only ever incarnates *insufficiently* and why he would criticize Taylor for assuming that a particular moral resource could make us 'live up' to these demands. Again: Derrida focuses on that which is excluded if one adopts one moral resource rather than another. Let us listen to Derrida on this structural moment of exclusion in the case of international law: "International law is respected nowhere. And as soon as one party does not respect [this law], the others no longer consider it respectable and begin to betray it in their turn. The United States and Israel are not the only ones who have become accustomed to taking all the liberties that they deem necessary with UN resolutions." (Derrida 2013, 111)

It's not the specifics of Derrida's statement that interest us here – although it would be interesting which rogue states he would have had in mind. What is of importance, rather, is Derrida's idea of political sovereignty that is at play: recall that a rogue state is the state that has the power to decide which state is rogue and, more importantly, which state is not. Here too one should proceed toward a careful reading of Derrida: 'as soon as' the international law is betrayed for instance is to be read alongside the mention of states that 'have become accustomed' to betray these laws – it's the custom that international law will have been betrayed. Due to the political moment swallowing up transcendence (whether it be in exclusive humanism or the 'moral resources' of a particular Christianity'), the 'take' on a worldview always already turns it into a 'spin': the idea that there is *more than one* worldview or frame is then turned into the thought that there is *but one* worldview or frame.

In Derrida's account of sovereignty, one again encounters his taste for aporias. Derrida states that the sovereignty of the nation-state depends on this state being able to decide upon and maintain the non-violence of the public realm through monopolizing violence. The 'peace' of the public realm thus depends upon the prior (monopolized) violence of the state. Or, as Derrida would have it: the condition of possibility of this peace lies in the condition of its impossibility, since peace is only ever possible through the presence of a certain violence (Derrida 2002b, 228–292).

What interests Derrida in such conceptions of the sovereignty of the state is its desire for oneness and indivisibility. It is these metaphysical notions – recall that the One, the Good, etc. in the metaphysical tradition have always been regarded as being one (as opposed to multiple), simple (as opposed to complex), etc. – that according to Derrida are secularized in political thinking. However, when it comes to modernity and its politics, the problem is of course that this sovereign nation-state clashes and conflicts with other nation-states no matter how unique and indivisible its sovereignty seems. Indeed, there is 'more than one' good in modernity and the good of this one does not necessarily accord nicely with the good of the other.

On the level of identity-politics, however, Derrida's thoughts of sovereignty are quite peculiar and differ considerably for Taylor's settling for 'but one' moral resource. Here too there is 'more than one' good, identity, moral resource: the 'right' to enter this culture rather than another always happens at the expense of being included in other groups, social imaginaries and cultures. 'Belonging' to this group is simultaneously to give up belonging to another group. The condition of possibility of inclusion is its condition of impossibility.

Yet it would be wrong to think that Derrida wants to do without sovereignty or identity. His opposition to Taylor who, as we will see, insists on such a 'common' and 'strong' identity, lies elsewhere.[7] For Derrida will insist that we cannot live without identity (as a certain Levinas and certainly Nancy has it) but will also insist that this craving for identity – to belong to this nation rather than to that one, this social imaginary rather than another – is *insufficiently* aware of its exclusivity and of the concomitant sovereign power of inclusion. The other always has more rights, *plus de droits que moi*. The only reasonable option for Derrida is to be aware that what is *better* than insisting on the 'common' identity or even the fraternity implied in the human rights, is to be aware that it is me, us, we 'that therefore are the real rogues' who deny these rights to others.

---

[7] Philosophically, Derrida is looking for an 'unconditionality without sovereignty' which would be a 'sovereignty without a sovereign,' without *one* being able to lay claim to power. Such a situation is hardly conceivable today, but one might think here how one asks for 'second opinions' in cases of health-issues. Here the sovereignty and power of *one* doctor is divested and distributed to *other* doctors while the very fact of authority and power remains. See e.g. Derrida (2003, 196).

It is obvious that these debates between Derrida and Taylor on the question of the end of metaphysics and the fate of identities will have to be settled on a metaphysical terrain.

5 Otherwise than Identity. Derrida and Taylor on Christian Identity-politics

Before switching to this metaphysical terrain, let us turn to a simple example Derrida has once given of his view on a sort of communitarian moral division of labor – where everyone takes care 'of their own' and only afterwards turns to others. Derrida replies:

> I, of course, have preferences. I am one of the common people who prefer their cat to their neighbor's cat and my family to others. But I do not have a good conscience about that. I know that if I transform this into a general rule it would be the ruin of ethics. If I put as a principle that I will feed first of all my cat, my family, my nation, that would be the end of any ethical politics. So when I give a preference to my cat, which I do, that will not prevent me from having some remorse for the cat dying or starving next door, or, to change the example, for all the people on earth who are starving and dying today. So you cannot prevent me from having a bad conscience, and that is the main motivation of my ethics and my politics (…) It is not because I am indifferent, but because I am not indifferent, that I try not to make a difference, not to make a difference ethically and politically, between my family and his family and your family. I confess that it is not easy. (Derrida 2001, 69)

The politics towards one's own, which always risks the ruin of ethics, is unavoidable even if insufficient, just as the 'transcendent' call toward action envisaged by human rights only ever incarnates in all too finite and determinate actions. Nothing can be ruined more easily than a universal ethics. However, Derrida here asserts that this kind of identity-politics does not escape him either, rogue that he is. It is this 'primacy of bad conscience' – no one can have remorse in your place – that separates Derrida from Taylor, who settles for such a 'common demeanor' and a common identity when it comes to the possibility of action at all.

We will in this section contrast Taylor's position with that of Jean-Luc Nancy in order to show that Derrida, on this question of identity, takes the more intermediate position. Whereas Taylor argues for a social imaginary or culture with a solid and stable identity, Nancy in fact argues for the opposite – the only identity of the human being is that he or she is 'without identity.' Derrida, however, argues for what we could call an 'otherwise than identity' and so tries to move beyond the sterile debate between communitarians and libertarians (in the European sense) as well as beyond the 'nature' (realism) and nurture (idealism) debate. Let us begin with Derrida who, in an interview with John D. Caputo, says:

> To be (...) concrete, take the example of a person or a culture. We often insist nowadays on cultural identity – for instance, on national identity, linguistic identity, and so on. Sometimes the struggles under the banner of cultural identity, national identity (...) are noble fights. But at the same time the people who fight for their identity must pay attention to the fact that identity is not the self-identity of a thing, this glass for instance (...) but implies a difference within identity. That is, the identity of a culture is a way of being different from itself, a culture is different from itself (...) Once you take into account this inner and other difference, then you pay attention to the other and you understand that fighting for your own identity is not exclusive of another identity, is open to another identity. And this prevents totalitarianism, nationalism, egocentrism. (Caputo 1997, 13)

Few quotes of Derrida are more important than this one. Three things are to be noted here. First, Derrida reiterates that we are not without identity and sometimes the fight for a recognition of one's identity – South Africa is a case in point – is deemed 'noble.' But even on a more basic level, there is obviously no point in denying one's identity: I cannot pretend *not* to be Belgian, European, and so on. Even the most cosmopolite of all the cosmopolites will speak one language rather than another. Secondly, this identity of the human is to be distinguished from that of a thing. A thing is 'self-identity': it is what it is. The table I see now will be pretty much the same table tomorrow. The table is *identical*. Human identity, however, is different: it is a 'difference within identity.' Derrida will not deny that there is an element of identity for the human as well: I will be pretty much the same in ten minutes than I am now. My identity and my self will not have changed. Yet, phenomenologically, something will have changed: I might have left the room, have breathed different air, thought about different things. These differences 'outside' me will have an impact on what happens 'within' me. The identity of my self depends on these encounters with otherness (and obviously others) more than we would realize: it is only once I stop breathing that I attain the self-identity of the thing (but then, obviously, there is no 'I' any longer). The third point, however, is most important. Derrida states that *once* we realize this being bound to otherness there is no reason not to suppose that, 'rogues that we all are,'[8] *all* are struggling for identity and that this struggle for identity is for 'them' as it is for 'us' dependent on otherness. It is such a connection of all with all that is intimated for Derrida in human rights, for instance, and

---

[8] Allusion is again to the paragraph, 'the rogue that therefore I am,' where Derrida takes pains to show that we must reverse the political thought that the rogue always concerns the other to the ethical recognition that the rogue might already pertain to us as well, see Derrida (2003, 95).

why it matters to extend these as much as possible (even though without Eurocentrism).

Taylor's idea of 'provincializing' Europe contrasts well with Derrida's thought on identity-politics. Commenting upon the shift between social imaginaries between the medieval and the modern era, Taylor argues that whereas the common identity of the Christian culture was somehow God-given, this quest now concerns 'the people' themselves: "for people to act together, in other words, to deliberate in order to form a *common* will on which they will act, requires a high degree of *common* commitment, a sense of *common identification*" (Taylor 2011, 43, italics mine). This shift, then – and this is one of the few places where Taylor acknowledges Derrida's thinking – concerns the 'invention' of the people, of a commonality when it concerns the identity and the will: "It is almost as if the American 'people' are invented as a nation by a law or legislative body that comes to be *after the event*, that is, after the revolution itself. It's a sort a creative rememoration of the event after the event – a temporal paradox of rereading the past through the present, a sort of historical bootstrapping" (Taylor 2007b, 35). Taylor then goes on to agree with Derrida's line of questioning, "who gives the authority to the people to invoke the people as their own authority?" (Taylor 2007b, 35)

Yet Derrida is here playing on the difference between a constative and a performative discursive modality (Derrida 2002c, 47-52): the establishment of this people as *one nation* depends at once on the constative 'we are free' and 'we have become free' and on the performative 'we ought to be free,' even though we are not entirely free yet. To become free, then, it is necessary to be with and without law, with and without authority as if the idea of *one nation* cannot happen without being *one nation under God*. If this is the case, the people are claiming and vindicating their own authority while deferring this very authority: just as it is free while not being free (the performative 'we ought to be free' overrides the constative 'we are freed from colonization'), just so it is unfree at the very moment of declaring its freedom (even 'after the event' it still seeks an authority higher than its own).

It is such a moment of indecision, of a back and forth between identity and difference, between what is 'common' to a self and to a culture and what 'unsettles' and 'destabilizes' this unity—even though this otherness would actually constitute the self—that Taylor neglects. For Taylor insists on a common identity even after modernity. In our secular age, religion, if it is to have a role in society and in the public realm, would, according to Taylor, constitute the cement or at least one of the binding factors of our political and cultural identity: if society is no longer 'under God' in the sense that this nation here would be the executor of God's will, "the new space for God in the secular world" (Taylor 2004, 193) is according to Taylor no longer solely to be seen in such political identity, but rather in some sort of mixture between national(ist) and personal or cultural identity. Religion has a place in the public realm for Taylor because it is "central to the personal identities of individuals or groups, and hence [can] always [be] a constituent of political identities" (Taylor 2004, 193–194). Although Taylor deems it "wise" to, *à la Derrida*, "distinguish our political identity from any particular confessional allegiance," he does come to the troublesome conclusion that the "reinvasion of the political identity by the confessional" (Taylor 2004, 194) is an ever-present possibility. *Unlike Derrida*, then, Taylor seems to be closer to this conclusion than he is at a distance from the wisdom to separate between religious and political identity. It seems fair to say that, for Taylor, this 'reinvasion' of the religious will take place rather than the principle of separation between religion and politics.

This does, however, not mean that Derrida would be on the other side of the communitarian spectrum. Such a 'libertarian' idea, where the only identity a culture or a group would share is that it is 'without identity', can be perceived in the works of Jean-Luc Nancy. For Nancy, the identity of a community may not lie in its identification with one or another confession, nation or another essence, be it the 'spirit' of a people or of humanity: "A community is not a project or a fusion, or in some general way a productive or operative project – nor is it a *project* at all" (Nancy 1991, 15). For Nancy, the 'essence' of community lies in its existence: it is not something that can be attained or be lost, but rather something that always is 'in the making' as it were, without a 'common will' or an essence ever realizing itself. Such a realization would in effect be the death of community: it would settle for one or the other particular communion (or project) and forget about the universal and ontological community in Nancy's sense. Such a community of singulars ('community without communion') is for Nancy not to be seen as the social bond (onto which one or the other project waiting to be realized could graft itself) but rather as a 'network' of openings *to* one another. This network shows itself for Nancy in the cut or wound present in all such projects presented by the happenings of death and finitude (which cuts through every community with the other).[9]

Both Nancy's later deconstruction of Christianity, as well as his recent works on community confirm this basic stance. This 'outside' of communion cannot be politically recuperated, nor can it be contained in a Christian or other confes-

---

9 See Nancy (1991, 26–34).

sional account of community.[10] Rather, Nancy is seeking how to phrase such community once these great unifiers and these great projects of, for instance communism and Christianism are fading away. In this regard, Nancy's anticommunitarianism does not give way to an individualism immediately: if Nancy, for instance, would agree for instance with Groucho Marx's famous quote that 'he would never belong to a club that allows him as a member,' then Nancy would be distrustful both of anyone who wanted to be a member of any club at all but also of the one who takes pride in the fact of being such an individual that he or she would find no club at all. Nancy's account of community seeks to overcome both the fact that the individual would be fused in, forgotten or oppressed by the community and the fact that the individual might pose him-or herself somewhat autonomously outside of any community.

It is clear, however, that in Taylor's account of the religions in the public realm Nancy would see nothing but a retreat into one or the other particular project or communion. It is less clear, however, how Derrida would ultimately regard both Nancy's and Taylor's positions. It is this that we will speculate upon in the remainder of this article by considering Derrida's response to Nancy's deconstruction of Christianity. Derrida's response to Nancy is, as ever, ambiguous:

> Just as it is neither enough to present oneself as a Christian nor to 'believe' in order to hold forth a language that is 'authentically' Christian, likewise it is not enough *not* to believe or believe oneself (...) non-Christian in order to utter a discourse (...) safely sheltered from all Christianity. This is not about being free of harm, safe, and saved, seeking one's salvation outside of Christianity. These values would still be Christian ones. (Derrida 2005, 220)

How to belong to a Christian community, then? If we apply this specific case to Derrida, Taylor and Nancy, then the following distinctions might emerge. Whereas Taylor thinks that some strong commitment and strong identity is enough to present oneself as 'authentically' Christian, Nancy thinks that to present oneself as a non-Christian is enough to be 'without' Christianity. But in Taylor's case, Derrida would argue that committing to one kind of Christian community is not sufficient to discriminate between the different social imaginaries of different kinds of Christian communities: we have in effect seen above that there is some slippage in the meaning of 'Christian' in Taylor's account – where a certain *kind* of Christianity needs to be overcome in order to arrive at a more essential

---

10 See Nancy (2010, 17–18) and Nancy (2008, 142–143). An important addition to this discussion is Nancy's recent (2013, 62, 75, 119 , 139, 141) on the thought of companionship as 'the work of inoperativity.'

Christianity. In Nancy's case, Derrida would point to a similar slippage: just as it is insufficient to 'believe' oneself Christian, it is not enough to think that one can abandon Christianity in one simple stroke: the identity of the 'anti'-Christian is constituted by the other just as much as the identity of the 'Christian'. Whereas Taylor sticks to the 'constative' of a constitution of a community ("we are Christian"), attaining to a fully realized Christian identity, Nancy would stick to the 'performative' ("we ought no longer to be Christian"), and so restlessly performing one's abstraction from any form of identity over and over again. Whereas Taylor's Christian identity would be haunted by the identity of the other – whether they be 'atheist,' 'Buddhist,' 'Confucian' or even those Christians of a different kind he seeks willingly to abandon —Nancy's deconstruction of Christianity is haunted by those remainders of the Christian tradition that Nancy willingly seeks to overcome.

Here Derrida's position would be more nuanced: for Derrida, there is nothing but an uncertain and always improper belonging to one or the other community or social imaginary. There is no way out of this: just as with the American revolution, we are stuck in the middle of a constative ("I am Christian") and a performative ("I want/ought to be Christian even when cross-pressured by other identities") when it comes to membership of a community. Whereas Taylor argues from out of the constative – because of this or that common characteristic we belong to this or that community – and Nancy from out of the performative – we never belong to this or that community because identity never is a given – Derrida argues that, when it comes to our belonging to one or the other community, we are *neither with nor without* identity. In the West, for instance, I cannot confidently say that I am a Christian and neither can I confidently say that I am not a Christian, because the Christian would be cross-pressured by secular views just as the atheist would be by religious views.

The difference with Taylor and Nancy is immense here: Derrida would argue that although the immanent frame, empirically, is closed to transcendence and turns into a 'spin,' it, ontologically, never can be closed and thus *is* open to the viewpoint of the other. For this 'between identities,' this uncommon and somewhat uncomfortable overlap, does not happen in the void for Derrida: it is not the anti-human, anti-life and heroic stance that Taylor wants to attribute to Derrida. On the contrary, it is the very movement of life that Derrida desires to follow here, for this back and forth between identities, between the 'idea' of Christianity and a 'certain kind' of Christianity, for instance, is not just abstract philosophical reasoning but demands that it be lived in "the exemplarity of the example" (Derrida 2007, 349). In such a moment of incarnation and such an example, Derrida argues, what was invisible, namely the difference between, for instance, the idea of justice and the insufficient forms in which this justice incarnates, *becomes visible*, as when Mandela went against the grain of the existing laws of Apartheid *in the name* of a more just law (Derrida 2007, 337). It is necessary, Derrida argues, that "the exemplary witnesses, those who make us think about the law they reflect, are those who, in certain situations, *do not respect* laws" (Derrida 2007, 349). It is out of respect for the law, in the name of justice, that laws can be suspended here or there.

If Derrida mentions Mandela here, as one of the 'exemplary witnesses,' it is because Mandela *inhabits* the space between the law of the South Africa he revolted against and the South Africa he, as one of the few, is willing to imagine. Here Taylor is right when pointing to Mandela as one of the 'conversions' possible in and proper to the secular age. One should not be too critical of his use of 'spectacular' examples as Mandela for the art of convincing might work more in an emotional rather than in a rational manner (Grondin 2012, 261–262). When it comes to what we are able to imagine socially, Derrida and Taylor would agree that we need figures like this, that, were it not for such a moment of incarnation, we would not be able to speak of the universality of such a thing as human rights and neither would we be able to judge these incarnations (whether they be 'Christian,' 'Confucian' or something else) forever insufficient. Without someone like Mandela, one would perhaps not have been able to dream of a South Africa without Apartheid and one might have been stuck in the laws of the communitarian white minority, just as one might get stuck in a Christianity 'of a certain kind' that no longer dreams of an effectivity pertaining to an extension of the Gospel. Derrida would insist, though, that Taylor turn away from these 'spectacular' examples in order to interpret them in a 'specular' way: it is not certain whether it is because of such moments of incarnations (empirical) that one can imagine a universality of these laws and of human rights (ontologically) or whether it is because of the fact of such universality (ontologically) that one is left with 'the exemplarity of examples' (empirically). Yet, whereas a 'spectacular' example is the utopia of an identity realized once and for all (at the expense of otherness), the ghostly incarnation Derrida advances is mindful both of an identity that is offered and comes into being, through the example, through the example, but also of a difference within these identities and incarnations which makes for the fact it never is fully realized (and thus remains open to other examples). This, again, is the difference between *but one* and *more than one* example (of identity, of worldviews, etc.): Mandela is *one way* of recognizing that there is more to the immanent laws than sheer immanence – it is a take – but can never be *the way* of incarnating the universal idea of justice in empirical laws – it is not a spin.

6 Conclusion

More often than not, one indeed gets the impression that the *telos* of Taylor's description of cross-pressures in the secular age is the release of these very pressures, as if to admit to cross pressures is also to admit the porosity of the immanent frame. Often, too, one feels that Taylor is somehow stuck in a *petitio principi* where what needs to be proven is already presupposed: the critique of scientific reductionism, for instance, is not immediately *pro* religious faith – it is not *because* science cannot prove this or that or *because* it has blind spots in general that one must believe.[11]

Yet, and to stick to the plurality of today's cross-pressures, our argument here has not been to dismiss Taylor's account but rather to find a *tertium datur* or an ally for Taylor in Derrida. It pertains to philosophy, though, to state when philosophical reasoning falls short and to point to problems in this reasoning. So, when we argue that Taylor aims ultimately to get rid of cross-pressures, that is, "when he seems to suggest that this pressure comes from the now-ignored transcendent *itself*, 'the solicitations of the spiritual'" (Smith 2014, 75 reference to Taylor 2007, 360), it is not to defend the view that Nancy has a better view on these pressures, namely that "an absolute transcendental of opening" (Karolis 2013, 692) of world and of identities would be a more genuine account of what it means to live in a secular age. It is to acknowledge rather that these cross-pressures themselves are real and that much needs to be done not to settle for one or the other identity and forget about such cross-pressures.

It is, on this account, that Derrida's account is to be preferred philosophically (and why Taylor's rather straightforward dismissal of Derrida remains inexplicable). It is, for instance, inexplicable that the realism Taylor so admires in Heidegger cannot for him be extended to Derrida's thought. For Derrida's account of our identity being bound to the other and to otherness is precisely what is real and is what constitutes the very movement of life.[12]

If anything is given to thought after our discussion of Taylor and the 'postmodernists' Derrida and Nancy then, it is that with their respective praise for plurality and the concomitant search for, in Taylor's terms, a motivator for human action (which Taylor solely seeks in religion), Derrida has somewhat of

---

[11] See Taylor (2007, 555).
[12] For Taylor on Heidegger, see Taylor (2005, 447–448) on Derrida and especially 448 on Heidegger as "an uncompromising realist". See however also Derrida (2008, 34), "the question of the living and of the living animal. For me that will always have been the most important and decisive question." For more on Derrida's realism, see Marder 2011.

a head-start. For Derrida's uncertain belonging to one or the other religious or otherwise community, rather than cuddling up in one's own community, at least has the advantage of being challenged by the other and by otherness. We have seen that Derrida would not disagree with Taylor's take on cross-pressures, nor with his take on a transcendence within immanence. Yet we have seen Derrida doubting whether it would be *just one* moral resource that would constitute the 'solicitations of the spiritual,' especially if these resources are exclusively religious and if they are to announce the end of our cross-pressures.

Derrida, in effect, would argue for an infinite cross-pressuredness of sorts, in that the right to belong concerns the other, first and foremost. If anything, this call issued by the other is a call *for action*, a motivator to transcend one's communal comfort zone as it were and therefore a right to put some pressure on us, and our social imaginaries: "An opening up is something that is decided (...) An opening up must occur where there is war, and there is war everywhere in the world today. Peace is only possible when one of the warring sides takes the first step, the hazardous initiative, the risk of opening up dialogue." (Chérif 2008, 59)

After all: someone has to set the example.

Bibliography

Caputo, John D. 1997. *Deconstruction in a Nutshell*. New York: Fordham University Press.
Chérif, Mustapha. 2008. *Islam and the West: A Conversation with Jacques Derrida*. Chicago: The University of Chicago Press.
Derrida, Jacques. 1994. *Spectres of Marx: The State of the Debt, the Work of Mourning and the New International* (translation by Peggy Kamuf). London/New York: Routledge.
Derrida, Jacques. 1997. *À Dieu à Emmanuel Levinas*. Paris: Galilée.
Derrida, Jacques. 1999. *Adieu to Emmanuel Levinas* (translation by Pascal-Anne Brault and Michael Naas). Stanford: Stanford University Press.
Derrida, Jacques. 2000. *Of Hospitality: Anne Defourmantelle Invites Jacques Derrida to Respond*. Stanford: Stanford University Press.
Derrida, Jacques. 2001. "On Forgiveness: A Roundtable Discussion with Jacques Derrida." In *Questioning God*, edited by John Caputo and Michael Scanlon, 52–72. Bloomington: Indiana University Press.
Derrida, Jacques. 2002. "Faith and Knowledge: The Two Sources of 'Religion' at the Limits of Reason alone." In *Acts of Religion*, edited by Gil Anidjar, 40–101. London: Routledge.
Derrida, Jacques. 2002b. "Force of Law." In *Acts of Religion*, edited by G. Anidjar, 228–298. London: Routledge.
Derrida, Jacques. 2002c. "Declarations of Independence." In *Negotiations. Interventions and Interviews 1971–2001*, edited by E. Rottenberg, 46–55. Stanford: Stanford University Press.
Derrida, Jacques. 2003. *Voyous*. Paris: Galilée.

Derrida, Jacques. 2003b. *Psyche: Inventions de l'autre II*. Paris: Galilée.
Derrida, Jacques. 2005. *On Touching – Jean-Luc Nancy* (translation by Christine Irizarry). New York: Fordham University Press.
Derrida, Jacques. 2007. "Nelson Mandela, in admiration." In *Basic Writings*, edited by David F. Krell, 330–352. London: Routledge.
Derrida, Jacques. 2008. *The Animal that Therefore I Am* (translation by Marie-Louis Millet). New York: Fordham University Press.
Derrida, Jacques. 2013. "Auto-Immunity: Real and Symbolic Suicides." In *Philosophy in a Time of Terror: Dialogues with Jurgen Habermas and Jacques Derrida*, edited by Giovanna Borradori, 85–136. Chicago: The University of Chicago Press.
Grondin, Jean. 2012. "Charles Taylor a-t-il des raisons de croire à proposer? Grandeur et limites d'une justification de l'option métaphysique de la croyance par des enjeux." *Science et Esprit* 64: 245–262.
Karolis, Alexander C. 2013. "Sense in Competing Narratives of Secularization: Charles Taylor and Jean-Luc Nancy." *Sophia* 52:673–694.
Marder, Michael. 2011. *The Event of The Thing: Derrida's Post-Deconstructive Realism*. Toronto: Toronto University Press.
Nancy, Jean-Luc. 1991. *The Inoperative Community* (translation by Peter Connor). Minneapolis: The University of Minnesota Press.
Nancy, Jean-Luc. 2008. *Dis-Enclosure: The Deconstruction of Christianity, I* (translation by Guy Malenfant et al.). New York: Fordham University Press.
Nancy, Jean-Luc. 2010. *The Truth of Democracy* (translation by Pascal-Anne Brault). New York: Fordham University Press.
Nancy, Jean-Luc. 2012. *L'équivalence des catastrophes. (Après Fukushima)*. Paris: Galiléé.
Nancy, Jean-Luc. 2013. *La communauté désavouée*. Paris: Galilée.
Nietzsche, Friedrich. 1976. *Menschliches allzumenschliches*. München: Carl Hanzer Verlag.
Smith James K.A., 2014. *How (not) to be Secular: Reading Charles Taylor*. Gran Rapids: Eerdmans.
Taylor, Charles. 1999. *A Catholic Modernity?* Oxford: Oxford University Press.
Taylor, Charles. 2002. "Conditions of an Unforced Consensus on Human Rights." In *The Politics of Human Rights*, edited by Obrad Savic, 101–119. London: Verso.
Taylor, Charles. 2004. *Modern Social Imaginaries*. Durham/London: Duke University Press.
Taylor, Charles. 2005. "Heidegger on Language." In *A Companion to Heidegger*, edited by Hubert Dreyfus and Mark Wrathall, 433–455. London: Blackwell.
Taylor, Charles. 2007. *A Secular Age*. Cambridge, MA: Harvard University Press.
Taylor, Charles. 2007b. "On Social Imaginaries." In *Traversing the Imaginary: Richard Kearney and the Postmodern Challenge*, edited by Peter Gratton and John P. Manoussakis, 29–47. Evanston, IL: Northwestern University Press.
Taylor, Charles. 2011. "Why we Need a Radical Redefinition of Secularism." In *The Power of Religion in the Public Sphere*, edited by Eduardo Mendieta and Jonathan Vanantwerpen, 34–59. Columbia: Columbia University Press.
Thomson, Iain. 2011. "Transcendence and the Problem of Otherworldly Nihilism: Taylor, Heidegger and Nietzsche." *Inquiry* 54:140–159.

Section 3: **Human Rights and Migration — (Post-)Secular Social Imaginaries in Contemporary Perspective**

Robin Vandevoordt, Noel Clycq and Gert Verschraegen
Studying Culture through Imaginaries

Some Reflections on the Relevance of Imaginaries for the Social Sciences

1 Introduction

Even though social imaginaries' philosophical relevance is ever more widely acknowledged, it remains a rather strange intruder for cultural sociologists and anthropologists. How individuals make sense of the world they live in through the structures underlying their thoughts, actions and experiences, how they evaluate each other's and their own behaviour, or how they use widely available narratives to understand an ever more complex stream of events: all these descriptions given by Charles Taylor (2004, 23) are exactly what the social-scientific study of culture is about. And yet some scholars working from within these social sciences have argued precisely that social imaginaries might help provide a way out of some of the impasses in which their disciplines have been caught (Appadurai 1996; Strauss 2006).

In this chapter, we therefore explore the conceptual and heuristic relevance of social imaginaries for cultural analysis. We begin by sketching some of the key problems and approaches in the social-scientific study of culture, before situating social imaginaries within this field. The last section, then, explores the contribution of imaginaries more empirically through the particular case of human rights. This essay, however, does not of course seek to present an exhaustive overview of social-scientific conceptions of culture.[1] Instead, a selection has been made to highlight some of the relative strengths and weaknesses of social imaginaries, thereby focusing particularly on the grey area between secular and religious imaginaries.

2 Studying Culture

The study of culture has formed itself around a number of debates on what it is that scholars should study, and how they should go about it. Scholars building

---
[1] For a general overview, see Alexander 2003 and Hall et al. 2010.

on the work of Emile Durkheim, for instance, conceive of culture as a relatively coherent ensemble of cognitive distinctions and symbolic forms structuring people's thoughts and experiences. These structures operate independently of individual agents' consciousness: actors can only use already existing cognitive schemes, frameworks or symbols to interpret the world they live in. How individuals think and act, is thus primarily determined by external social forces. The main function of these social structures, moreover, consists of integrating individual members, by stimulating obedience and loyalty towards the group and its behavioural rules. Scholars taking inspiration from Max Weber's writings, on the other hand, argue that culture is made of the subjective processes by which individual agents make sense of the world they are living in. For them, cultural analyses should therefore concentrate on the symbolic actions and utterances by virtue of which individuals express themselves and make sense of the expressions created by others. Within this tradition, cultural analysis aims to make sense of social actions and expressions, to specify the meaning they have for the actors, and to elucidate how they use particular symbolic forms and ideas both to understand their environment and to act strategically within it.

Besides these pertinent discussions on the nature of culture and how it should be studied, the 1980s and 1990s saw the rise of a more historically oriented debate revolving around the relative coherence of cultural systems. Precisely through its strong reliance on ethnography, cultural anthropology, for instance, has traditionally been inclined towards full submersion in particular local communities, which are then contrasted, as individual units, with one another. A similar assumption of coherence and internal homogeneity can be traced even more easily in many Durkheimian approaches, as they often concentrate their enquiries on the integrating functions of a shared culture, albeit ever more broadly (taking humanity or human rights as its core) or ephemerally (focusing on singular rather than recurring events). To a certain extent, such assumptions also underlie much of the work undertaken in Weberian research, particularly when relying on the construction of ideal-types, whether they be related to class, nationality or professional cultures.

Why is this such a problem? Surely there still is *some* cultural coherence to be found within particular groups, and at particular points in time? And is that not the most important task of cultural scholars, to explore the nature and construction of the more solid building blocks out of which contemporary subjects structure their identities? The primary problem though, is not so much that these approaches have suddenly lost their relevance, but rather that they are increasingly less well-equipped to deal with some of contemporary culture's most important characteristics. Mass migration has fed into super-diverse societies where intercultural contact is now part of an everyday reality for ever more people, and where 24/7 satellite news and social media provide individuals with an ever wider range of repertoires, narratives and frames with which to make sense of the world, and upon which to construct their identities. As boundaries and borders can no longer be easily demarcated, the key assumption that in any particular culture, individuals exhibit more or less similar behaviour, adhere to the same set of core values and interpret the world with the same symbolic tools, is no longer tenable. In other words, it has now become obvious that the traditional concept of culture as a relatively coherent ensemble of beliefs, cognitions or shared senses of meanings, has serious limitations.

The problem with the more classical approaches to culture – which are still being used across the social sciences – thus seems to be that their tools are not sufficiently up-to-date to analyse the cultural complexities caused by the exponential process of globalisation. That is, how can we analyse how individuals and groups make sense of the global flow of ideas, images and narratives streaming into their lives? What impact do their encounters with diversity have on how they imagine society and their own place in it? According to some of the leading authors in cultural anthropology and sociology, we are therefore still in need of new methodological and theoretical tools to deal with this globalised condition of cultural complexity and super-diversity (e.g. Marcus 1995; Appadurai 1996, 2013; Hannerz 1992).

It is precisely these questions, of course, which feed into this chapter as we explore how social imaginaries may help to formulate responses to these debates. To assess the particular merits of social imaginaries, however, we first need to situate the notion more firmly within the wider conceptual field of cultural analysis. As much contemporary research still relies heavily on the classical paradigms, we will first describe these in more detail (2.1 and 2.2), before discussing two of the most influential recent attempts to correct their fallacies (2.3 and 2.4).

2.1 Emile Durkheim and the Ritualist and Mentalist Traditions

To obtain a better insight into how the Durkheimian perspective works, it is well worth revisiting one of the classic studies in cultural sociology, Durkheim's *The Elementary Forms of the Religious Life* (1914). In this ambitious book, Durkheim set out to explore the minimal, most crucial elements of religion, by examining what he considered to be its most simple, 'primitive' forms. By focusing on anthropological accounts of Aboriginal and Indian tribes, Durkheim sought to identify some of the most fundamental mechanisms at work in *any* religion whatsoever. One of the most crucial structures he found, was a ubiquitous distinction between the sacred and the profane, the latter referring to everyday life and its recurring routines, and the former denoting everything that was assigned an exceptional meaning, setting it apart from normal life. This distinction not only helped community members to classify particular objects, such as spears and totems, but also to understand the basic meaning of places, events, actions, symbols or even names. The Aborigines, for instance, interrupt their harsh hunting-gathering lives every now and then with abundant, excessive rituals in which they wear exceptionally colourful costumes, and engage in ecstatic dances. Nothing of the world in which they live, according to Durkheim, can be understood unless one grasps how the categories of the profane and the sacred are continuously assigned to any object or subject they encounter (Weyns 2014).

There are two dimensions in this particular vision, both of which have persisted in different sub-branches in the cultural sciences. Firstly, this work has influenced a more cognitive, neo-Kantian tradition in cultural research (Douglas 1996; Zerubavel 1999). Durkheim agreed with Kant that we can only perceive the world through pre-existing categories that structure our thoughts and experiences. In contrast to Kant, however, Durkheim argued that these categories are not inherent to an ability for universal reason with which every individual subject is endowed. Instead, these perceptual categories are produced and determined by social forces – thus effectively sociologising Kant's epistemological argument. In other words, how individuals understand and experience the world is structured by external social forces. Furthermore, while most societies draw distinctions between the sacred and the profane, the particular substance of these classifications (what belongs to either category) corresponds to the social structure of any particular society. In this sense, to study any particular culture means primarily to relate its underlying mental structures to the social structure of its community (Malkki 1995).

Besides this more cognitive, mentalist branch, scholars have also focussed on religion's social functions. According to Durkheim, the Aborigines' sacred rituals served to shock and inspire awe in individual members by displaying the exceptional power of the group – an experience he described as 'collective effervescence.' Through their strong emotional impact, such experiences enforce individuals' obedience and loyalty towards their group. According to Durkheim, then, the category of the sacred – just like the Western God-idea – is in fact nothing more than society or community imagined in an abstract form. Objects, events and symbols carrying a sacred meaning produce bonds between individual members, precisely through the shared experience of ritual sacredness. It is this powerful force which turns individual beings into *moral beings*, belonging to a wider community.

Similar analyses have been made well into the 21st century, some of them building on the paradigm of 'civil religion.'[2] This paradigm was founded upon the classic work by Robert Bellah (1967) on how the ritual functions of religion seem to persist in American patriotism. As a collective moral identity, America is celebrated through sacred buildings (the Lincoln Memorial as a cathedral of the nation-state), persons (the founding fathers) and sacrosanct cultural narratives (freedom and the American Dream). Furthermore, individuals find themselves 're-integrated' every now and then through national rituals such as the Fourth of July, the chanting of the national anthem at small- and largescale events, and by high school students pledging alliance to the flag before beginning their morning classes. Precisely by their sacredness – these symbols are indisputable, set apart from normal everyday objects and actions – individuals are rendered moral members of an integrated community.

The combination of these two strands in Durkheim's work, to conclude, is aptly captured by the concept of *conscience collective* (or 'collective consciousness' as it is usually translated). This notion refers not only to a shared understanding of the world through a series of distinctions (in the sense of consciousness), but also to the moral force of the group producing these distinctions (in the sense of conscience). One can see that it is precisely in this notion that the Durkheimian approach shows some close affinities to Taylor's conception of social imaginaries as both epistemological and moral in nature – but we will return to this later on in more detail.

2.2 Max Weber and the Interpretative, Ideational Tradition

A different strand of cultural research has been built upon the work of Max Weber and the tradition of hermeneutics associated with Wilhelm Dilthey and Heinrich Rickert. To study culture, according to these scholars, one needs to interpret and understand (*Verstehen*) what behaviour subjectively means to individuals themselves, instead of 'explaining' their behaviour through external social forces. Gilbert Ryle (1971) provided this argument with the well-known example of two different persons blinking an eye. For one of them, this 'act' may be nothing more but a spastic, involuntary movement of his eyelid, whereas for the other, blinking might actually mean something more, an affirmation of acquaintance or an inside joke. While the externally visible behaviour is identical in both cases, only the latter is a form of cultural communication, precisely

---

2 E.g. Furseth 1994 and Williams 2013.

because of the particular meaning such a blink has for the individuals involved. In this sense, the interpretive approach is more 'subjective' than its Durkheimian counterpart, as in the latter, subjective elements may only be included as the effects of external social forces, whereas the former takes these elements to the heart of the analysis (Weyns 2014).

The ultimate goal of most Weberian perspectives, however, lies in the construction of 'ideal types.' In their everyday conduct, individuals are guided by specific value-ideas, and it is the task of cultural scientists to identify the precise logic of these value-ideas by enlarging them as perfect 'types' of such singular rationalities. In a more contemporary form, this thought figure can be recognised in the symbolic boundaries approach, a growing body of research pioneered by cultural sociologist Michèle Lamont. Taking Weber's (1946, 300–301) classic distinction between status and class as a point of departure, this approach conceives of culture in terms of a limited number of symbolic value-ideas to which individuals assign relative importance, and by means of which they construct their identities as adhering to specific status groups. In her classic comparative study of the culture of the American and French middle class, for instance, Lamont (1992) distinguishes between the cultural (a refined taste for manners and high culture), moral (honest, correct behaviour towards others) and material (professional and practical success) criteria respondents use for evaluating their own and other's behaviour. An ideal-typical 'culture' person, for instance, considers it more important that people have a well-developed taste for style and high culture, whilst ascribing lesser value to a professional career or traditional moral virtues such as modesty, courage and loyalty. In reality, of course, individuals generally cannot be confined to any one 'ideal type.' Instead, they are continuously involved in 'boundary work,' as they try to use these different value-ideas strategically in different situations (Lamont and Molnar 2002). Precisely this focus on boundary *work* makes this approach at least a more promising alternative for analysing culture in its complex global conditions: creative work is involved in drawing contingent boundaries – instead of these boundaries being self-evidently determined by a coherent mental structure corresponding to one particular community. As we will see later on, it is through this focus on subjective, creative processes, that Appadurai's reading of social imaginaries can be understood as an idiosyncratic variant of this Weberian strand of research.

An altogether different, genealogical strand of research taking cues from Weber's writings, deals with the historical emergence, spread and impact of particular value-ideas, such as the protestant work ethic and its influence on the development of capitalist reason. The causal assumptions Weber makes therefore seem to invert Durkheim's theories: it is not so much *social structures* that define our vision of the world, as it is our *particular vision* of the world that steers society in a certain direction. This ideational conception of culture thus emphasises the substance of culture (as value-ideas), rather than its functional qualities in structuring our perceptions through classificatory forms. In turn, however, these particular value-ideas may ultimately end up imprisoning subjects within their particular logic: hence Weber's grim vision of capitalist-instrumentalist reason turning into an 'iron cage' with dim prospects for those trying to escape it. Such a focus on the socio-historical trajectory of value-ideas in terms of their substance or content can be recognised in the analyses of Adorno and Horkheimer (1997), as well as some of the work by Foucault (1979) and Anderson (1983).

2.3 Bourdieu: Combining Durkheimian Mentalism and Weberian Status Struggle

Ever since Durkheim and Weber wrote their classics, several scholars have sought to bridge the gap between them. Judging by its increasing popularity in recent decades, one of the most influential attempts to do so has been Pierre Bourdieu's work as a whole. Bourdieu (1977, 1986) constructed his sociology around three key concepts: habitus, cultural capital and field. Habitus refers to the ensemble of cognitive schemes and practical dispositions (i.e. inclinations) that enable us to interpret our actions and the world around us. How we see the world and give meaning to our actions, feelings and others, is, in other words, primarily determined by our habitus. In line with the Durkheimian paradigm, Bourdieu argues that our habitus is itself structured by external social forces. These external social forces, however, are no longer simply related to wider society as an integrated whole, but to differentiated social fields such as religion, politics, education, and so on. Each of these fields produces and reproduces its own logic, by imposing a set of implicit rules for social conduct. In Bourdieu's terms, fields have their very own *orthopraxy* and *orthodoxy*, that is, particular conceptions as to which practices and thoughts are right or wrong.

Within these fields, however – and this is where Weber comes in – actors are engaged in a continuous competition to acquire 'power,' either through material or symbolic forms of 'capital.' According to Bourdieu, actors thus strategically use their command of the rules and logic of particular fields to improve or maintain their position. The lion's share of Bourdieusian cultural analyses focuses precisely on these perennial struggles for power, whether they consist of consumption and lifestyle or the use of dialect and language. One of the cornerstones of his theory, furthermore, is that these battles are fought primarily by means of implicitly acquired, unarticulated frameworks of experience and thought: rather than consisting of explicit discourses, these frameworks consist of implicit *doxa*. These schemata may be implicit partly because they are 'embodied,' as opposed to merely cognitive or mentalist: they are rooted in practical routines, dispositions and inclinations.

A good example of his theory can be found in his co-authored study of the (French) education system (Bourdieu and Passeron 1977). Middle-class children, they argue, have often internalised particular forms of social interaction which enable them to deal with 'authority' and 'play' in a certain way: they have developed an appreciation for more intellectual rather than physical games, as well as a sense for subtle verbal debates in the standard language as opposed to more direct and vulgar language, and they have learned to accept non-violent forms of authority (such as teacher's). As middle-class children have generally internalised these assets well before entering the class room, it provides them with an immediate advantage within the social field of education. These children have acquired a different habitus which structures the way they behave, think and experience the world, and which is, in turn, itself structured by their objective (socio-economic) position in society.

2.4 The 'Practical Turn'

For authors starting from this paradigm (Reckwitz 2002; Swidler 2001; Knorr Cetina 1981; Sewell 1992), the smallest analytic unit should not be located in ideas, pre-formed cognitive structures or social fields, but in embodied practices themselves. At least at first sight, these approaches seem to offer little new to Bourdieu's adaptations of Durkheimian mentalism – that is, making these objective social structures include not only cognitive schemes but also practical dispositions. However, the most fundamental contribution these approaches make lies in their perspective on causal mechanisms. Instead of focusing on how meaning is imposed on practices – as Durkheimian and Bourdieusian researchers often do – these scholars tend to focus on how meaning emerges from practices, that is, how practices have a logic of their own from which wider senses or arrangements of meaning eventually develop. The key point is therefore that, at least in some cases, meaning-structures are not entirely formed in advance, neither in the heads of individuals (as Weberians would have it), nor in the form of elaborate societal structures (as Durkheimians would). William Sewell Jr. (1996), for instance, argued that there had not been a consistent, well-defined conception of the French Revolution until the storming of the Bastille. It was only after this concrete event, that the meaning of the revolution crystallised into a solid form which was to structure people's thoughts and actions for years and centuries to come. Precisely this enlarged emphasis on practices-as-such distinguishes these approaches from Bourdieu's work; for him, the inscription of culture remained 'in last instance' structured by already differentiated social fields – even though his notion of habitus was meant to include more room for individual strategies and capabilities.

Instead of focusing on recurring structures or 'regularities,' these scholars thus concentrate more on practical "arrangements of people, artefacts and things" (Schatzki 2001, 6) in which structures may or may not be reproduced. An often-cited source of inspiration is Anthony Giddens' (1984) structuration theory, which no longer conceives of structures as reproducing themselves above the heads of individual agents as an immanent social law (e.g. Sewell 1992). Instead, social structures are enacted time and time again in singular events, and this endows every event with a contingent 'structuring' force, that is, it can both reproduce the prevalent social structure, as well as develop a new, slightly deviant logic of its own. By focusing on concrete practices, these approaches thus seek to bypass the fallacies of both mentalist-structuralism and subjectivist-ideationalism. Furthermore, the relative flexibility of these approaches may allow them to deal more aptly with the consequences of globalisation as they take specific practices as their core material, rather than relatively fixed, coherent cultures belonging to any well-delineated social group. Such a practical approach thus enables researchers to explore, in principle, an endless range of situations in which super-diversity and media practices converge,[3] and in which identities can be construed.

3 Social Imaginaries

3.1 Conceptions of Social Imaginaries

How then, can social imaginaries contribute to the debates and problems in the social-scientific study of culture? To fully assess the concept's relevance, it is useful to have a look at the more empirically grounded variants of the term, rather than strictly limiting ourselves to Charles Taylor's specific reading. One of the most often cited influences on the Chicago-based Centre for Transcultural Studies (CTS), in which the concept emerged most programmatically, is Cornelius Castoriadis' (1975) *The Imaginary Institution of Society*. In that work, Castoriadis

---

[3] See for instance the growing importance of 'everyday life' as practices in audience studies, instead of reception studies (Bird 2003) and, more generally, the emerging concept of 'media practices' (Couldry 2004).

tackled orthodox Marxists' tendency to give causal primacy to social and material structures over cultural and ideational ones. In his view, ideas and attitudes were not so much determined by material structures, as the other way around: researchers should focus on how acts of creative imagination are continuously reshaping the world into new forms. In that sense, his account appears to be a rather peculiar variant on the idealist threads in Weber's thought, focusing on the emergence of new ways to deal with already existing ideas.

Probably the most widely cited work within this strand of literature, however, is Benedict Anderson's (1983) *Imagined Communities*. There, Anderson reconstructs the rise and spread of the nation-state as an increasingly self-evident model for organising public affairs and structuring collective identities. While the design of his account is remarkably Weberian, focusing on the rise and spread of a substantial idea, a more original dimension of his work is more practical in its outlook. According to Anderson, one of the most crucial factors in enforcing the nation-state model was the development of print capitalism, as it allowed individuals over a wide area to orient themselves communally on the same selection of news, thereby enabling a similar perspective on current affairs, and stimulating the adoption of a shared language. In order to create the sense of shared destiny and community typical for the nation-state, individual citizens had to be able to imagine themselves as occupying the same social sphere and temporality, giving them the feeling that the same things were 'happening to them,' on the same shared national trajectory and the same temporal horizons. Through shared practices such as reading the newspaper they could 'imagine' themselves to be in a community of other citizens reading the paper – an *imaginary* community, as most members never actually meet one another, let alone develop personal, reciprocal bonds as one does with close relatives or neighbours.

By focusing on imaginaries in this manner, Anderson simultaneously moved the notion away from merely creative practices onto the construction of *collective identities* – an emphasis which was generally followed by Appadurai and Taylor. Through his emphasis on the role of these collective identities, Anderson's work also contains some Durkheimian elements. In this sense, nation-states can be thought of as functional equivalents of religion, that is, those elements that 'integrate' modern societies through a 'conscience collective,' a shared sense of community which is both epistemological (how to perceive the world through language and the printed press) and moral (structured around normative ideals and values).

In a sense, Arjun Appadurai (1996, 2013) extends the historical work of Anderson by applying the notion of imaginaries to contemporary global cultures. Whereas print capitalism was crucial for the rise of the nation-state, we have now entered an era in which digital media and mass migration are bound to have an equally profound impact on the way we make sense of the world we live in. Rather than being socialised in a relatively homogenous culture, which would enable us to have a self-evident 'sense' of the world we share with others, individuals now deal with a myriad of narratives and images flowing into their lives, both through the media and through everyday contact with other cultures. For Appadurai, this means primarily that the imagination will acquire a much more constitutive, central role in societies, as individuals and groups now have to deal creatively with all those ideas flowing into their world, and construct individual and collective identities out of the mass of stimuli. Culture therefore becomes less predictable: people can take cues for constructing their identity from an ever larger repertoire of narratives, ideas and images. In this sense, for instance, the rapid emergence of the Indignados and Occupy-movements and their spread across the globe is as exemplary as the Arab Spring.[4] As with Castoriadis and Anderson, there is a strong Weberian undertone in Appadurai's perspective, as his research design focuses on the subjective, substantial components of culture, that is, on how individuals and groups make sense of their environment, and on how imaginaries spread themselves across the globe.[5]

Charles Taylor's (2004) writings on imaginaries, then, is presumably the most abstract and broad-ranging of the authors discussed here. Taylor defines social imaginaries as "the ways people imagine their social existence, how they fit together with others, how things go on between them and their fellows, the expectations which are normally met, and the deeper normative notions and images which underlie these expectations" (2004, 23).

As with Anderson, this definition explicitly thematises the construction of a 'we-group,' a collective identity that provides an inarticulate answer to the question 'who we are.' As such, it allows at once for the more Durkheimian focus on integration and the *conscience collective*, on whatever level it may occur (e.g. ethnic-cultural group, nation, or even humanity as a whole), and for a more Weberian focus on boundary work, in which our own identity serves to distinguish ourselves from others.

Specific to Taylor's conception of imaginaries, however, is that it refers to the wider background[6] of concrete actions and practices, which "extends beyond the

---

4 This distinguishes Appadurai's perspective from those of Castoriadis and Gaonkar, as the latter two assume a particular repertoire of imaginaries to any particular society.
5 See also Appadurai (2013), and the allusion to Geertz' famous essay on the Balinese cockfights in his *Deep Democracy*. This focus on substantial ideas is also characteristic for other uses of the term, see for instance the book-length studies by Ivy (1995) and Steger (2008).
6 A notion which refers to Heidegger and Wittgenstein (Taylor 1993).

immediate background understanding that makes sense of our particular practices," into "a wider grasp of our whole predicament: how we stand to each other, how we got to where we are, how we relate to other groups, and so on" (2004, 25). Social imaginaries are thus less about a practical understanding of a particular action or situation, and more about something that lies beneath these understandings, an often unarticulated notion of a 'moral or metaphysical order' which provides both the epistemological and moral context in which such an action makes sense. An analysis of social imaginaries hence not only takes into account the more immediate, yet implicit knowledge and taken-for-granted schemes that actors employ in everyday situations, but especially focuses on the broader socio-historical contexts, practices and interpretations within and by which these actions acquire a broader political and moral meaning. Taylor illustrates these points with the example of a 'demonstration': participants share not only a practical sense of what a demonstration looks like and how it ought to be organised, but also have a wider understanding of its legitimacy and functions in a vital democracy, as well as at least an unarticulated awareness of its iconographic resonances through history (e.g. Tiananmen in 1989, or the French Revolution, as factual and moral models of demonstrations).

According to Taylor (2004: 25), these practices and understandings are inextricably woven into each other's fabric: "If the understanding makes the practice possible, it is also true that it is the practice that largely carries the understanding." Here Taylor (2004, 30–1) seeks to bridge the divide between materialism and idealism:

> In fact, what we see in human history is ranges of human practices that are both at once, that is, material practices carried out by human beings in space and time, and very often coercively maintained, and at the same time, self-conceptions, modes of understanding. These are often inseparable, in the way described in the discussion of social imaginaries, just because the self-understandings are the essential condition of the practice making sense that it does to the participants. Because human practices are the kind of thing that makes sense, certain ideas are internal to them; one cannot distinguish the two in order to ask the question: Which causes which?

However, Taylor (2004, 26) does seem to suggest at least three concrete ways in which social imaginaries can come about: they can trickle down from elite theories (e.g. how Grotius' and Locke's writings gave rise to the notion of a free public sphere); they can be improvised or creatively interpreted by particular groups (cf. Appadurai's conception of imaginaries); and they can develop unintentionally and incrementally out of concrete practices (e.g. 'the economy').

This saddles us with a fundamental question: how is it that Taylor claims to reconcile these different causal notions into one particular concept? As we have seen earlier, the four traditional and recent conceptions of culture generally elaborate one type of causal explanation – or better, tend to focus their analytical attention on one type of causal explanation. For Durkheimians, it is ultimately society itself that structures how we think, including our moral and epistemological sense of the world. For Weberians, social actions and societal developments are primarily steered by specific ideas or constellations of ideas. Bourdieu in turn sought to bring these together by drawing attention to the importance of embodied practices, in which individuals act strategically through their command of the rules of a particular field. Practice theories, lastly, tended to decouple these embodied practices from the structuring forces of particular fields, thus stimulating scholars to concentrate even more on the practices themselves, and on the immediate understandings embodied by them.

How then can we situate Taylor's notion of social imaginaries within these accounts? And what, if anything, does it contribute? Taylor agrees with practice theories and Bourdieu's work that understandings are mutually imbedded in concrete practices, rather than merely cognitive or ideational.[7] However, while Taylor acknowledges the role of practices, these practices themselves are not at the heart of his enterprise, nor are the immediate background understandings embodied by them – as is the case with many practice theories. Instead, Taylor's main point of interest is the wider historical and moral background underlying those immediate understandings, a background which is in no way reducible to the structuring logic of any particular social field. It is at precisely this point, that the specific contribution of Taylor's social imaginaries comes to the fore: he reconnects the flexibility of practice theories to an intellectual background which is not reducible to a totalising social force, but is, rather, bound up with particular, substantial ideas.

Consider, for instance, Armstrong's practical case study of the rise of a positive collective LGBT-identity in San Francisco (as discussed in Swidler, 2001). According to her practice-theoretical reading of the events, this identity only emerged in and through the organisation of a parade, a shared practice which enabled individuals to develop a collective identity. Taylor's notion of social imaginaries, however, would incline us to concentrate on the implicit background to the movement and its parade, that is, the broader historical context of civil movements which have inspired minorities to claim public recognition ever since the 1950s; or the 'expressive' turn in American culture from the late 1960s onwards, and not least the US's identification with a moral order that is based on merit, cultural equality and freedom. From Taylor's perspective, to

---

7 For the links between Taylor and 'practice theorists' see Reckwitz 2002.

grasp the 'imaginary' at work in this social practice means focusing our lens on the wider moral order in which the parade takes place, both as a concrete action, and as something that is mutually understood as a legitimate practice.

Compared to Anderson's and Appadurai's conceptions of the term, Taylor's imaginaries thus appear to be the most abstract, by paying closest attention to the unarticulated understandings of a wider moral order. This renders his account closer to the Durkheimian notion of a *conscience collective:* modern social imaginaries refer to a mechanism that reunites individuals and groups through a shared image of both in an (ideal) moral order. In his impressive study *A Secular Age*, for instance, Taylor explicitly refers to Durkheim in his typology of paleo-Durkheimian, neo-Durkheimian, and post-Durkheimian social forms (Taylor 2007, 489–492).[8] Taylor's use of Durkheimian theory is reflected in the level of abstraction in the cases upon which he builds his argument, such as the rise of the 'age of authenticity' (compared to Appadurai's study of activist-alliances, for instance) or the emergence of the public sphere. While Appadurai's approach enables scholars to focus on the creative work done by individuals and groups to construct a particular vision of the world out of the chaos of globalised cultures, Taylor urges us to look for the overarching images bringing together seemingly isolated agents.

While this Durkheimian slant accounts for some of the strengths in Taylor's approach, it also renders it more difficult to assess the originality and added value of his use of the term. In this sense, it is not always obvious to imagine what the contribution of imaginaries may be, for instance, to the vast body of literature on civil religion and modern rituals. It might be argued that Taylor in fact concentrates on the functional equivalents of religion in Durkheim's sense, that is, what unites people through a shared epistemological and moral understanding of their world. And furthermore, Taylor's conception may not be of great help in addressing the contemporary heterogenisation of cultural narratives and visions of a just moral order: it seems to be better equipped to analyse relatively coherent communities, rather than cultural practices situated within an age of globalisation.

---

8 By coining this Durkheimian typology, Taylor aims to historicize the complex relation between society and religion. While 'paleo-Durkheimian' refers to early or premodern social forms in which religion is deeply embedded in the entire social structure, neo-Durkheimian social forms are typical for societies where religion is partially differentiated or disembedded from the traditional social structure of kinship and village life and comes to serve as an expression of a larger social identity, such as the nation state or the global village. Neo-Durkheimian social forms, however, are characterized by individualized religious experience which has difficulties relating to overarching social formations.

However, what is new in comparison to Durkheimian studies, is the hermeneutic focus on the historical path of particular cultural horizons, instead of an attempt merely to identify their social functions. In this sense, Taylor has reconstructed the rise of the current economic sphere (2004), the changing conceptions of the Western self (1989), the shifts within collective religious life (2007), and, more generally, the modern social imaginary. In all these cases, Taylor's approach underlines how particular social practices are embedded in specific social-historical contexts and how interpretations and ideas always work in the context of other ideas. Ideas and interpretations historically shift in meaning, and are part of broader societal settings and historical-semantic domains that shape the meaning(s) of a specific utterance or action. In this sense, Taylor's thoroughly historicising approach parallels the work of authors like Koselleck (1985, 2006) who have connected the rise of the modern cultural imaginary to a series of semantic changes in central concepts such as democracy, autonomy, private rights or the public sphere, all of which testify to changed modes of identity formation and the formation of cultural horizons that have informed our contemporary self-understanding.

3.2 The Relevance of Social Imaginaries

How then, can we assess the heuristic relevance of social imaginaries to the socio-scientific field of cultural analysis? Based on our analyses above, we argue that the concept harbours at least two potential contributions to the socio-scientific study of culture. To be sure, we do not contend that a perspective on social imaginaries is more 'true' or 'accurate' than other forms of cultural analysis in any absolute sense. Rather, we consider the potential of these approaches to serve as heuristic tools which may help draw scholars' attention to particular phenomena, and improve their understanding.

Firstly, defining imaginaries as "the ways people imagine their social existence" (Taylor 2004, 23) enables an approach that is both more flexible and more narrowed down than traditional cultural perspectives. It is more specific in the sense that its core analytic unit is not a coherent *ensemble* of beliefs, narratives and mental structures, nor a wide range of cultural repertoires available to individuals. Instead, social imaginaries are designed to examine particular ideas and narratives flowing through the social world, most notably those ideas that embody visions of one's own society and the relations among its members. In turn, this narrower focus may stimulate scholars to trace these imaginaries across contexts, places and cultures, thus allowing for more flexibility to include a range of seemingly unrelated phenomena. In other words, it is precisely imaginaries' *substantial fluidity* which renders them a useful heuristic tool for cultural analysis, well-adapted to the complexities of contemporary culture.[9]

As such, one of the main advantages of building an approach around the concept of social imaginaries, is the tendency of these to cross social 'fields' (and sub-disciplinary boundaries). Rather than limiting debates on the secular, for instance, to the sociology of religion, one can thus explore the (historical) path of unifying visions in ethnic-cultural groups, nationalism, human rights or even international sports such as cricket (Steger 2008; Ivy 1995; for an example of the latter see Appadurai 1996). This is a particular advantage compared to Bourdieusian approaches. To give an example, scholars using such a framework in the cultural sociology of religion, tend to focus their attention on the workings of local churches and state institutions (Edgell 2012), whereas an approach centred around social imaginaries may be tailored much more to dealing with how traditional religions are increasingly under threat from less obvious competitors such as alternative spirituality, national identity, political orientation or even sports teams (cf. Luckmann 1967). As we mentioned earlier, this relative openness renders such an approach closer to the Durkheimian tradition of tracing the functional equivalents of religion as a form of social and moral integration (e.g. the civic religion paradigm), albeit with a more substantial, hermeneutic emphasis on its ideational content (focusing on what symbols mean rather than what their social function is) and its historical trajectory.

Secondly, and particularly through Appadurai's (2013) work, scholars could be urged to focus not only on embodied meanings in practices, but also on the *creative* capacities of individual agents to deal with imaginaries of different, overlapping institutions and social fields. This is a particular point about which both Bourdieu's critics (Lamont and Lareau 1988; Lahire 2003) and scholars using Bourdieu's theories have complained persistently. Even though the latter's notion of 'habitus' was originally designed to bridge the gap between voluntaristic agency and structural determination, his theories have been widely criticised for implicitly emphasising structure over agency, through the structuration of individual habitus by social fields. Furthermore, one may reflect with Appadurai on the usefulness of the term habitus, as individuals are ever less clearly socialised within one particular social field: "culture becomes less what Bourdieu would have called a habitus (a tacit realm of reproducible practise and dispositions) and more an arena for conscious choice, justification, and

---

[9] Some excellent studies using 'imaginaries' through its substantial fluidity are: Anderson 2010; Salazar 2010 and Dejaeghere and McCleary 2010.

representation, the latter often to multiple and spatially dislocated audiences" (1996, 44).

Based on their fluidity and emphasis on creative processes, social imaginaries may thus help to theoretically integrate a number of apparently unrelated case studies, such as human rights, refugees, education and migration, on a more theoretical level. However, it should be noted that a wide variety of case studies have of course been undertaken using the symbolic boundary vocabulary (Lamont and Molnar 2002), and if such studies allow enough space for local contexts (rather than working with a priori social categories), these studies may well provide a much more subtle, complex tool for analysing how individuals and groups make sense of one another in a more diverse world. At the heart of their enterprise are, indeed, meaning-making processes, which include a variety of evaluative structures and repertoires. Moreover, by explicitly putting boundary *work* at the heart of their research, they equally emphasise the creative aspect so important to the 'imaginaries' approach, albeit in an admittedly less frivolous tone. Similarly, this fluidity helps to situate imaginaries among more recent efforts to render the concept of culture more apt to deal with globalisation, whether through multi-site ethnography (Marcus 1995), transnationalism (Hannerz 1996) or urban anthropology (Atkinson et al. 2007).

Thirdly, imaginaries may help to redraw and reinforce the link between practices and ideas. As we discussed in section 2.4, scholars working on the sociology and anthropology of culture increasingly focus on the implicit understandings that are embodied in concrete practices. Taylor's work, in particular, makes it possible to cast an eye on the bigger picture, and add a greater level of abstraction to the analysis of embodied meaning – which is often, though not always, lacking in studies following the 'practical turn' (Gorski 2013). One could, for instance, try to acquire a better understanding of the behaviour of refugee movements by including in the analysis not only the 'power field' in which they are engaged with competing movements and the state, but also the (relatively recent) emergence of the 'rights'-perspective. It was only when asylum became the most important migration channel, that refugee movements started to shift from religious charity and political affiliation to an imaginary based on the rights of refugees as members of a global community. Similarly, imaginaries may stimulate scholars to trace the historical roots of the assumed legitimacy of human rights movements, or even the rise of right-wing populism and global terrorism.

4 Human Rights and the Sacralisation of the Individual

In this section, we provide a brief case study on how the imaginary of human rights can be read as one of a variety of creative reactions to the cultural complexities stemming from globalisation and increased diversity. Although the 'juridical revolution' of the twentieth century has formulated human rights – most eminently in the United Nations Declaration – as legal rights and instruments by which governments can be held criminally responsible in international law and prosecuted in international (or regional) courts when violating their citizens' fundamental rights, human rights are also predicated on a deeper, more fundamental shift in the modern social imaginary (e.g. Hunt 2007; Madsen and Verschraegen 2013). Ultimately, that is, the idea and the practices of human rights rely on a continuous effort to imagine humanity as a community of equals. The emergence of human rights can hence be seen as a key step in the more recent reimagining and restructuring of the secular, especially the political, and the religious social imaginaries (Taylor 2004, 2007). In consonance with Taylor's view on the modern, post-secular social imaginary (which is far too complex to present adequately here), human rights seem to fit into post-Durkheimian social forms, in which there is a de-linking of religious identity and sacralised cultural forms from overarching social formations (e.g. nations) and from collective religious authorities such as churches (Taylor, 2007, 473–481).

Here we would like to make the idea of a human rights imaginary more specific by drawing on recent work by Hans Joas (2013). By reading the emergence of human rights as the outcome of a long-term process of sacralising the individual person, Joas provides a convincing socio-historical account of how post-secular imaginaries come into being and evolve (see also Madsen and Verschraegen 2016). Just like Taylor, Joas takes as his point of departure the work of Emile Durkheim. The latter was one of the first sociologists to relate individual rights to a historical shift in the social imaginary. In contrast to the established natural law thinking or liberal theory of the 19th century, Durkheim no longer saw rights as vested in individuals previous to and irrespective of their involvement in society, but grounded them in an understanding of a double process of secularisation of society and sacralisation of the human person. What lies at the basis of the emergence of individual human rights, Durkheim wrote, "is not the notion of the individual as he/she is, but the way in which society treats and conceives, the esteem in which it holds the individual" (Durkheim 1950, 103). Underpinning this idea is a process of secularisation through which godly powers have been relocated as authority immanent within society and eventually within the human person itself:

> The human person is conceived as being invested with that mysterious property which creates an empty space around holy objects, which keeps them away from profane contacts and which draws them away from ordinary life. And it is exactly this feature which induces the respect of which it is the object. Whoever makes an attempt on a man's life, on a man's liberty, on a man's honor inspires us with a feeling of horror, in every way analogous to that which the believer experiences when he sees his idol profaned. (Durkheim 1975, 61)

From this Durkheimian vantage point, Joas explains how the abolition of torture throughout the eighteenth and nineteenth centuries and the humanisation of the criminal justice system can indeed be read as the outcome of an increasing 'sacredness' of the human person. Earlier work in cultural and legal history and sociology (e.g. Hunt 2007) already described how the elevation of the cultural ideal of 'the human person' became visible in changing attitudes towards 'bodily integrity,' the increasing sense of the separation and sacredness of human bodies, which led to a humanisation of penal law and penal practice. This humanisation of penalisation can be seen as a first, yet fundamental step forward in the process of 'inclusion' in the broader category of 'humanity,' inclusion here meaning the integration of those social categories – slaves, criminals, handicapped people, etc. – which previously had not been self-evidently included within the category of human beings. The outward expansion of human rights in the twentieth century, both in terms of the range of claimants covered and the range of enforceable claims, can also be understood in these terms. Extensive rights for women, children, the elderly, sexual and cultural minorities and people with disabilities were gradually put into place, and also extended to non-citizen residents, as more and more often these rights were defined on universalistic grounds from which no 'human beings' were to be excluded.

The development of human rights thus illustrates the basic Durkheimian insight that secularised and individualised social orders also sacralise a culture's core, which in turn defines the social identity of a society and regulates the relationship between individuals and the community. In the *Elementary Forms of the Religious Life*, for instance, Durkheim noted how during the French Revolution "society and its essential ideas became, directly and with no transfiguration of any sort, the object of a veritable cult (...) things purely laical by nature were transformed by public opinion into sacred things" (1975, 245). In this sense, the gradual emergence of human rights – from the French revolution to the era of contemporary global modernity – can be interpreted in terms of a fundamental shift in our moral imaginary and self-understanding. Such an understanding provides us with ample tools to understand a range of contemporary moral practices and discourses. The way we talk, think and feel about torture, for instance, can easily be understood as part of a long-term cultural process to increasingly treat the individual body, at some level, as 'sacred' in Durkheim's sense, as being set apart and not to be violated. Likewise, the emergence of a global 'human rights culture' with a strong emphasis on individual personhood can be interpreted as the relocation of sacrality from the religious realm of the gods to the secular realm of individual human activity.

Although Durkheim already laid out the main contours of this process of increasing the value of the person, Joas (2013, 69–96) has added important insights by examining how the human rights imaginary arose as a *creative, collective attempt* to give meaning to some of the most violent and traumatic experiences of modern history, such as slavery and the Holocaust. It is true that the literature on human rights has often pointed out the link between human rights violations and war, genocide or other atrocities, yet Joas adds to this knowledge by spelling out the preconditions for the successful transformation of experiences of violence into a commitment to human rights. Cruelty, suffering and bondage are not sufficient to transform negative experiences into universalist values and norms. In fact, human history is packed with cases of collective violence which have not led to progress in human rights (the crimes of Stalinism, to give but one example). The question that arises then is why and when a process of 'coming to terms' with traumatic experiences of collective violence can take place. By what mechanisms do violent experiences, ranging from rape to paramilitary death squads or genocide, become embodied into norms, practices and institutions expressing moral universalism?

Joas develops an answer by putting forward a conceptual triangle, which he immediately applies to the most important human rights movement of the nineteenth century, abolitionism (the movement to abolish slavery). Firstly, a framework of discursive traditions has to be available and deliver moral standards by which existing practices are to be condemned. In the case of the genesis of abolitionism, it only became possible to regard a prevailing practice such as slavery as a sin because a universalist morality – extending to 'the least of my brothers' – was already inherent in Christianity. The abolitionist movements in Great Britain and the United States were indeed supported mainly by evangelical religious groups who condemned slavery (in the 17th and 18th century applied mostly to Africans) as 'un-Christian' and were scandalised by the opposition of slaveholders to the evangelisation of the slaves.

Yet it took a specific historical conjuncture to put such universalist moral schemes into practice. Although an intense moral motivation to extend rights to slaves was present in Christian protestant culture, it required, secondly, some socio-structural changes to make the inclusion of slaves into humanity meaningful in the societal context of that time. As Thomas Haskell (1985) has famously pointed out, it was only because of the rise of worldwide industrial capitalism and the increasing global interlinkage of social relations that a 'humanitarian sensibility' became possible. It was primarily a change in cognitive style – specifically a change in the perception of causal connection and consequently a shift in the conventions of moral responsibility so that we feel responsible for misdeeds elsewhere – that underlay the new constellation of attitudes and activities that we now group under the banner of human rights. "Together," Joas writes, "the first and second components open up a space in which it becomes possible to articulate experiences that previously went unheard" (2013, 92).

Nevertheless, a third component was needed for the abolitionist movement to become politically successful. Without the creation of a public sphere going beyond the borders of the nation-state and a network of activists operating on a transnational basis, abolitionism would never have succeeded in transforming the image of slavery from a legitimate or necessary economic activity into a serious violation of individual human rights.

Even though Joas did not use the term 'imaginaries' himself, his work provides us with better insight into what the term might add to more traditional cultural approaches. On the one hand, Joas complements the Durkheimian reading of human rights as a collective imaginary which is functionally equivalent to religion, with the creative, historical efforts to make sense of atrocities both culturally (how to identify with the subjects of these atrocities?) and normatively (by drawing out the lines of desired possibilities for the future). On the other hand, Joas has provided a more substantial link between human rights as emerging from embodied experiences (e. g. slavery) and practices (e. g. in international law), with its emergence from wider historical imaginaries such as Christian universal morality and the idea of a public sphere.

5 Conclusion

We began this chapter by sketching a number of ongoing debates in the social-scientific study of culture. First, we described two perspectives on the relative importance of structure and agency. In the Durkheimian variant, culture imposes itself upon individuals through mental structures, whereas the Weberian variant conceives of culture as a more fluid ensemble of singular ideas that are creatively used by individuals to make sense of their environment. Second, there have been recurrent debates on the relation between the mental (in the Durkheimian sense) or discursive (in the Weberian sense) dimensions of culture on the one hand, and its practical, embodied aspects on the other (as in Bourdieu's work and in practice theories). Third, and perhaps more importantly for our purposes, over the last few decades, the landscape of the study of culture has been drastically altered in attempts to address the consequences of globalisation. As sense-making practices are increasingly diversified through mass migration and media, traditional methods relying on the assumption of internal homogeneity (such as ethnography or even national or ideal-typical comparison) seemed to become too blunt for contemporary settings.

In this chapter we attempted to explore the particular heuristic value of social imaginaries through a discussion of the term in Anderson, Appadurai and Taylor, and its relevance for understanding human rights. We concluded that imaginaries may be a valuable tool in at least three ways: first, because of the term's *substantial fluidity*, social imaginaries help concentrate on particular imaginaries emerging, spreading and influencing people's behaviour. The concept is not necessarily linked to any differentiated field (such as education, politics or economy), but to singular sets of meanings revolving around a particular topic, vision or practice, such as human rights or the nation-state.

Second, when conceived of in Appadurai's sense, imaginaries may stimulate scholars to focus on the creative interpretative capacities of individuals and groups in a context of cultural complexity. The emphasis, then, lies not so much on how these repertoires and narratives are used strategically as 'tools' in a particular setting, but rather on how a relative, possibly even temporary unity is constructed from among the chaotic wealth of cultural material/sense-making frameworks (cf. Appadurai 2013, part II).

Third, imaginaries as conceived of by Taylor may help to redraw the relationship between practices and ideas. Whilst the term may lend itself to concentrating on embodied meanings in micro-practices and situations, imaginaries may help relate these meanings to the wider historical context in which they took place, again comparably irrespectively of any differentiated field or ideal-typical group to which they belong. In this sense 'human rights' can be seen as a particular ensemble of embodied practices (through civil society and law-making processes) with a much wider historical rooting in the wake of the Second World War.

Bibliography

Adorno, Theodor W., and Max Horkheimer. 1997. *Dialectics of Enlightenment*. London/New York: Verso.
Alexander, Jeffrey, and Steven Seidman, eds. 1990. *Culture and Society: Contemporary Debates*. Cambridge: Cambridge University Press.
Anderson, Benedict. 1991. *Imagined Communities: Reflections on the Origins and Spread of Nationalism*. London: Verso.
Andersson, Mette. 2010. "The Social Imaginaries of First Generation Europeans." *Social Identity: Journal of the Study of Race, Nation and Culture* 16 (1):3–21.
Appadurai, Arjun. 1996. *Modernity At Large: The Cultural Dimensions of Globalization*. Minneapolis: University of Minnesota Press.
Appadurai, Arjun. 2013. *The Future as Cultural Fact: Essays On The Global Condition*. London/New York: Verso.
Atkinson, Paul Anthony, Sara Delamont, Amanda, Coffey, John Lofland and Lyn H. Lofland. 2007. *Handbook of Ethnography*. London: Sage Publications.
Bellah, Robert N. 1967. "Civil Religion in America." *Daedalus* 96 (1):1–21.
Bird, Elizabeth S. 2003. *The Audience in Everyday Life: Living In A Media World*. London/New York: Routledge.
Bourdieu, Pierre. 1977. *Outline of a theory of practice*. Cambridge: Cambridge University Press.
Bourdieu, Pierre. 1986. *Distinction: A Social Critique of the Judgment of Taste*. Cambridge: Cambridge University Press.
Bourdieu, Pierre and Jacues Passeron. 1997. *Reproduction in Education, Society and Culture*. London: Sage.
Castoriadis, Cornelius. 1997. *The Imaginary Institution of Society*. Cambridge, MA: MIT Press.
Couldry, Nick. 2004. "Theorising Media as Practices." *Social Semiotics*, 14 (2):115–132.
Dejaeghere, Joan, and Kate McCleary. 2010. "The Making of Mexican Migrant Youth Civic Identities: Transnational and Spaces and Imaginaries." *Anthropology and Education Quarterly* 41 (3):228–244.
Douglas, Mary. 1966. *Purity and Danger: An Analysis of the Concepts of Pollution and Taboo*. New York: Pantheon.
Durkheim, Emile. 1950. *Leçons de Sociologie*. Paris: Presses Universitaires de France.
Durkheim, Emile. 1975. "Individualism and the Intellectuals." In *Durkheim on Religion*, edited by W.S.F. Pickering, 77–98. London: Routledge.
Durkheim, Emile. 1995. *The Elementary Forms of the Religious Life*. New York: Free Press.
Edgell, Penny. 2012. "A Cultural Sociology of Religion: New Directions." *Annual Review of Sociology*, 38: 247–265.
Foucault, Michel. 1990. *The History of Sexuality. Volume 1: An Introduction*. New York: Vintage Books.
Furseth, Inger. 1994. "Civil Religion In A Low Key: The Case of Norway." *Acta Sociologica* 37: 39–54.
Gaonkar, Dilip Parameshwar. 2002. "Toward New Imaginaries: An Introduction." *Public Culture* 14 (1):1–19.
Geertz, Clifford. 1973. *The Interpretation of Cultures*. New York: Basic Books.

Giddens, Anthony. 1984. *The Constitution of Society: Outline of the Theory of Structuration.* Berkeley: University of California Press.
Gorski, Philip S., ed. 2013. *Bourdieu and Historical Analysis.* New York: Duke University Press.
Hall, John R., Laura Grindstaff and Lo Ming-Chen. 2010. *Handbook of Cultural sociology.* London/New York: Routledge.
Hannerz, Ulf. 1992. *Cultural Complexity: Studies in the Social Organization of Meaning.* London/New York: Routledge.
Hannerz, Ulf. 1996. *Transnational Connections: Culture, People, Places.* London/New York: Routledge.
Hunt, Lynn. 2007. *Inventing Human Rights: A History.* New York: WW Norton and Company.
Joas, Hans. 2013. *The Sacredness of the Person: A New Genealogy of Human Rights.* Washington D.C.: Georgetown University Press.
Ivy, Marilyn. 1995. *Discourses of the Vanishing: Modernity, Phantasm, Japan.* Chicago: University of Chicago Press.
Knorr-Cetina, Karin. 1981. *The Manufacture of Knowledge: An Essay on the Constructivist and Contextual Nature of Science.* Oxford: Pergamon Press.
Koselleck, Reinhart. 1985. *Futures Past: On the Semantics of Historical Time.* Cambridge, MA: MIT Press.
Koselleck, Reinhart. 2006. *Begriffsgeschichten.* Frankfurt am Main: Suhrkamp.
Lahire, Bernard. 2003. "From the Habitus to an Individual Heritage of Dispositions. Towards a Sociology at the Level of the Individual." *Poetics*, 31 (5–6):329–355.
Lamont, Michèle. 1992. *Money, Morals and Manners: The Cultures of the French and the American Upper-Middle Class.* Chicago: Chicago University Press.
Lamont, Michèle and Annette Lareau. "Cultural Capital: Allusions, Gaps and Glissandos in Recent Theoretical Developments." *Sociological Theory* 6 (2):153–168.
Lamont, Michèle and Virag Molnar. 2002. "The Study of Boundaries in the Social Sciences." *Annual Review of Sociology* 28:167–195.
Luckmann, Thomas. 1967. *The Invisible Religion: The Problem of Religion in Modern Society.* New York: Macmillan.
Malkki, Liisa. 1995. *Purity and Exile: Violence, Memory and National Cosmology Among Hutu Refugees in Tanzania.* Chicago: University of Chicago Press.
Madsen, Mikael Rask and Gert Verschraegen. 2016. "Toward a New Sociology of Human Rights?" *Humanity: an International Journal of Human Rights, Humanitarianism, and Development* 7 (2):273–293.
Madsen, Mikael Rask and Gert Verschraegen. 2013. "Making Human Rights Intelligible: An Introduction to Sociology of Human Rights." In *Making Human Rights Intelligible: Towards a Sociology of Human Rights*, edited by Mikael Rask Madsen and Gert Verschraegen, 1–22. Oxford: Hart Publishing.
Marcus George E. 1995. "Ethnography in/of the World System: The Emergence of Multi-Sited Ethnography." *Annual Review of Anthropology* 24:95–117.
Mauss, Marcel. 1973. "Techniques of the Body." *Economy and Society*, 2 (1):70–88.
Reckwitz, Andreas. 2002. "Toward A Theory of Social Practices: A Development in Culturalist Theorizing." *European Journal of Social Theory* 5 (2):243–263.
Ryle, Gilbert. 2009. *The Concept of Mind.* London/New York: Routledge.

Salazar, Noel. 2010. *Envisioning Eden: Mobilizing Imaginaries in Tourism and Beyond.* Oxford: Berghahn.
Schatzki, Theodore. 2001. "Introduction: Practice Theory." In *The Practice Turn in Contemporary Theory*, edited by Theodore Schatzki, Karin Knorr-Cetina and Elke von Savigny, 1–14. London/New York: Routledge.
Sewell, William H. Jr. 1992. "A Theory of Structure: Duality, Agency and Transformation." *American Journal of Sociology* 98:1–29.
Sewell, William H. Jr. 1996. "Historical Events as Transformations of Structures: Inventing Revolution at the Bastille." *Theory and Society* 25:841–881.
Steger, Manfred B. 2008. *The Rise of the Global Imaginary: Political Ideologies From the French Revolution to the Global War on Terror.* Oxford: University Press.
Strauss, Claudia. 2006. "The Imaginary." *Anthropological Theory* 6 (3):322–344.
Swidler, Ann. 2000. "What Anchors Cultural Practices." In *The Practice Turn in Contemporary Theory*, edited by Theodore Schatzki, Karin Knorr-Cetina and Elke von Savigny, 74–92. London/New York: Routledge.
Taylor, Charles. 1989. *Sources of the Self: The Making of the Modern Identity.* Harvard: Harvard University Press.
Taylor, Charles. 1993. "Engaged Agency and Background in Heidegger." In *The Cambridge Companion to Heidegger*, edited by Charles Guignon, 317–336. Cambridge: Cambridge University Press.
Taylor, Charles. 2004. *Modern Social Imaginaries.* Durham/London: Duke University Press.
Taylor, Charles. 2007. *A Secular Age.* Harvard: Harvard University Press.
Weber, Max. 1946. *From Max Weber: Essays in Sociology*, translated and edited H.H. Gerth and Charles Wright Mills. Oxford: Oxford University Press.
Weyns, Walter. 2014. *Klassieke sociologen en hun erfenis.* Tielt: Lannoo.
Williams, Rhys H. 2013. "Civil Religion and the Cultural Politics of Identity in Obama's America." *Journal for the Scientific Study of Religion* 52 (2):239–257.
Zerubavel, Eviatar. 1999. *Social Mindscapes: An Invitation to Cognitive Sociology.* Harvard: Harvard University Press.

Nicole L. Immler
Human Rights as a Secular Social Imaginary in the Field of Transitional Justice

The Dutch-Indonesian 'Rawagede Case'

1 Prologue

On 14 September 2011 the imaginary about the Dutch colonial *past* changed to being a colonial *present*, a present that still needs to be dealt with, when the Civil Court in The Hague obliged the Dutch government to apologize and to pay compensation to some of the victims of its colonial policy in Indonesia.[1] For the first time the government had to acknowledge its responsibility for a massacre by its military, which killed most of the male population (alleged resistance fighters) of the village of Rawagede, today Balongsari, in West Java during the Indonesian War of Independence in 1947. At that time the Dutch were fighting a decolonisation war, trying to keep their colony (the Dutch East Indies), while Indonesia – after the Japanese occupation during World War II had ended Dutch rule – had declared its independence and an end to 350 years of colonial power on 17th August 1945. It was international pressure and the realisation that the war could not be won that pushed the Dutch finally to formally acknowledge Indonesian sovereignty on 27th December 1949.

Although the decision has been called a "milestone," legally and historically speaking, as the statute of limitation was (partly) barred (Veraart 2012, 258–259), critics have noted an absence of human rights discourse, interpreting this as a significant element of silencing (Lorenz 2015, 228). They see no effort by the Dutch state to deal with this past in the broader sense (Lorenz 2015, 232), no endeavour to reveal the historical truth about the colonial past but rather to hide its systematic nature (Eickhoff 2013, 53), seeing a continuum of a hitherto selective and euphemistic way to cope with one's colonial past, characterized by the very absence of any universal moral standard such as human rights (Raben 2002, 101).

---

[1] https://www.recht.nl/rechtspraak/?ecli=ECLI:NL:RBSGR:2011:BS8793 (14 September 2011).

I will argue, however, that those assumptions are based upon a too narrow interpretation of human rights. Departing from a definition of human rights that describes alongside its *legal* nature also its *utopian* character – and thereby following up on ideas of Charles Taylor and Samuel Moyn – this chapter analyses how human rights function as a *social imaginary* on the individual level and their impact in the political but also broader social and cultural realm.

While human rights have developed into a global moral imaginary (Taylor 2002), a new field of research and practice has been established: Transitional Justice, also called "one of the defining global movements of our time" (Neumann and Thompson 2015, 23).[2] It studies the long-term effects of human rights violations and the instruments to deal with past atrocities, such as criminal trials, apologies, historical commissions, and reparations. Although literature and practice are dominated by strong beliefs in those measures, there is still little empirical evidence of their intended effect (Olsen, Payne, and Reiter, 2010).

This chapter explores what the concept of *social imaginaries* has to offer for a critical, bottom-up approach in the field of Transitional Justice. It will be argued that it makes the situatedness of those claims more visible: that we see less a negotiation about the *past* between the Dutch state and its former colonial subjects in the East, and more an inquiry into *present-day* post-colonial Netherlands.

2 Social Imaginaries

Social imaginaries, as defined by Charles Taylor, are "the ways people imagine their social existence, how they fit together with others, how things go on between them and their fellows, the expectations that are normally met, and the deeper normative notions and images that underlie these expectations." It is about the "images, stories and legends," thus the narratives shaping people's lives, desires and ideas. "The social imaginary is that common understanding that makes possible common practices and a widely shared sense of legitimacy." Taylor gives a concrete example: "Let's say we organize a demonstration. This means that this act is already in our repertory. We know how to assemble, pick up banners, and march. (...) We understand the ritual." (Taylor 2002, 106 and 108)

---

[2] It is a discipline dominated by historians (establishing truth about the violation of human rights) and lawyers (to act upon those facts); next to countless NGOs lobbying in this respect.

While Taylor describes the spaces of the imaginary, which people see themselves in and act upon, the anthropologist Arjun Appadurai noted that such efforts to cultivate voice and to make oneself visible are also about exercising 'the capacity to aspire,' as he has called it. He described how people via certain social actions exercise and extend their *capacity to aspire:* "Aspirations have certainly something to do with wants, preferences, choices, and calculations (...) Aspirations are never simply individual (but) always formed in interaction and in the thick of social life." And he notes: "looking at aspirations as cultural capacities, we are surely in a better position to understand how people actually navigate their social spaces" (Appadurai 2004, 67 and 84).

As the idea of the social imaginary is in the first place a philosophical concept that is rarely studied from the bottom up, this article endeavours, by using the Dutch-Indonesian case, to explore how social imaginaries – and particularly imaginaries of human rights – are lived. As Claudia Strauss emphasizes, there is a need for a more "person-centred approach (...) so that we are talking about the imaginaries of real people, not the imaginaries of imagined people." Following up on Strauss this article will engage with an actor's perspective "to counter the tendency to see imaginaries as more homogeneous or fixed than they are," and to modify public collective representations (Strauss 2006, 339).

Human rights are often experienced as a legal category only. By shifting the frame from the *legal* to the *imaginary* perspective – human rights as an imaginary, as "the heartfelt desire to make the world a better place,"[3] as Samuel Moyn has called it (2010, 225) – this article aims to reveal the implications of a legal human rights framework on imagining justice from an actor's perspective. I maintain that using the lens of *social imaginaries* will clarify how personal aspirations resonate with political discourses and respective social contexts. It will allow us, as Taylor writes (2002, 106), to identify deeply embedded (moral) assumptions that shape societies, to consciously think about them, understand their impact and challenge their legitimacy.

---

3 "When people hear the phrase 'human rights,' they think of the highest moral precepts and political ideals. And they are right to do so. They have in mind a familiar set of indispensable liberal freedoms, and sometimes more expansive principles of social protection. But they also mean something more. The phrase implies an agenda for improving the world, and bringing about a new one in which the dignity of each individual will enjoy secure international protection. It is a recognizably utopian program: for the political standards it champions and the emotional passion it inspires, this program draws on the image of a place that has not yet been called into being. It promises to penetrate the impregnability of state borders, slowly replacing them with the authority of international law." (Moyn 2010, 1)

After a brief historical overview of how the human rights discourse developed into a global moral and secular imaginary (3), it will be shown how imaginaries of justice have developed in recent decades into a right to compensation (4), formulating – based upon empirical research on the Dutch-Indonesian case[4] (5) – what we gain by applying the concept of *social imaginaries* in the Transitional Justice field (6): This will reveal whose imaginaries of justice we talk about; it will situate and therewith scrutinize the human rights imaginaries in a postcolonial setting, and identify the presence of the past, key to understanding what is at stake when negotiating the colonial past via court cases in Europe.

3 Human Rights as Secular Social Imaginary in a Globalizing World

In today's globalized society intercultural understanding is an obligation and not an option, wrote Arjun Appadurai (2004, 62) about the significance of Charles Taylor's work that highlights the ethical obligation to extend recognition to people with different worldviews. In his classic essay *Multiculturalism and the Politics of Recognition* Taylor described how our identity is shaped by the recognition of others and the need to restore identities: "Nonrecognition or misrecognition can inflict harm [by] imprisoning someone in a false, distorted, and reduced mode of being" (Taylor 1994, 25). Recognition is a basic need to have feelings of self-worth and self-esteem, and thus constitutes a "vital human need" (Taylor 1994, 26); while being and feeling acknowledged oneself is also the precondition to acknowledging others.

At the same time Taylor emphasized that this multicultural diversity needs to be managed, without privileging religious, non-religious, or anti-religious views, and suggested that secularism would provide such a neutral language. In his book *A Secular Age* (2007) he argues that the modern world has not seen the disappearance of religion, but rather its diversification and in many places its growth. There he developed an alternative notion of what secularization actually means, namely managing the diversity – particularly suggesting that human rights would offer this kind of secular and shared language that could connect people.

---

[4] This research was made possible by a Marie Curie Fellowship for the project *Narrated (In)Justice: compensation policies and trans-generational narratives of (in)justice*, conducted within the program 'Understanding the Age of Transitional Justice: Narratives in Historical Perspective' at the NIOD Institute for War, Holocaust and Genocide Studies in Amsterdam.

Human rights have become a fundamental aspect of what Charles Taylor has called the "modern moral order." According to Taylor, this order has developed since the 17th century in Western society, from the theory about the mutual benefit through social contracts (Locke and Grotius), via ideas about the natural rights of man ('all men are created equal'), towards the human rights practice that became widespread after World War II: "the notion of rights that are prior to and untouchable by political structures (...) the clearest expression of our modern idea of a moral order underlying the political – the ideal of order as mutual benefit – which the political has to respect" (Taylor 2002, 124).

For Taylor it is the imaginative capacity that is key in the human rights discourse. Other authors share this idea. The historian Lynn Hunt has linked the emergence of human rights to the growing sensibility and empathy in the 18th century trained by reading realist novels: "their innovative prose techniques, imitating nonfictional forms of letters and memoirs, allowed the illusion of access to another's interior life in ways that created the condition for political identification" (Hunt 2007; Jolly and Jensen 2014, 7) and compassion with a fellow human being. Specifically, these novels encouraged readers to identify with weak characters struggling against oppression, thereby making them understand all humans possess equal rights.

This imaginative capacity in a literal sense, a kind of humanitarianism, was however not yet secular nor oriented on individual rights, as the historian Samuel Moyn stressed. He highlighted the fact that human rights, as we know them today, had their breakthrough only in the social utopia movements of the 1970s, remaining *the last utopia* after earlier ones, such as socialism, had collapsed: human rights "survived as a moral utopia as political utopias died" (2012, 214). Describing human rights as a secular utopia he puts – similarly to Taylor – emphasis on the power of the moral social imaginaries that govern societies in Western Europe to this day.

But before becoming a *secular utopia*, human rights first had to be stripped of certain religious, cultural and political loadings. Moyn shows that, differently than often said, human rights were after 1945 not (yet) a cross-cultural concept. Although the UN Declaration (1948) was co-written by many authors and activists from all around the globe, human rights in the 1950s was a loaded concept, hijacked by groups that were the most diverse and dominated by their constituencies as well as Cold War rhetoric. Following Moyn it is precisely the kind of 'neutral' character it gained in the 1970s that is part of its success, when human rights became "the core language of a new politics of humanity" beyond the political spectrum of right and left (Moyn 2012, 227).

While in the 1970s human rights were foremost an instrument of *external moral criticism* (criticizing others), they have developed since the 1980s (based on experiences with the dictatorships in Latin America) into an instrument also of *internal criticism*. As such it has developed into a political resource for internal transformation processes as a basis for establishing a democratic successor state – based upon the idea that dealing with past wrongs becomes the precondition for a 'just and democratic society.' This was called also the 'homecoming of human rights' (Oomen 2013).

In this sense the concept of human rights has developed: from *a quasi religious-charismatic* and *moral concept* on the individual level in the 1970s, providing only a new venue for idealism and hope, and offering a "substitute utopia" for mobilizing people (exemplified by individuals writing Christmas cards to political prisoners via Amnesty International), into a *more secular,* and *administrative* language of institutionalized globalized *politics* in the 1990s (Moyn 2012, 146). Through the rise of human rights discourse, global concerns have become a part of local experience, and vice versa, as it has become common to "remember now atrocities as human rights violations" (Levy and Sznaider 2010, 82).

Human rights became a key concept of our (Western) society, but there are challenges to the concept. Are human rights, as Taylor suggests, a neutral and shared language to communicate recognition between different groups, a language of secular dialogue in a globalized society? Do human rights, as Levy and Sznaider state, stimulate a new understanding by translating local experiences into a global value system? In the last decade human rights have been the subject of an increasingly interdisciplinary scholarly debate.

Critics have argued that human rights are also about blaming, about who is right and who wrong, which in consequence rather divides people instead of improving a dialogue, and rather creates or reaffirms borders instead of breaking them down (Kennedy 2014). Some argued that the individualistic interpretation of human rights (as used by Moyn), is too narrow; embodying, for example, a certain Western value system embedded in liberalism. Here US-Western historiography on Human Rights is blamed for inscribing a history suggestive of a European tradition, while neglecting the possibility that the various decolonization struggles were human rights struggles as well (Slaughter 2007, Simpson 2013). While in Europe the struggle for human rights means foremost the protection of individuals from state violence, in former colonies it long meant defence of their right to national self-determination, which required subordination of the rights of the individual (civil and political) to the collective aim.

Relatedly, some critics interpret Taylor's idea of the moral order to be too Western, excluding collective and also religious worldviews. Postcolonial scholars noted that similarly the concept of recognition (as advocated by Taylor) needs to be extended to questions of agency, socio-political power structures, and redistribution, bringing "the politics of dignity and the politics of poverty into a single framework" (Appadurai 2004, 63), indicating that there are more than ethical dilemmas in a post-colonial setting. Taylor himself specified some risks when he emphasized that cultural values and identities must never be negotiated through social processes with former colonizers, as internalized self-deprecation has become "one of the most potent instruments of their own oppression" (Taylor 1994, 26).

Many scholars asked for a critical reflection on the *universalization* of the human rights concept, pinpointing that the abstract principles need to be *transculturally* justified, but also to be translated into *local practices:* "this is the paradox of making human rights in the vernacular: in order to be accepted, they have to be tailored to the local context and resonate with the local cultural framework" (Merry 2006, 49). The imaginative capacity of the human rights discourse as well as its "translation problem" (Bachmann-Medick 2012), both play an important role in the explored case.

4 The Age of Transitional Justice: How Imaginaries of Justice Have Changed

When the book *The Guilt of Nations* (Barkan 2000) was published, it was the first overview of a new era that could in retrospect be called *The Age of Transitional Justice.* The historian Elazar Barkan collected several case studies of how various nations have dealt with their difficult historical pasts and analysed them in a shared frame, showing that the acknowledgement of historical wrongs has become a major concern, dominating 'public attention and political issues,' in a changing Europe since 1989, but also worldwide. After the fall of the dictatorships in Latin America and the end of Apartheid in South Africa, a new kind of politics developed, connected with an increasingly powerful human rights movement, enabling, after victims of World War II, victims of communism and colonialism also to articulate their histories and make their own claims (Torpey 2006a). Although the cases have been as diverse as 'Nazi gold,' restitution efforts in Eastern Europe, and proclamation by indigenous groups of cultural patrimony over territories appropriated by European settlers, Barkan shows patterns in which he recognized a certain "willingness of nations to embrace their own guilt" (2000, xvii).[5] For this change of mind he located a specific moment in

---

[5] Barkan sees "a potentially new international morality" (2000, ix) within a global economy, calling it the triumph of liberal Enlightenment, others are more skeptical, seeing it rather as

time: "About March 5, 1997, world morality – not to say, human nature – changed," namely when "Switzerland announced its intention to sell a substantial amount of its gold to create a humanitarian fund of 5 billion dollars (...) to be dispensed to Holocaust victims who lost their money in Swiss banks" (Barkan 2000, xv). This is often recalled as the very moment when the financial dimension of the Holocaust, the extensive robbery of goods, came onto the international agenda, initiating hopes of numerous Jewish families to finally gain justice.

This moral shift can be located also in the Dutch debate, when archive funds brought to light the active involvement of Dutch institutions in the lootings (a newspaper series on "*German* art robbery" became one on *Dutch* art robbery)[6], but also how civil servants had auctioned among themselves discovered Jewish jewellery in the 60's.[7] This incident, indicating a clear lack of historical and moral consciousness, became a debate changer; an international affair became a Dutch affair, and instead of solely sympathy with the victims now also Dutch collaboration gets identified. While the Holocaust since the 1970's was an accepted *psychological* reality, only now did it become a *material* reality that raised anger and turned many into claimants.[8] The claims of those years can be read more generally as an expression of a new family self-assurance: a story of uncertainty and shame has become a story of 'moral victory,' including the faith to reunite families (Immler 2013, 98).

Fifty years earlier, ideas about justice were quite distinct: the first institutionalized process of Transitional Justice were the Nuremberg Trials (1945/46), the prosecution of the German National Socialist elite under pressure of the Allied forces. The trials established "a transcendent memory of what constitutes 'crimes against humanity'" (Jolly and Jensen 2014, 7). While the field was dominated first by lawyers, law, and legal rights (criminal prosecutions), successively other instruments became important, such as historical commissions, reparation programs, apologies, commemorations, and education programs. Therefore the German case is exemplary, how all those elements added up on each other. The *Vergangenheitsbewältigung* was not an event but a long-term process in which also ideas about justice have changed. Therefore historian Constantin

---

a substitute for progressive politics that is linked to the collapse of socialism and the decline of the nation-state (Torpey 2006).

6 *NRC*, 31 October 1997, 7, 14 and 21 November 1997.

7 *Groene Amsterdammer*, 10 December 1997.

8 Nicole L. Immler, 'The perception of the Dutch compensation policies from a transgenerational perspective,' lecture, National Holocaust Museum, Amsterdam, 4 October 2017; unpublished manuscript.

Goschler preferred to call it a *justice in transition* instead of *transitional justice*, highlighting the process instead of the result (2009, 47).

While there is consent that after conflicts, both legal and non-legal instruments are necessary to rebuild social trust and a stable society, in the last few years there has been a worldwide shift from *retributive justice* (legal-, perpetrator- and state-centred approach) towards *restorative justice* (dialogue-oriented, victim- and community-centred approach). Exemplary therefore stands the *Truth and Reconciliation Commission* (TRC 1995–99) in South Africa, which ranked bringing truth and fostering forgiveness higher than prosecuting the perpetrators.

Reconciliation scenarios gained a prominent position during the 1990s, visible particularly when the slogan 'revealing is healing,' amnesty for truth, and Bishop Tutu's idea of 'Ubuntu' (to acknowledge each other's humanity) became a main narrative in discussions on transition, while human rights advocates rather aimed for prosecutions, punishments and reparations. This points to an interesting tension within the Transitional Justice field at large, in which the *politics of reconciliation* – associated with religiously loaded terms such as forgiveness, impunity, and closure – has become a dominant discourse, though 'at odds' with the secular and juridical framework that originally shaped and defined the field (VanAntwerpen 2008). Another tension is that while in the West the TRC is often seen as a success model (it enabled a political transition without civil war), in South Africa there is increasing suspicion as the morality of Transitional Justice rhetoric and the redistribution of wealth did not go hand in hand (Gready 2011).[9] Meanwhile the conviction arose that *reparations in the broader sense* (symbolic and material) were also needed to restore victims' dignity and to create future peace and stability (De Greiff 2006).

While *before* World War II, states that had lost a war paid reparations to the winner as economic compensation, *afterwards* states also paid compensation for injury sustained by individuals. While the frame in the 1970s was 'acknowledging past victimhood' in the context of national 'war welfare policy,' since the 1990s it's rather about acknowledging guilt, embedded in an emerging global human rights narrative and an "international system of public shame" (Barkan 2000, 320). While compensation in the past has been more a kind of gesture, today the idea of recognition requiring a monetary complement is increasingly

---

[9] The TRC "highlighted what had changed already most (gross civil and political abuses) and not what had changed least (economic and social rights concerns)", what Paul Gready called "an act of colonisation of human rights, narrowly construed (…) elevating to power a particular set of civil-political rights (…) Other ways of understanding of human rights are available" (Gready 2011, 8–10).

manifest in (inter)national legislation. A good example is the Rome Statute (1998), which grants victims of gross human rights violations the right to request reparation at the International Criminal Court in The Hague, embracing the so-called 'Van Boven/Bassiouni Principles', which were negotiated since the early 1990s to harmonize victims' rights, and which set a new internal standard for reparations when adopted by the UN in 2005.

Reparations developed from compensating for 'damage' within private law towards addressing questions of 'human dignity' and 'social rehabilitation' in civil law, from a selective into a more inclusive process: the humanisation of international law, addressing the human, the individual in his community.[10] The de facto development towards a right to compensation and the shift in public and legal discourse from *victims* to *claimants* is seen as a success story of empowerment and citizenship.

However, in the last decade scepticism grew: questions arose as to whether the politics of recognition and transitional justice instruments (aiming to transform societies into 'better' democracies) really provide what they promise, since in a globalized society even more complicated elements might be at stake. While some scholars see in reparation claims indeed mere extensions of backward-looking identity politics, endangering the social fabric of society by causing fragmentation (Torpey 2006b), others see them rather as a tactic used by groups to enhance their citizenship, questioning enduring inequalities and demanding a pluralistic politics (Nobles 2006). The following analysis of the Dutch-Indonesian case will provide here some insights.

5 The Dutch-Indonesian Case: How the Colonial Past Became a Colonial Present

First rumours about violent excesses by the Dutch military in former Dutch-Indie prompted, already in 1948, an unofficial report by the government, followed in 1969 – after a veteran's TV-testimony – by an official report (*Excessennota* 1969), giving an overview of four years of diplomatic dispute and armed conflict during which some 150,000 Indonesians (civilians and soldiers) and about 5,000 Dutch soldiers died. Since then those so-called 'excesses' (76 were listed) were repeatedly thematized, owing to document or photo findings. Also, several books were published on this issue, but all without major effect. While after the first 1995 RTL-4 documentary about 'mass executions on Java,' a legal procedure was

---

10 Theo van Boven, interview with author, Utrecht, 13 March 2013.

still called "unfeasible",[11] the year 2007 saw, next to a Dutch TV documentary on 'The massacre of Rawagede' on its 50th anniversary, a legal claim in preparation; by the *Committee for Dutch Debts of Honour* and a Dutch lawyer for international humanitarian law, Liesbeth Zegveld. She helped to establish the dialogue with the Dutch government. As the government insisted on considering the case as barred, the claimants stepped in 2008 in front of the court, on behalf of Indonesian civilian victims who suffered from acts committed by Dutch soldiers. It concerned one male survivor and eight (survivor-)widows in their 80s.

5.1 The Court Cases

At the Civil Court in 2011 Zegveld framed the historical details of the events in a broader sense by speaking of human rights violations, referring to civil law (a state has an obligation to protect its citizens), and standards established in regard to World War II policies, thereby questioning the practice hitherto of statute of limitation in regard to colonial crimes: "These cases [such as compensation to Jewish Holocaust survivors] go further back than Rawagede, so how come that no statute of limitation is put upon them?" she explained as one of her main strategies.[12] Zegveld thereby bridged two different memories – World War II and Colonialism – to gain understanding by the Court and its audiences; and won.

It was a unique decision: the Dutch government was ordered to apologize and to pay compensation (20,000 Euros) to one survivor and nine remaining widows. The claims of (survivor-)children were neglected, as the court called them "descendants" and considered them to be "less directly affected."[13] On 9 December 2011 the ambassador Tjeerd de Zwaan issued the first official apology by the Dutch government at the victims' monument in Rawagede. The payments followed. However, contrary to its intention of closing a case – by highlighting the exceptionality of the historic event as well as by excluding the younger generation – the court case provoked a whole new dynamic.

Meanwhile, the decision on Rawagede serves as a quasi-model for other cases of Indonesian widows, whose husbands had been victims of similar military summary executions, such as those in Sulawesi in 1946/47.[14] Moreover, chil-

---

11 Cees Fasseur, in: *Trouw*, 17 Augustus 1995.
12 Liesbeth Zegveld, in: *Jakarta Post*, 13 September 2013.
13 https://www.recht.nl/rechtspraak/?ecli=ECLI:NL:RBSGR:2011:BS8793 (14 September 2011).
14 Based upon an informal agreement with the Dutch government: https://zoek.officielebekendmakingen.nl/stcrt-2013–25383.html (10 September 2013).

dren of executed Indonesians in the villages of Suppa and Bulukumba in South Sulawesi, now elderly, also stepped in front of the same court in 2014, claiming "equal treatment", by arguing it is unjust for the Dutch state to make a distinction between the widows and the children, as "it is about the same incident, same place, same process."[15]

What in 2011 was still *unthinkable*, four years later became *possible*. In an interlocutory judgment on 11 March 2015, the court held the Dutch State liable for the damages of both the widows and the children of men who were summarily executed in the former Dutch East Indies.[16] What in 2011 was considered as acceptable by standards of reasonableness and fairness, was now seen as contrary to good faith. Do we see here a success story of human rights?

5.2 The Court Decision Scholarly Discussed

While the Dutch present themselves in the international arena as a human rights country, Dutch scholars remarked that human rights are foremost a matter of export than of introspection, namely considered as something that others lack rather than something that has to be actively cultivated at home (Oomen 2013). In this context, scholars, when evaluating the Rawagede decision, have been scrutinizing whether the character of the legal decision and the reaction on part of the Dutch state is characterized by a human rights discourse.

At first sight the reasoning in the first 'Rawagede-decision' was extraordinary. While the historical facts juridically speaking were considered as barred, the Court reconsidered them for moral reasons: referring to the "very exceptionality" of the historical injustice, that those events relate to a period in Dutch history that has not yet been settled and of which the victims are still alive, referring here also to the "generous refund policy towards victims of World War II." Thereby post-war and post-colonial history were linked for the first time in an official legal document (Veraart 2012, 252–55), performing what has been called in literature "multidirectional memory," an expression of the fact that memories of different historical wrongs are often intertwined and help each other to surface (Rothberg 2009). However, the Court immediately diverged from the World War II precedents when excluding the children.

---

[15] Shafiah Paturusi (82), interview with author, Amsterdam, 19 August 2014.
[16] De Rechtspraak, https://recht.nl/rechtspraak/?ecli=ECLI:NL:RBDHA:2015:2442 (11 March 2015).

Legal scholars have asked whether this lack of trans-generational awareness is legitimate, that is to suspend the statute of limitation only partially, namely exclusively to the benefits of first generation victims, which would mean neutralizing the precedent they impose (Veraart 2012, 258).

As historian one had to ask whether this reference to World War II policies is not per se misleading, suggesting a similarity, while actually choosing a different procedure: descendants were excluded, no historical commissions were established, no state reports were drafted; all common practices in the restitution and compensation policies of the late 1990s towards (Dutch) Jewry. Here descendants also had a legitimate status; otherwise it would have fostered the argument that the government deliberately had waited that long to reduce the number of claimants (Immler and Jouwe 2015).

The dissimilarities are even larger when one reads the analogy as a reference to the German *Vergangenheitsbewältigung*, the comprehensive persecution, memory, compensation and education culture in Germany, as historian Chris Lorenz did. He sees no effort for a *Vergangenheitsbewältigung* in the broader sense, but rather an effort to silence the past as the Dutch state refused until then to fund systematic historical research on Dutch war crimes in Indonesia: "reconciliation is hoped for *without* truth-finding," an endeavour he called the "production of ignorance" (2015, 232).[17] He emphasized what "at first sight looks like a fine example of 'politics of regret' and of 'reparation politics' based on human rights, including both a financial settlement with the victims and the explicit apologies offered by the state responsible for the massacre," turns out on closer analysis "to be pretty deceiving": stating an absence of human rights discourse, and interpreting it as a significant element of silencing (2015, 228). In his view, the Rawagede decision stated false facts, when calling Rawagede an "exceptional crime" instead of a "war-crime," and focusing on exceptionality instead of investigating its possible systematic nature.

Moreover he argues that providing compensation would close the case before the 'historical truth' has even been properly examined. Other scholars question whether the colonial past has been judged upon. Indeed, Rawagede has become the image for the brutality of the Dutch military, but the colonial character of those military missions were not deconstructed (Eickhoff 2013, 53). A finding that continues, in a way, what has been said beforehand about the selective and euphemistic way Rawagede and other massacres have been dealt with, corre-

---

17 This comprehensive research meanwhile has started (in September 2017), financed by the Dutch government: *Decolonisation, violence and war in Indonesia 1945–1950;* https://www.ind45-50.org/en.

sponding to what Remco Raben has described as a striking characteristic of the Dutch way of coping with their colonial past, namely the very absence of any universal moral standard such as human rights (2002, 101). Particularly inconsistent here is the fact that perpetrators from World War II are still prosecuted, while there was no prosecution for the Dutch criminal deeds in Indonesia. Although since 1968/71 human rights violations and war crimes are exempted from a statute of limitation, crimes committed by Dutch military in Indonesia are excluded as a follow-up to the amnesty laws agreed upon in the context of the sovereignty handover in 1949; a repeal of the amnesty law would ask to renegotiate the sovereignty, an argument made since then (Lorenz 2015, 229).

Similarily, historian Bart Luttikhuis has argued that the *legal approach* rather stimulates thinking about single incidents instead of its systematic and comprehensive nature. He asked whether legally sanctioned apologies do not have "adverse effects," namely confining public debate to "specific types of incidents that fall within the parameters of legal responsibility and legal evidence" (2014, 92; transl. NI). He argues that the legal approach is rather misleading in terms of providing knowledge about the past (as the juridification reduces the history to single provable facts), also diminishing the apology owing to its forced nature (namely furthering a guilt-discussion instead of a responsibility-discussion) and its restrictedness to certain cases. This would not just undermine the performative power of the gesture but also hinder "the chance of successful reconciliation." Thus, he speaks of a failure of memory politics (2014, 105). Similarly as Lorenz, who sees only a "strategic way of handling human rights" on the part of the Dutch government, namely defined by national interests (2015, 232), Luttikhuis is sceptical whether the many small and limited debates on clear defined crimes will help to integrate the colonial past into the Dutch *"master narrative"* (2014, 99).

All those arguments hint towards the limitations of the court cases doing justice neither to the historical events nor being useful in terms of memory and reconciliation politics. Those postulations are however based upon a narrow *legal* interpretation of human rights. Taking also the *imaginative* capacity of human rights into account, I like to suggest that an analysis from a bottom-up actor's perspective – who spoke for whom, and why – can provide a different reading of the Rawagede case. In retrospect it is foremost the court decision that attracts scholarly attention, while from an actor's perspective also the process itself is crucial and telling. Zooming in on some actors will show the broader social implications of those legal decisions, which will allow a better understanding of how global discourses (on human rights and Transitional Justice) and personal experiences relate to each other.

5.3 Bottom-Up: Actors, Motives, Ideas of Justice

One key actor in this case is Jeffry Pondaag, who represents the 'widows of Rawagede' in the *Committee for Dutch Debts of Honour*. When asked by the judge at the Court for his motives to engage, he firmly demanded acknowledgement of the executions in Indonesia performed by the Dutch troops and recognition of their victims. But interviewing Pondaag shows his aim is much broader. He wants to give the victims a voice and a face also to confront the Dutch with their colonial past.

Pondaag, born 1953 in Jakarta, is not directly related to the village, but as an Indonesian having lived nearly 50 years in the Netherlands he wants to correct the image of this shared Dutch-Indonesian history: "My concern is the perception (...) The Dutch must realize what they have done."[18] In 1969, the year of the *Excessennota*, he arrived as a 16-year-old boy with his divorced Dutch mother in the Netherlands. There he was confronted by countless stereotypes ("They say we are terrorists, extremists and troublemakers") and a surrounding that was not aware that his past was also a shared past. Also within his family he was challenged by opposing stances towards the past and urged to navigate between the Indonesian voices of his family, a father fighting on the Indonesian side, and his Dutch father-in-law, an East Indies veteran, who always kept silent. Pondaag, who still holds an Indonesian passport, feels himself to be "a stranger" in his family, as other family members who as Dutch collaborators had to flee Indonesia now embrace the Netherlands, while he feels they had been treated unfairly.

It was also the ambivalent presence of the theme in the media that irritated him: all the reports, in which more and more facts emerged, made him angry as the revelations had hardly any consequences. Some of those documents, carefully stored in his personal archive, he made available on the *Committee's* homepage.[19] It is more than archiving a desire for justice; it is building an archive as such, to provide information to an "ignorant audience". His concern is the little knowledge about the colonial past in present-day Dutch society, and the legacies of this ignorance in the form of what he calls discrimination, racism, and institutionalized structural inequality.

In this respect it is a statement that the *Committee for Dutch Debts of Honour* (or *Komite Utang Kehormatan Belanda* as the Indonesian branch is called) was established on a symbolic date, 5th May 2005. While the Dutch then celebrate an-

---

[18] Jeffry Pondaag, interview with author, Heemskerk, 13 November 2014 and Amsterdam, 5 February 2015 (with Nancy Jouwe).
[19] http://www.kukb.nl/new/index.php.

nually their liberation from the German oppression, after having commemorated the end of World War II the day before, Pondaag has different thoughts: "The 5th of May Liberation Day? Why? In the same days Dutch soldiers left to 'occupy Indie.' In their terms 'liberating Indie.'" The most celebrated Dutch commemorative ritual is for him rather evidence of historical amnesia. The name was a conscious choice; referring to the organisation *Japanese Honorary Debts*, which has lobbied for the acknowledgement of Dutch citizen victims of the Japanese occupation of the Dutch East Indies (now Indonesia), but with a clear difference: "They only stand up for the Dutch living here, the Indo-Europeans. But what about those people there [in Indonesia], what I am doing, who are they?" The Dutch have clear expectations towards Japan or Germany as a former occupier, while according to Pondaag they do not carry out their duties as former occupiers in Indonesia. This kind of cross-referencing, using analogies to stress double standards, he sees as a tool increasingly used by journalists, creating a moral standard in the media – a tool he copies. He accuses foremost the state and its representatives. While ignorance on state level hurts, even more painful is to admit personal discrimination. He feels hurt by his colleagues' denigrating remarks about Muslims. Although he is Christian, it feels like misrecognition as Indonesian. The colonial hierarchies are still bothering him: "I am concerned that we are not considered as human. There is a ladder, isn't it? Then you first get the Dutch, then the Europeans, then the half-breeds, then the Chinese and then we come, the indigenous people, let's say, the natives. That's how we were called." He feels a similar neglect when the Dutch royal family uses yearly on Prince's Day a golden carriage with the symbols of colonialism on its doors. What for them is a symbol of tradition, for him is a "shameless" symbol of exploitation that should be put in the museum. These are just some of many examples he uses, which show how present public debates resonate with a felt neglect of the colonial past. Pondaag's driving force for the court case is to create better living conditions for the former victims in Indonesia, but he is also convinced more knowledge about the colonial past will lead towards a transformation of Dutch society. His aspiration is to tell the untold.

Here we see a trend: compensation claims are increasingly a *frame* in which not only historical injustice, but present-day injustices are negotiated, in which legacies of discrimination and inequality (in the form of prejudices, inequities and emotions), misrepresentations and gaps in history books, are made explicit.

Literature has described how since the 1980s various groups used their colonial past for their emancipation in Dutch society, supported by the government who invested via cultural policies in identity-politics as a form of integration-policy (Oostindie 2011). But this culturalism has been pushing socially sensitive issues (such as class, participation etc.) into the background. It seems that those concerns return now also in the form of compensation claims; and not accidentally at a moment in time when migration and asylum politics are daily on the news.

5.4 Human Rights: From an Individual towards a Multi-Directional Aspiration

Jeffry Pondaag's remarks make clear that in the first instance he is guided by his own diaspora experience. For Pondaag going to court was "the last instrument," as all other ways did not work out to establish truth and to force people to listen. His lawyer, Liesbeth Zegveld, translated his anger, his experience and his knowledge into the language of law and gave him therewith a voice. Without her he would never have had the chance to sue the Dutch state, but without him the case would never have started.

Differently from the before mentioned scholars, he is convinced that an increasing number of court cases will help to show the real nature of the violence and to reach the more general broad Dutch public. By keeping on fighting one court case after the other, repeating his arguments again and again, establishing new facts about new victims in new places, he tries to change an established narrative. Just as collective memory needs "continuously performing" (Rigney 2008, 93), also counter-memories need a more permanent presence in the public space to become effective.

What looks like the fight of two individuals against the Dutch state has become, however, a larger movement. Human rights lawyer Zegveld is motivated by her conviction that a state has to take responsibility for unlawful actions in his name. Passionately she defends civilians, who in violent conflicts became so-called 'collateral damage,' taking it seriously that for those the violent past is still a hurtful present.[20]

Since 2000 she has followed up on different cases of (mass)murder, whether more recent ones such as Srebrenica, or old colonial issues; providing legal assistance to Indonesian victims, to Dutch soldiers who had refused to join the colonial army, and to families of killed train-hijackers, Moluccans, who had fought for some acknowledgment of their post-colonial situation by the Dutch state. Zegveld, one could say, personifies the 'Age of Transitional Justice' in the Netherlands, as it is her success and her popularity in the media that feeds the process.

---

[20] Liesbeth Zegveld, 'Sorry?', https://www.maartenonline.nl/sorry-zeggen.html (May 2015).

While Zegveld, by connecting those cases, tests the limits of law, Pondaag builds imaginative alliances against the Dutch government; when speaking also for those who in the late 1940s refused to go as soldiers to Indonesia and/or were therefore punished with prison and social ostracism. Here the Rawagede claim functioned as catalyst. Some Dutch soldiers, who were involved in the so-called 'police actions,' asked the Dutch government, in a public letter in end 2007, to recognize the outrage and to offer an apology.[21] A veteran's son told me that his father welcomed the Rawagede verdict because it felt just for him. Although projection might play a role here, it indicates his own feelings and relief about it: "I felt his shame about what had happened and of what he has been part of. And I felt it bodily, a kind of vicarious shame, it felt terrible; but we did not speak."[22]

The court cases became a reason to talk; within families, in and across communities. Children of conscientious objectors, men who had refused to fight in Indonesia and therefore went underground or were convicted, asked Pondaag and Zegveld for advice on how to get a proper acknowledgment for their fathers. Members of the Indo-European community also did this; mixed Indonesian-Dutch who had worked for the colonial administration, were harassed, and had stayed in internment camps for months.[23] They had to leave Indonesia after independence and since then struggle for recognition of what they had lost, materially as well as in social status.

Also former Dutch UN officials, such as Theo van Boven – who as former head of the human rights section had fought decades long at the UN for a right to compensation for victims of mass atrocities – is personally relieved about the Rawagede decision. He had worked in the foreign ministry in The Hague in the early 1960s, a time in which West New Guinea, still being Dutch territory, was integrated into Indonesia (1962), and during which upcoming dictatorships elsewhere in the world were a cause of concern. He feels still embarrassed about his own blind eye at that time regarding human rights violations in Indonesia: "We were just liberated from the Nazis, what I still can remember, with our newly gained freedom we then oppressed (...) the national feelings in Indonesia, and opposed the independence with armed resistance (...) with serious war crimes, executions."[24] For him the Rawagede decision symbolizes one small step in the homecoming of human rights.

---

21 *Trouw*, 11 December 2007.
22 Frans K., informal talk with author, 16 November 2014.
23 https://javapost.nl/2015/02/03/indonesische-vechtjas/.
24 Theo van Boven, interview with author, Utrecht, 13 March 2013.

Although the discussion on Rawagede at the beginning reached mainly specific audiences, the ideas of what is possible are slowly expanding, also in Indonesia.

The Rawagede decision immediately inspired activists representing victims of Indonesian state terror. Just two days after the ruling, Haris Azhar, coordinator of the ‚Commission for Missing Persons and Victims of Violence' (KONTRAS), stated in the *Jakarta Post* that the ruling carries "several important lessons," such as that human rights violations have no expiry date, and he has hope that the court's decision might change the way Dutch people saw Indonesians: "Usually an admission of past mistakes leads to deeper understanding about the country and its people."[25]

Bedjo Untung, who has for years weekly joined a demonstration before the parliament in Jakarta, gained new hope for change. The oft-heard argument that human rights pressures from the Dutch would display a kind of neo-colonial attitude he considers to be inadmissible: "this rhetoric allies with the military instead with the victims."[26] He experiences in this decision a democratic state, where judges are independent, and where such a debate can be held about one's own past.

The Rawagede decision had its *resonance* of course also at the local level.[27] In the village itself a young woman was excited that her grandmother's hard life finally was acknowledged: "When I heard from Uuk's story, I feel sad. Imagine, if I had a small baby, suddenly my husband died and I was alone. It must have been very hard."[28] Another young woman put it differently: "My grandmother is famous. You can find her on YouTube."[29] In such ways now history became vivid. Also in other parts of Indonesia young people became alert, such as Hadiamin M. from Sidrap in South Sulawesi, who saw a report on Rawagede on TV and then realized the similarities with his grandmother's story; suddenly he was able to situate the story that so far had little resonance in the family.[30]

Furthermore, the Rawagede decision has set a *precedent* for similar cases elsewhere. It has influenced victim representatives of the independence war in

---

25 *Jakarta Post*, 16 September 2011 and *Jakarta Globe*, 14 September 2011.
26 Bedjo Untung, interview with author, Jakarta, 29 October 2015.
27 These insights are based upon interviews conducted by the author (facilitated by a translator and photographer Suzanne Liem) in October 2015, covering 8 victim-families in Rawagede and 12 in Sulawesi; including 5 local experts.
28 Granddaughter from Ibu Tijeng, interview with author, Balongsari (Rawagede), 20 October 2015.
29 Granddaughter fom Ibu Wanti Dodo, interview with author, Balongsari, 23 October 2015.
30 Hadiamin en Ibu Manna, interview with author, Sidrap, 30 October 2015.

Kenya to file a suit against the British state, deciding for a court case after political negotiations were blocked.[31] It was also a landmark decision in October 2012, when three former Mau-Mau fighters won against the UK government for having experienced 'unspeakable acts of brutality' under colonial power. As a consequence more than five thousand Kenyans received compensation from the British government for torture suffered under their colonial regime.[32] Thus, the realm of what seems possible has increased; extending the spaces in which people can allow themselves to imagine and desire justice. It has introduced the idea of a "victim oriented and relativist approach towards statutory limitations in civil cases;" nonetheless legal scholar Larissa van den Herik sees its main importance "at the meta level in that it functioned as a leverage for the Dutch state and society to revisit its colonial past" (2012, 705 and 693).

These examples show that the Dutch court cases touch a much broader public than represented in the media, which stages foremost two opposing parties, visible in headlines such as "Indonesians filed a complaint against the Dutch state,"[33] while in fact the court cases address several parties inside and outside Dutch society. While compensation rhetoric and claims are based upon clear identities and dichotomies, the use of human rights language creates a space in which relational thinking could happen, connecting members of different groups, also establishing links between different forms of injustice, past and present. This *relational element* of the human rights discourse has so far hardly been part of a scholarly reflection, which is more than pinpointing 'double standards,' but rather examining its powerful inspirational character.

5.5 A Relational Human Rights Discourse

Pondaag was long portrayed as an angry nagger, gripped by the past. This was an attempt by his opponents to delegitimize his claims – reflecting their strong faith that a reconciliatory attitude is 'healthy,' while resentments are not seen as 'socially productive' (Brudholm 2008). Those critics overlooked that imagining justice is also a creative and future-oriented process. It means also exercising "the capacity to aspire," as the anthropologist Appadurai has called it (2004, 84). Claiming, as a kind of speech act, enables actors to articulate aspirations and thereby to navigate social spaces.

---

[31] Zegveld, in: *Jakarta Post*, 13 September 2013.
[32] *The Guardian*, 29 October 2014.
[33] *Volkskrant*, 8 September 2008.

As described above, Pondaag's imaginaries of justice became that of a larger group; gaining not just slowly the sympathy from various journalists, and researchers, but also initiating a multidirectional process within which members of different groups can identify themselves. It is developing towards what Barkan has called "dialogue" (2000, 319), inviting several parties to express their views on the violent past: "the dialogue of restitution brings new pluralistic perspectives of the national historic and current identities to the public view and thus redefines the nation" (2000, 322).

Thus, what started as the passion from an individual has developed into a small, but heterogenic, social movement, in which different cases of (historical) injustice became equally legitimate claims by making use of an overarching human rights frame. The power of the human rights discourse lies in its *relational perspective*. It helped to make and understand the Rawagede claim in the first place: the possibility of reference to World War II policies and double standards enabled winning the case in the court room. But the decision has also affected the imaginaries about justice – of what is possible – from many diverse individuals, carrying a *multidirectional memory* (Rothberg 2009) that empowers different groups. Pondaag, an outsider challenging the establishment, has become the embodiment of a multidirectional memory of historical injustice, a figurehead for many of those who feel themselves neglected.

However, despite these developments, all his achievements and media publicity, Jeffry Pondaag's main narrative maintains still "I am not listened to," followed by numerous examples of neglected letters, ignorant responses or failed dialogs. While Pondaag extended the 'capacity to aspire' for others, creating spaces and feelings of liberation, he did not manage to achieve this for himself. Here we see the effects of the 'two walls of silence' problem (Dan Bar-On 1995): firstly, one has to allow oneself to speak; then one needs the empathetic listener, who really listens. Forcing the state to listen via legal claims is not what listening is about. It seems that in Dutch society Pondaag's voice is still too marginal to give him the feeling that people do listen. This is an impression he shares with others I talked to during my research. Although many Dutch families have links with the colonial Dutch-Indies, they articulate a felt absence of this past in public life. Is this the case?

Compared to World War II, memory of colonialism is often perceived as silent, despite comprehensive research. This has several reasons, one of which is a certain public rhetoric, for example Prime Minister Balkenende's well-known statement in 2006 in parliament, when he called the "VOC [Dutch East Indies Company]-mentality" a virtue of Dutch identity, associating it with a successful commercial spirit. Critics saw here proof of 'colonial amnesia' (Stoler and

Strassler 2000): taking pride in economic achievements and neglecting the injustices intrinsic to imperialism.

Dutch scholars are divided. While some see a continuous engagement with the colonial past, though pointing out foremost the lack of systematic research on the structural and colonial nature of the violence (Eickhoff 2013, 53), others see a conscious silencing of this past by particular groups, such as the veterans, their institutions and political representatives, and academia (Scagliola 2012, 427–436). Others blame instead Dutch memory culture, arguing that the colonial violence, though not silenced in public discourse, is not perceived as such owing to the way the Dutch frame their memory. This framing, says Paul Bijl, following Ann Stoler, ensures that national and colonial history are kept apart. Seeing themselves as the "better" imperialists (Bijl 2012, 449), not being as bad as the British or the Belgians, and perceiving themselves still foremost as victims of World War II, downplaying their collaborator role therein, makes it "virtually impossible" to see their own colonial acts of violence (Lorenz 2015, 23). In regard to both historical periods the Dutch still have difficulties integrating the wrongs of the past, and more specifically the role of perpetrator, in their image of themselves and their national history.

Thus, what is needed? More historical research (as historians argue) or a reassessment of the memory and human rights culture (as other scholars argue), or a moral debate as activists like Jeffry Pondaag suggest ("The king has to apologize (…) the soldiers were sent in the name of the royal family")?

Pondaag's feeling of "not to be listened to" is nourished by his impression of the colonial past, its social, cultural and religious legacy, still being a taboo. A taboo however is not characterized by the absence of facts, but that factual findings are not discussed and no moral judgment is put on them. Via a "communicative refusal to comment" the taboo is declared a "non-issue" and ignored (Keppler 1994, 181). Such observations made in the study of family memory (Immler 2013, 92) are similarly true in the public realm; as shown earlier in the Jewish case. This makes it clear why a moral judgment is crucial in such debates about past wrongs, in the scholarly and in the political field.

6 What Does the Concept of 'Social Imaginaries' Add to Transitional Justice Research?

Two decades ago these recent court cases in The Hague on colonial injustice might have been called a utopian program, today they gain slowly ground. Each court decision is another step towards becoming a social imaginary in the sense of Taylor, namely shared by a substantial community. However, imaginaries always start small, shared by a few, and only over time do they become institutionalized. Limiting the entitlement to compensation to a few widows still alive was meant to consider the past as passed, while accepting also the children is one step further in regard to accepting intergenerational responsibilities. Thereby the colonial *past* has successively become a colonial *present*. Here the case has shown that the decision as to which past is passed, is not one of experience only, but also about continuously performing. But who performs?

6.1 Whose Imaginaries of Justice Do We Here Talk about?

When scrutinizing 'whose imaginaries of justice we here talk about' it has to be realized that it was not Indonesian victims forcing the Dutch state into two consecutive lawsuits, but an Indonesian living in the Netherlands. Desires for justice play here also on a different level; one could call it the *diaspora element* of reparation claims. It is striking that often members of the Diaspora are key in making reparation claims (Wiebelhaus-Brahm 2016);[34] most visible in diaspora communities such as the Jewish, the Armenian or the slavery descendants' communities; identifying themselves via claims, while people within their countries often have other priorities or no means.

Thus, if compensations have become a key aspect of a globalized world, advocated by people living in migrant or diaspora conditions, this begs to discuss reparations not just in the frame of *historical injustice* (colonized versus colonizer) but *present day injustice* felt in an increasingly globalized society ('We are here, because you were there'). The current social and political atmosphere in which such pluralism is contested, as well as the 'hybrid individual' (Paul Gilroy), feeds an increasing desire of individuals to be acknowledged with their own cultural, religious, ethnic and (post)colonial background. In this context reparation claims have become a popular frame, though – as this article argues – partly misleading, directing our attention to the wrongs of the past instead of to its legacies in the present, which motivated the claims in the first place.

Following up on Taylor's and Moyn's work, one can say that if this *imaginative* character of human rights were to colour today's compensation debate, then this asks us to shift the focus: to consider compensation not foremost as an *instrument of acknowledgment*, addressing the past, but an *instrument of dialogue*,

---

[34] Nonetheless, the "agency of diasporas in building pressure for and articulating a vision of transitional justice has been underexplored" (Wiebelhaus-Brahm 2016, 23).

addressing the present. This shift would contribute to what Andreas Huyssen has asked for, a debate on continuities, creating awareness of the solid links between past and present forms of injustice, rather than following the idea of human rights practices "righting past wrongs via redress or restitution claims" (2010).

This change of perspective would make the compensation debate – which often gets stuck in essentialising dichotomist categories of the past (victims/perpetrators) or future-oriented reconciliation rhetoric – much more effective, when understanding its situatedness: in the Dutch case, an increasingly pluralized society in which compensation claims have became a popular *frame* to address not *historical* but *present-day* injustice, not to perform *trauma* but to practice *citizenship*, criticising the lack of political sensitivity and vision in regard to a pluralized society in which all members have their own stories that want to be told.

6.2 Imaginations of Justice Differ

What reads partly as a success story of human rights from a Dutch point of view has a shadow-side. There are also difficulties of 'doing justice' based upon a human rights discourse that suggests being secular and neutral. Activist Pondaag and lawyer Zegveld consider identification of the historical wrongs, apologies by state officials and compensations as *universal* elements of a recognition process, and both suggest those elements to various groups as a 'proper acknowledgment.' However, in the West Javanese village of Rawagede we have seen that the compensations paid to a few individuals disturbed the social balance, leading to severe personal threats and social upheavals (for more details: Immler 2018): "Why only the living widows?" family members of already deceased widows asked, considering that, as heirs, they had an equal right to this money. In order to acknowledge that alongside the individual, there was also collective victimhood, half of the money collected was divided between all 181-victim families buried at the monument. The head of the local widow *Foundation*, Sukarman, explains: "Collectivity is an unwritten custom."[35] While Zegveld and Pondaag saw this as a violation of the widows' rights and also as a form of corruption, a case for the Indonesian justice system,[36] Sukarman saw for himself no other way out: "They see me as representative of all the victims. (...) Otherwise they [the neglected descendants] would have burnt my house." In his view, he has just *translated* the decision of international law

---

35 Sukarman, interview with the author, Balongsari, 22 October 2015.
36 Zegveld, in: *Jakarta Post*, 13 September 2013.

into local realities, where colonial violence is not felt as an individual experience but by a whole community.

But it is more than that. Sukarman has also *acted upon* a different human rights discourse, one that rather celebrates civil victims as a collective of heroes fallen for Indonesia's independence instead of mourning them as individual victims. In his context, human rights refer first of all to the right of national self-determination in the decolonisation struggle. This becomes visible not just in his speeches at Rawagede's monument, but also in the interviews with other protagonists, acting on behalf of the widows. Batara Hutagalung, the Indonesian partner of the *Committee for Dutch Debts of Honour,* welcomed the court decision as it introduced the idea that "a state can be blamed guilty," but had difficulties in accepting that the Court acknowledge the widows because they had been Dutch nationals ('onderdanen') at the time. For him this amounted to a renewed neglect of Indonesia's independence on 17 August 1945.[37] Moreover, he considers an individual perspective counterproductive, knowing of too many such massacres.

One such was in Suppa, a small village in South Sulawesi, where Andi Monji (72) witnessed as a boy his father being shot and the loss of several other family members. In 2014 he testified in The Hague as a representative of many child survivors in South Sulawesi.[38] From his perspective, a victim community was driven apart, because at first only the widows were eligible for recognition and reparations while the children were not. These distinctions made by the Dutch Court do not reflect his social reality. For him, going to court meant also restoration of the social fabric back home.

Those interviewees feel uncomfortable about the individual approach, as for them justice entails a collective and relational aspect. Here, Transitional Justice becomes visible as a very local experience. Just as Appadurai has emphasized: "Aspirations are never simply individual [but] always formed in interaction and in the thick of social life" (2004, 67). Some scholars however see the global human rights discourse as a successful tool for Indonesia to reach beyond national history writing. Katharine McGregor has shown that for Sulawesi it has facilitated discussion of war crimes in terms of individual victimhood, which helped victims to receive attention, whereas staying within customary systems and national historiography silences them (2014, 295–302). Here frictions become evident.

---

[37] Hutagalung, interviewed by the author in Jakarta, 18 October 2015.
[38] Monji, interview with author, Suppa-Pinrang, South Sulawesi, 13 and 14 October 2015.

Individual court cases and individual compensations, both have, as seen in Rawagede, unintended consequences that hint towards multiple problems when the idea about 'having a right to justice' is translated into a (non-western) village context, described rather as dominated by a 'having a duty to share' culture. When membership of an "extended family is itself regarded as a fundamental human right," and everyday culture is dominated by "community, duties, and religion," human rights relations are, according to legal scholar Tom Zwart, in a way "more direct, personal, and reciprocal, and therefore more horizontal than they are in the West" (2012, 551 and 555). However, it is also not as simple as 'the collective has profited, therefore so has the individual.' While widow Ibu Tijeng is content that the compensation enabled her to rebuild her old house, her granddaughter feels her oma has been instrumentalised as the village's "money-machine;" she would have preferred an empowering, self-determined process.[39] By watching the sharing practice she developed a clear idea of what feels unjust to her and how things "ought to go" (Taylor 2002, 106).

Here the Dutch-Indonesian case displays some of the tensions in the field of Transitional Justice between local customs and Dutch rule, in which the acknowledgement of injustice, owing to the legal system, goes along with a form of individualisation that can damage existing social structures; while the local collective 'solution' is not accepted either. As other cases have shown as well, this is a documented difficulty in Indonesia and scholars have argued for more involvement of local grass-roots initiatives in such recognition processes, to take more into account its collective and cultural dimension (Bräuchler 2009, 3 and 10).

7 Conclusion

In the Netherlands the Rawagede decision and its follow-ups became symbolic of a new 'moral order.' While the Civil Court is still scrutinizing historical facts, already we see how those legal claims initiated a broader public and scholarly debate on the nature of the colonial past and about the self-image of the Dutch. We can observe how the aspiration of one individual has developed into a *multi-directional aspiration*, empowering imaginaries about justice from members of diverse groups who feel neglected. At the same time it has become clear that those compensation claims are increasingly a *frame* in which not only historical injustice, but present-day injustices are negotiated. Here the article

---

[39] Ibu Tijeng, daughter and granddaughter, interview with author, Balongsari, 20 October 2015.

pinpoints the *diaspora element* in the reparation claims: that an Indonesian in the Netherlands translated his felt neglect of himself and his history into a claim on behalf of the formerly colonized. Therewith the claims go far beyond the acknowledgment of historical injustice, but address the failures of a pluralized Dutch society, in which many post-colonial migrants still feel not fully acknowledged members. It was Taylor who emphasized that this multicultural diversity needs to be managed through a secular language, suggesting human rights (2007). In this case study it becomes clear how compensation claims are such a tool to thematise diversity. In this sense the claims are far more than a negotiation about the *past* between the Dutch state and its former colonial 'subjects' in the East, but also an inquiry into *present-day* post-colonial Netherlands. It is the idea of a pluralized society that is at stake.

In Indonesia the claims stimulated ideas about human rights at various levels. But it also became clear that Dutch imaginaries of justice do not always match local realities in Indonesia. They need to be more *translated* to the local. More research about how individuals relate themselves to the larger collectives they live in and how this shapes (and is shaped by) their social imaginaries about justice – without idealizing or overstating the cultural dimensions of these imaginaries – could offer in the future a complementary approach in the Transitional Justice field. This will not just pre-empt some of the unintended and unwanted consequences, but also identify the assumptions informing 'our' understanding of justice.

Transitional Justice as a discipline and field is in itself a secular social imaginary: the belief that transformative justice exists. The idea that justice can be gained has been manifested in the last decade within international legislation, but – as shown above – there are more challenges than to bring legal-proof evidence for the victim's entitlement, but how to *do* justice so that it's *felt* that justice has been done.[40] ntroducing an alternative human rights perspective, focusing on its *imaginative* aspect, has revealed about whose imaginaries of justice we talk and in which way in both countries imaginations about justice differ. It has exposed the situatedness of the claims and the normative challenges of the human rights idea, and its need of translation; adressing translation not just as a problem but a potential (Bachmann-Medick 2012, 358). This hopefully delivers some input to further discuss, as Paul Gready has formulated, in which way

---

40 Imaginations about the past often have more truth than archival evidence, something to be more aware of in the struggle with facts and numbers. Recognition has a strong 'imaginary' component, intrinsically linked to performing the idea of family (Immler 2013, 97–99).

"transitional justice is, or could be, at the forefront of reimagining how we think about human rights" (2011, 9).

Bibliography

Appadurai, Arjun. 2004. "The Capacity to Aspire: Culture and the Terms of Recognition." In *Culture and Public Action*, edited by Vijayendra Rao and Michael Walton, 59–84. Palo Alto: Stanford University Press.

Bachmann-Medick, Doris. 2012. "Menschenrechte als Übersetzungsproblem." *Geschichte und Gesellschaft* 38: 331-359.

Barkan, Elazar. 2000. *The Guilt of Nations: Restitution and Negotiating Historical Injustices*. New York: Norton.

Bar-On, Dan. 1995. *Fear and Hope: Three Generations of the Holocaust*. Cambridge, MA: Harvard University Press.

Bijl, Paul. 2012. "Colonial Memory and Forgetting in the Netherlands and Indonesia." *Journal of Genocide Research* 14(3–4):441–461.

Bräuchler, Birgit, ed. 2009. *Reconciling Indonesia: Grassroots Agency for Peace*. London/New York: Routledge.

De Greiff, Pablo. 2006. *The Handbook of Reparations*. Oxford: Oxford University Press.

Eickhoff, Martijn. 2013. "Weggestreept Verleden? Nederlandse Historici en het Rawagede Debat." *Groniek* 194:53–67.

Frei, Norbert, José Brunner and Constantin Goschler, eds. 2009. *Die Praxis der Wiedergutmachung: Geschichte, Erfahrung und Wirkung in Deutschland und Israel*. Göttingen: Wallstein.

Gready, Paul. 2011. *The Era of Transitional Justice: The Aftermath of the Truth and Reconciliation Commission*. London/New York: Routledge.

Herik, Larissa van den. 2012. "Addressing 'Colonial Crimes' through Reparations? Adjudicating Dutch Atrocities Committed in Indonesia." *Journal International Criminal Justice* 10(3):693–705.

Hunt, Lynn. 2007. *Inventing Human Rights: A History*. New York: W.W. Norton & Company.

Huyssen, Andreas. 2010. "Natural Rights, Cultural Rights, and the Politics of Memory." http://hemi.nyu.edu/hemi/en/e-misferica-62/huyssen.

Immler, Nicole L. 2013. "Die Anwesenheit des Abwesenden: Schweigen im Familiengedächtnis." In *Jenseits des beredeten Schweigens: Neue Perspektiven auf den sprachlosen Augenblick*, edited by Sandra Markewitz, 73–99. Bielefeld: Aisthesis.

Immler, Nicole, and Nancy Jouwe, 1 April 2015. "Koloniaal Verleden Gaat ook Latere Generaties aan" (*Colonial History also Affects Descendants*). In *Trouw*.

Immler, Nicole L. 2018. "Narrating (In)Justice in the Form of a Reparation Claim: Bottom-Up Reflections on a Post-Colonial Setting – The Rawagede Case." In *Understanding the Age of Transitional Justice: Crimes, Courts, Commissions, and Chronicling*, edited by Nanci Adler. New Brunswick: Rutgers University Press, 149–174.

Jensen, Meg and Margaretta Jolly, eds. 2014. *We Shall Bear Witness: Life Narratives and Human Rights*. Madison: The University of Wisconsin Press.

Kennedy, Rosanne. 2014. "Moving Testimony: Human Rights, Palestinian Memory, and the Transnational Public Sphere." In *Transnational Memory Circulation, Articulation, Scales*, edited by Chiara De Cesari and Ann Rigney, 51–78. Boston: Walter de Gruyter.

Keppler, Angela. 1994. *Tischgespräche: über Formen kommunikativer Vergemeinschaftung am Beispiel der Konversation in Familien*. Frankfurt am Main: Suhrkamp.

Lorenz, Chris. 2015. "Can a Criminal Event in the Past Disappear in a Garbage Bin in the Present? Dutch Colonial Memory and Human Rights: The Case of Rawagede." In *Afterlife of Events: Perspectives on Mnemohistory*, edited by Marek Tamm, 219–241. New York: Palgrave Macmillan.

Luttikhuis, Bart. 2014. "Juridisch Afgedwongen Excuses: Rawagedeh, Zuid-Celebes en de Nederlandse Terughoudendheid." *BMGN – Low Countries Historical Review* 129(4): 92–105.

Merry, Sally Engle. 2006. "Transnational Human Rights and Local Activism: Mapping the Middle American." *Anthropologist* 108(1):28–51.

McGregor, Katharine. 2014. "From National Sacrifice to Compensation Claims: Changing Indonesian Representations of the Westerling Massacres in South Sulawesi, 1946–47." In *Colonial Counterinsurgency and Mass Violence: the Dutch Empire in Indonesia*, edited by Bart Luttikhuis and A. Dirk Moses, 282–307. London: Routledge.

Moyn, Samuel. 2010. *The Last Utopia: Human Rights in History*. Cambridge, MA: Harvard University Press.

Nobles, Melissa. "Reparations Claims: Politics by Another Name." *Political Power and Social Theory* 18:253–258.

Neumann, Klaus and Thompson, Janna. 2015. "Introduction: Beyond the Legalist Paradigm." In *Historical Justice and Memory*, edited by Klaus Neumann and Janna Thompson, 3–24. Madison: University of Wisconsin Press.

Olsen, Tricia D., Leigh A. Payne and Andrew G. Reiter, eds. 2010. *Transitional Justice in Balance: Comparing Processes, Weighing Efficacy*. Washington D.C.: United States Institute of Peace Press.

Oomen, Barbara. 2013. *Rights for Others: The Slow Home-Coming of Human Rights in the Netherlands*. Cambridge: Cambridge University Press.

Oostindie, Gert. 2011. *Postcolonial Netherlands: Sixty-five Years of Forgetting, Commemorating, Silencing*. Amsterdam: Amsterdam University Press.

Raben, Remco. 2002. "Koloniale Vergangenheit und postkoloniale Moral in den Niederlanden." In *Verbrechen Erinnern. Die Auseinandersetzung mit Holocaust und Völkermord*, edited by Volker Knigge and Norbert Frei, 90–110. München: Beck.

Rigney, Ann. 2008. "Divided Pasts: A Premature Memorial and the Dynamics of Collective Remembrance." *Memory Studies* 1(1):89–97.

Rothberg, Michael. 2009. *Multidirectional Memory: Remembering the Holocaust in the Age of Decolonization*. Redwood City: Stanford University Press.

Scagliola, Stef. 2012. "Cleo's 'Unfinished Business': Coming to Terms with Dutch War Crimes in Indonesia's War of Independence." *Journal of Genocide Research* 14(3–4):419–439.

Simpson, Bradley R. 2013. "Self-Determination, Human Rights, and the End of Empire in the1970s." *Humanity: An International Journal of Human Rights, Humanitarianism, and Development* 4(2):239–260.

Slaughter, Joseph R. 2007. *Human Rights, Inc.: The World Novel, Narrative Form, and International Law*. New York: Fordham University Press.

Stoler, Ann Laura and Karen Strassler. 2000. "Castings for the Colonial: Memory Work in 'New Order' Java." *Comparative Studies in Society and History* 42(1):4–48.
Strauss, Claudia. 2006. "The Imaginary." *Anthropological Theory*, 6(3): 322–344.
Taylor, Charles. 1994. "The Politics of Recognition." In *Multiculturalism: Examining the Politics of Recognition*, edited by Amy Gutman. Princeton: Princeton University Press.
Taylor, Charles. 2002. "Modern Social Imaginaries." *Public Culture*, 14(1):91–124.
Taylor, Charles. 2007. *A Secular Age*. Cambridge, MA: Harvard University Press.
Torpey, John. 2006a. *Making Whole What Has Been Smashed: On Reparations Politics*. Cambridge, MA: Harvard University Press.
Torpey, John. 2006b. "Modes of Repair: Reparations and Citizenship at the Dawn of the New Millennium." *Political Power and Social Theory* 18:207–226.
VanAntwerpen, Jonathan. 2008. Religion, Secularism, and the Language of Transition: http://www.global.ucsb.edu/orfaleacenter/luce/luce08/documents/VanAntwerpen_reconciliation.pdf.
Veraart, Wouter. 2012. "Uitzondering of Precedent? De Historische Dubbelzinnigheid van de Rawagede-Uitspraak." *Ars Aequi*, Vol. April:251–259.
Wiebelhaus-Brahm, Eric (2016). Exploring Variation in Diasporas' Engagement with Transitional Justice Processes. *Journal of Peacebuilding & Development* 11(3):23–36.
Zwart, Tom. 2012. "Using Local Culture to Further the Implementation of International Human Rights: The Receptor Approach." *Human Rights Quarterly* 34(2):546–569.

Christiane Timmerman, Gert Verschraegen, Kenneth
Hemmerechts, Roos Willems
Europe and the Human Rights Imaginary

The Role of Perceptions of Human Rights in Europe and
Migration Aspirations

1 Introduction

During the last decade, debates about the meaning of Europe have been prominent in various disciplines (Christiansen et al. 2001; Malmborg and Stråth 2002; De Teyssier and Baudier 2006; Wilson and Millar 2007). With the enlargement of the European Union (EU) to 28 Member States, discussions about what exactly Europe is and where it is going are gaining importance (Stråth 2006). EU enlargement as well as growing internal and external immigration have greatly increased Europe's social, cultural and religious heterogeneity. Within Europe, there are different reactions to these evolutions. On the one hand, populist and nationalist politics draw strong boundaries between 'Europe' and the 'other,' which is illustrated by the agitated debates on the regulation of Muslim immigration and the accession of Turkey. On the other hand, more "cosmopolitan" European politics calls for "openness" as well as political and social integration of ethnic, cultural and religious minorities, based on the principle of shared "humanity" and human rights (Checkel and Katzenstein 2009, 11–15). Within this debate, religion often takes on "a new and deeply politicized role" (Checkel and Katzenstein 2009, 14): while some actors defend a non-confessional, secular European identity, others point to the Christian foundations of Europe and the EU.

Yet the concept of a European identity and its relation to human rights and democracy is relevant not only to European societies but to the outside world as

---

This research was carried out thanks to the support of the European Commission, Directorate-General for Research, 7th Framework Programme for Research – Socio-economic Sciences and Humanities (grant agreement nr. 244703). The information and views set out in this publication are those of the author(s) and do not necessarily reflect the official opinion of the European Communities. Neither the European Communities' institutions and bodies nor any person acting on their behalf may be held responsible for the use that may be made of the information contained therein. The EUMAGINE project is co-funded by the European Community FP7 2007–2013, under the Socio-economic Sciences and Humanities programme.

https://doi.org/10.1515/9783110435122-010

well (Wilson and Millar 2007). In view of the fact that human rights and secular democracy are central features of the EU, the question arises of whether Europe is also regarded as such by non-EU states and their citizens. Although Europe today is largely associated with the idea of democracy, the rule of law and a commitment to human rights (for example, the individual's right to religious freedom), there has been little research on how the association with human rights and democracy shapes the perception of the EU abroad, and to what extent these perceptions may influence the willingness to migrate to Europe. The international EUMAGINE research project which ran from 2010 until 2013 and covered four major emigration and so-called transit countries, studied the links between such outside perceptions of democracy and human rights in Europe and the migration desires of persons in non-EU countries.

The basic assumption of the EUMAGINE project was that migration aspirations, decisions and behaviour are linked to perceptions of democracy and human rights. This hypothesis builds on two observations. First, we recognize that the term 'human rights' as well as the terms 'political rights,' 'civil rights' and 'social rights,' have become a preferred jargon or terminology to express the aspirations of the present-day individual and polity. Second, given the fact that the actual enjoyment of rights depends to a large extent on a well-functioning state and public institutions (e.g. schools and hospitals, a well-regulated labour market, independent courts and commissions to protect the rights of individuals and minorities), migration to more mature states can be regarded as a legitimate channel to gain access to job opportunities, a decent education or the opportunity to teach or practice one's religion. To the extent that people 'imagine' themselves as having equal rights to any other human being, they might consider migration to a country where human rights are better protected than in their own country a genuine possibility.

Drawing selectively on the EUMAGINE project, this chapter will address the question of how migrants and non-migrants from source countries perceive human rights and democracy-related issues in their home country and in Europe, and how these perceptions affect their migration aspirations. In the next section (2) we will set the scene by outlining the emergence of human rights and how this can be linked to migration aspirations and decisions. Building on Benedict Anderson and Charles Taylor's notion of collective imaginaries, we will argue that human rights can be conceived of as a global secular imaginary that emerged after World War II, and will sketch how Europe and the European Union became associated with ideas of human rights and democracy. We will pay particular importance to the question of how far human rights can be seen as standards that can be endorsed by both religious and non-religious people. In the third section, we will explain in greater detail how the human rights imaginary might fuel aspirations to migrate, and in the fourth section we outline the analytical framework of the EUMAGINE study and clarify the data used, operationalization and methods. We present its main results regarding the impact of perceptions of human rights and democracy on migration aspirations in the fifth section, and conclude by returning to our main question or hypothesis, stating namely that there is a link between the perceptions of democracy and human rights in Europe and the home country and that these perceptions influence the formation of migration aspirations to Europe.

2 The Global Human Rights Imaginary and Europe

In their seminal writings, Benedict Anderson and Charles Taylor have eloquently described how, for the past two hundred years, modern societies have imagined themselves as bound up with the nation as a sovereign, geographically-limited territory. In Anderson's account (1991), the emergence of 'nationalism' has enabled citizens to imagine themselves as tied together through shared practices of narrating, forgetting and remembering, even though they may never encounter each other in real life. For Taylor as well, modern social imaginaries typically arise at the level of the nation-state (e.g. 2004, 109–142), yet he leaves open the possibility that imaginaries emerge at a substantially larger scale. Since a social imaginary in Taylor's thinking involves the different ways in which "people imagine their social existence, how they fit together with others (...) the expectations that are normally met, and the deeper normative notions and images that underlie these expectations" (2004, 23), it should not necessarily relate to the 'we' of the sovereign nation. To the extent that people connect to each other in the global – or, in Taylor's words, "metatopical" – economy, media and the internet, there is a clear extension of the social imaginary in space (2004, 178).

It can be argued that since the middle of the twentieth century, a major shift in the social imaginaries has been underway: the rise of a *global human rights imaginary* that expands and transforms earlier imaginaries grounded in conceptions of the nation and nation state. Collective imaginaries today increasingly refer to the level of global society or the 'we' of a single human community. As expressed by the 1948 UN Universal Declaration of Human Rights, we imagine ourselves to be part of one humanity in which every human being, irrespective of his or her nationality, holds certain fundamental rights. In Taylor's account, rights are, of course, a crucial element of modern social imaginaries, but are mainly located at the interface between the individual, society and state

(2004, 20–22). This classical image corresponds to the modern liberal paradigm of national citizenship, in which individual legal rights, membership of a state and national identity were conceived of as strongly linked. Yet, arguably this classical institutional form of national citizenship has been fundamentally transformed by the emergence of a 'post-national' paradigm of social order, in which individual rights are strengthened in comparison with the 'Westphalian' principle of absolute state sovereignty (Jacobson 1996; Soysal 1994).

As is well-known, Europe has played a crucial role in the institutionalization of this transnational rights regime. After the disastrous experiences of World War II, totalitarianism and genocide, Europe took the lead in institutionalising human rights. In 1950 the Council of Europe established a human rights regime under the *European Convention on the Protection of Human Rights and Basic Freedoms*, which entered into force in 1953. In the postwar period, the association between the European region and the human rights idea grew stronger, as human rights – and in particular their political and civil rights component —were used by the founders of the European project to defend and define the essence of (Western) Europe and fend off the spectre of communism (Moyn 2010, 75–83). Although the legacy of European colonialism stood in the way, to some extent, of this image throughout the 1950s and 1960s, a strong commitment to the issue of human rights is now generally seen as one of the principal characteristics of the European Union, both in its foreign and migration policies and in its internal strategies. Since the sixties, Europe has developed one of the most effective international systems of human rights implementation; fundamental freedoms of European citizens are guaranteed by the *European Court of Human Rights* (ECHR – founded in 1959), which gives individual EU citizens the possibility to appeal to the European Court in Strasbourg against perceived injustices in civil and state administration (Christoffersen and Madsen 2011).

The association between Europe and the idea of human rights is older, however, given the multiple links to Europe's political, religious and philosophical history (e.g. Alston 1999). It is often assumed that the history of human rights is somehow related to European (and by extension: North American) religious and cultural traditions, including Christianity. "Elements within Christianity which, in one way or another, may have fostered the development of secular human rights include for example the Protestant critique of political clericalism or the conceptual distinction between 'spiritual' and 'temporal' authorities as it was worked out in the aftermath of the medieval investiture Contest" (Bielefeldt 2006, 104). Even though the historical significance of the Christian tradition cannot be denied, it would be highly problematic to see this as the indispensable cultural roots of human rights (Bielefeldt 2006, 104). The whole conception of human rights is precisely that it is supposed to be shared: human rights are standards that can be endorsed by people who hold different religious and philosophical views (e.g. Cohen 2004). In fact, once a concept such as freedom of religion has been established, it often provides "a new hermeneutic standpoint from which innovative readings of one's own tradition – including for example a theological appreciation of those ideas – become possible" (Bielefeldt 2006, 104). This conception of a shared framework was present from the early start of the doctrine of human rights in the forties, as shown by the books by Mary Ann Glendon (2001) and Johannes Morsink (1999) on the drafting of the Universal Declaration of Human Rights. The different delegates, coming from various cultural and religious backgrounds, all worked towards a declaration that neither of the parties present could fully lay claim to. Jacques Maritain, a Catholic philosopher who participated in some of the deliberations that led to the Declaration, responded as follows to public astonishment that people of radically opposed views had agreed on rights: "Yes, we agree about the rights, but on condition that no one asks us why" (Glendon 2001, 19). It is precisely by creating agreement not based on common philosophical or religious ideas but on widely shared practices and norms, that it was possible to develop a conception of human rights which can be shared by adherents to different cultural and religious traditions.

Although the concept of human rights goes back to the late 1940s, it took a while before the idea of human rights really gained ground (e.g. Moyn 2010) In fact, a genuine global rights imaginary only came into being in the late 1980s, when human rights organizations began to flourish and international criminal tribunals became reality. Today, the global human rights regime has fundamentally redefined the world's understanding of the legitimate relationship between individuals and the state. The international legal protections of human rights law apply in principle directly to individuals, outside the authority of their governments. Most states, advocacy groups, and international organizations now express deference for the 'sanctity' of basic individual rights and individual dignity, and have incorporated the Universal Declaration of Human Rights and other enshrined principles concerning rights and responsibilities into their daily *modus operandi*. The global imaginary of human rights, however, has also transformed the way in which everyday citizens worldwide understand their 'rightful' place within society. Human rights increasingly function as a global discourse and cultural repertoire through which individuals can represent their rights and aspirations to themselves and to the international community. They offer "a language structure of words and shared understandings which agents appeal to when acting out their social lives" (O'Byrne 2012, 833). Charles Taylor would probably describe the structure of this human rights imaginary by using the concept of the "Direct-Access Society" (Taylor 2004, 155–162), a society of "radical horizontality (…) where each member is immediate to the whole" (Taylor 2004, 157). Whereas traditional groups or premodern states could easily lay claim to their members' identities and aspirations, persons can now think, act and cooperate "outside of any prior political order" (Taylor 2004, 156) and demand direct, unmediated access to societal goods and networks. According to Taylor, these modes of "imagined direct access" are a crucial feature of contemporary society and "link people translocally and internationally into a single collective agency" (2004, 160).

3 Perceptions of Human Rights and the Aspiration to Migrate

The EUMAGINE project analysed how the global imaginary of universal rights, in the form of a 'direct access' to societal goods, is linked to migration aspirations. More specifically, it focused on the effect of perceptions of democracy and human rights, such as corruption, safety and security, freedom of expression, job opportunities, social security and quality of health care/schools, on the willingness to migrate to Europe.

A central and obvious feature of the relationship between perceptions of democracy and human rights, on the one hand, and migration aspirations on the other, concerns the question of whether the state in which one lives is capable of guaranteeing individual rights and access to goods such as decent education and health care. Although the language of human rights presupposes a raft of universal, basic rights, the actual delivery of rights is very much dependent on one's membership of a specific state or polity (e.g. Madsen, Verschraegen 2013, 8–9). At present, access to rights such as the right to education, access to decent health care or the right to work is commonly administered by a state and limited to national citizens or those legally on the territory (although limiting conditions may be attached to the latter status).

This tension between the global aspirations of human rights and the actual delivery of rights through national citizenship evidently creates the possibility of using migration as an instrument for guaranteeing one's rights. To the extent that the actual enjoyment of many human rights presupposes a well-functioning state and public institutions (independent courts, formal and regulated labour markets, well-funded schools and hospitals, social security systems, etc.), migration can be considered as a legitimate channel to gain access to cultural and religious freedom, job opportunities, social security and a decent education. In fact, the structure of modern markets and businesses, and the logic of transnational fields such as science, education and health care, transforms international mobility of persons into quite normal and expected behaviour. Migration can be seen as "an attempt to take advantage of opportunities for inclusion. In terms of the economy, the law, education or health, and of modern organisations, migration is something individuals can be expected to do to adjust to the forms of inclusion on offer to them." (Bommes 2012, 27) So, on the one hand, migration is part of normal, i.e. socially expected, mobility in modern society. The case of internal migrations within the territory of a state makes this clear. Moving elsewhere within a country in order to enhance one's education, chase economic and career opportunities or re-unite with family is a normal event that hardly mobilises social attention. To some extent, migration within Europe has also become a routine practice that is largely seen as socially legitimate (cf. Recchi 2015). On the other hand, however, international – or non-European – migration is "manifestly treated as improbable and as a problem, particularly in those countries with fully developed nation states and welfare states, when migration crossing state boundaries is involved" (Bommes 2012, 27). It can be considered as an unforeseen and largely unwelcome side-effect of the attractiveness of European welfare states, which provide a high level of security, welfare and rights protection to their citizens.

It is not surprising that there is continued disagreement in the existing literature on how the relation between trans-national migration, human rights and the sovereignty of the nation-state should be assessed. On the one hand, cosmopolitan or trans-national scholars such as Soysal (1994) or Jacobson (1997) have argued that the combined effect of trans-national migration and the emergence of a stronger human rights system brings about the erosion of the traditional basis of nation-state membership, namely 'citizenship.' In such a transnational, cosmopolitan regime, mobility in and of itself might be defined as a human right. To the extent that human rights constitute – to use Hannah Arendt's words – 'a right to have rights,' individuals have a right to take advantage of opportunities to gain access to work, money, social rights, education or health, if they cannot enjoy these rights within their own polity. On the other hand, scholars such as Bosniak (2006), Joppke (2010) or Morris (2010, 2013) emphasize that states continue to control immigration and still largely determine access to residence or the right to seek employment. Furthermore, they note that the effective ability to migrate or to move – and even more so, to have access to opportunities for movement – is highly unequally distributed and has become a major stratifying force in our contemporary world (e.g. Shamir 2005). There is a genuine 'mobility gap' stretching from the severely restricted ability of Nigerian citizens to visit family members in Paris or London to the largely unrestricted possibilities to be mobile open to the global business elite.

But whoever may be right, the human rights discourse remains a powerful imaginary which can fuel the willingness and aspiration to migrate. As 'the jury' on the exact relation between human rights and migration 'is still out,' more empirical insight into the way in which human rights perceptions, motivations and behaviours are formed is more than welcome.

4 THE EUMAGINE Project

4.1 Conceptual Framework

The EUMAGINE project was the first of its kind to systematically carry out empirical research on the relation between perceptions of human rights and democracy, and migratory aspirations from the viewpoint of potential migrants and non-migrants. Various previous studies (e.g. de Haas 2010; Timmerman et al. 2013a) on international migration point to the importance of discourses and imaginations about migration and possible destination countries in generating and perpetuating migration aspirations. The discourses and imagined ideas related to democracy and human rights may focus on an individual (the specific rights of immigrants and asylum-seekers) or on a more general level (human rights in a free marketplace and a social welfare state characterized by the rule of law and democratic limited government). The extent to which policy regarding the rights of immigrants (e.g. limitation of procedural guarantees in matters of immigration or the right to family reunification), human rights in general and democratic government in the EU and its Member States, may have an effective impact on immigration patterns, will depend on the specific discourses and imaginations. Within contemporary scholarship, however, the attention to transnational human rights and democracy focuses primarily on the institutional aspects and the appeal to institutional mechanisms by individuals. The effects of democracy and human rights in other domains, such as their role in migratory movements, is still largely unstudied (Battistella 2005; Caloz-Tschopp and Dasen 2007).

In the EUMAGINE project, Europe as well as other potential destinations were conceived of as socially and discursively constructed locations, leaving space for respondents to elaborate their perceptions freely. The idea that geographic areas are imaginary and discursive constructions logically follows from the fact that the majority of potential migrants have never actually visited these places and usually possess limited information about possible destination countries (Efionayi-Mäder et al. 2001). Media discourses and discourses of returned migrants, friends and family abroad are important sources for creating perceptions and imaginations regarding the democracy and human rights situation of possible asylum and migration destinations (Koser and Pinkerton 2004). In this context, the EUMAGINE project specifically explored the perceptions of persons in source countries about human rights and democracy, and analysed the link between these perceptions and migration aspirations in particular.

The main hypothesis underlying the project was that perceptions of the human rights and democracy status in the home country and in Europe impact on individuals from so-called 'cultures of emigration,' where migration has become deeply rooted in people's behavioural repertoire (Massey 1998). This culture of emigration – observable in popular discourses, media discourses, cultural artefacts and social networks – weighs heavily on potential migrants' perceptions, aspirations and behaviour (Collyer 2006; Pang 2007; Timmerman 2008). For this reason, the EUMAGINE project operationalized perceptions of human rights and democracy issues, which are socially and culturally constructed, in a process mediated by, among other things, various discourses on and representations of Europe and migratory flows in the regions of origin. The project deliberately aimed to analyse the perceptions not only of migrants who already decided to move to Europe, but also the perceptions of non-migrants.

The EUMAGINE project was based on a specific analytical framework which informed the project design (see Figure 1). Attempts to migrate to Europe are presumed to be preceded by the development of perceptions of human rights and democracy in Europe and in the home country, and aspirations to migrate. These aspirations could include very vague wishes to go to Europe or elsewhere, or more specific preferences in terms of destinations and modes of migration (e.g. through family reunification, family formation, temporary work programmes, asylum or illegal entry). Migration-related perceptions and aspirations develop within a specific cultural, political-juridical and economic setting, which has been referred to as 'the emigration environment' (Carling 2002), and which is equally important to research given that persons in an emigration environment have specific perceptions of human rights and democracy-related issues.

Three levels of explanation are identified in this project: the macro, meso and microlevels (Faist 2000, 30–35) (Figure 1). The macrolevel includes the factors that are common to all potential migrants, such as national policies on emigration and immigration, the overall economic and political situation in the country, the mass media, and the extent of human rights and democracy. The mesolevel encompasses the factors in-between the individual level and that of society at large (Goss and Lindquist 1995). Most important are the local and transnational networks through which people collect information and exchange ideas. Finally, the microlevel concerns characteristics of individuals, such as, among others, gender and political allegiance (Carlson and Listhaug 2007), but also age, educational attainment, labour market situation, political-juridical status and so on. An important force in the framework is the feedback arrow, stressing the dynamic nature of migration-related perceptions and aspirations. Each act of migration has an impact on the context in which subsequent migration decisions are made (Massey 1998).

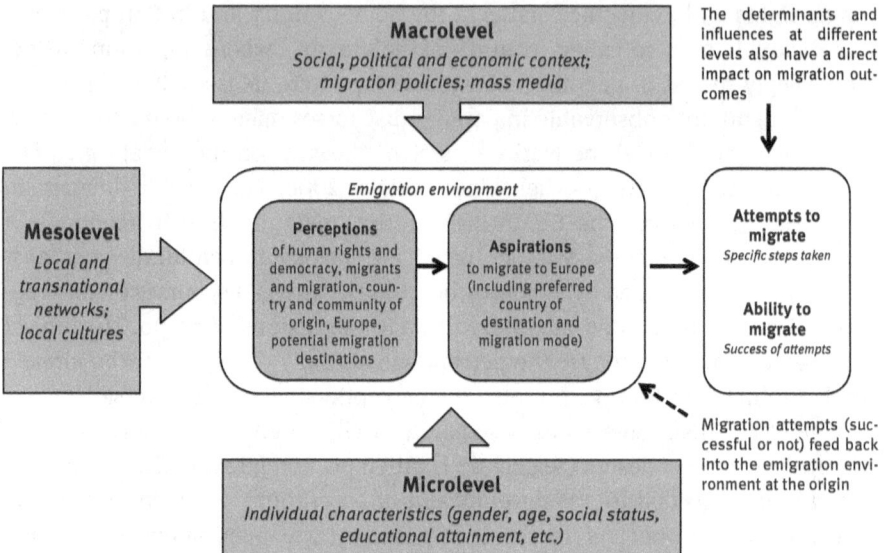

Figure 1: EUMAGINE conceptual framework (Source: Timmerman *et al.* 2010)

Two major assumptions underpin the core notion that macro and mesolevel discourses affect individual perceptions at the microlevel. First, it was assumed that these perceptions and aspirations are socially and culturally embedded – that is, largely influenced by the context in which they are structured. Within this framework, the main hypothesis was that policy, media and popular discourses on human rights and democracy have an impact on the imagination of migration as a valuable life project ('migratory imaginations') as well as on imaginations of specific destination countries ('geographical imaginations'). Second, it was hypothesized that these perceptions and imaginations correlate positively with migratory aspirations. Hence if attitudes towards and conceptions of immigration countries or regions are positive, they are more likely to feature in migration aspirations and to be chosen as migration destinations. Conversely, if individuals hold negative views of migration as a life project or of immigration destinations, they are less likely to aspire to migration or to opt for emigration to such places.

By assigning a potentially influential role in the shaping of migration aspirations to prospective migrants' perceptions, it was assumed that migrants' individual choices and their capacity to act upon their aspirations were also of importance. At the same time, it was fully acknowledged that various factors in the migration environment can interfere with the direct relationship between motivations and behaviour, including the existence of social networks, the availability of economic resources, trafficking and other migration-inducing factors. Therefore, while the agency of potential migrants was taken as a starting point for the research project, much attention was also paid to processes unfolding in their personal, direct environment.

4.2 Perceptions of Democracy and Human Rights versus Aspirations

Aiming to present a dynamic, non-Eurocentric analysis of the impact of perceptions of human rights and democracy on migration aspirations in important source countries, the EUMAGINE project focused, as stated earlier, in particular on the contribution of such perceptions to migration aspirations in emigration and so-called 'transit' regions outside the EU. Several themes were addressed: (1) the relation between perceptions among persons living in selected source countries of the human rights and democracy situation in the EU and in their own country and their migration aspirations; (2) the influence of human rights and democracy-related perceptions on migration compared with the effect of other migration determinants; and, (3) the extent to which migration is perceived as a valuable life project.

The project included four countries known to be important emigration countries to Europe and to have a specific human rights and democracy situation: Morocco, Turkey, Senegal and Ukraine. Each one is in and of itself a hub for immigration and so-called 'transit' migration, while emigration geared towards the EU and a variety of other countries continues. Except for Turkey, all three countries have negative net migration rates, and remittances constitute a significant share of the gross domestic product (GDP). Remittances are most prominent in Senegal, followed by Morocco and Ukraine, whereas in Turkey the share of remittances in GDP is only 0.15 per cent (Berriane et al. 2011; Demba Fall et al. 2011; Korfalı et al. 2011; Vollmer et al. 2011).[1]

---

[1] Aiming to gain insight into the diversity of perceptions, aspirations and motivations within each country, four types of research areas were chosen in each country. The research areas char-

A detailed questionnaire was developed over a ten-month period, including extensive pilot testing in each research area. Questions covered household migration histories, individual migration aspirations, perceptions of human rights and democracy, and a range of other topics. For the survey, a representative sample of 500 respondents aged 18–39 was identified within each of the 16 research areas, using a stratified cluster sample with random walks (Ersanilli 2012, 3–11).[2] In order to perform statistical analysis, the data were weighted to account for differences in the selection probability of respondents.[3]

The qualitative data collection took place among 320 informants (80 for each of the four countries, 20 in each research area), through in-depth semi-structured interviews. There was a purposeful selection of respondents according to gender, age, occupational status, migration experience and migration aspirations (De Clerck et al. 2011; De Clerck 2012).

The dependent variable in the quantitative analysis was the aspiration to migrate to Europe. In the survey conducted in the EUMAGINE project, respondents were asked whether they wanted to migrate to another country ("Ideally, if you had the opportunity, would you like to go abroad to live or work?"). In a follow-up question, respondents who said that they have aspirations to migrate to an-

---

acterized by high-emigration rates were Todgha Valley in Morocco, Emirdağ in Turkey, Darou Mousty in Senegal and Zbarazh Rayon in Ukraine; the research areas economically similar but with low emigration rates were the Central Plateau in Morocco, Dinar in Turkey, Lambaye in Senegal and Znamyanska Rayon in Ukraine; the research areas with a strong immigration history were Tangiers in Morocco, Fatih in Turkey, Golf Sud in Senegal and Solomyansky rayon in Ukraine; and finally the research areas with a specific human rights situation were Tounfite in Morocco, Van Merkez in Turkey, Orkadiéré in Senegal and Novovodolaz'ka Rayon in Ukraine.
2 A representative sample was selected of 500 respondents within the 16 research areas (8000 respondents in total), limited to those between 18 and 39 years old because this cohort is most likely to perceive emigration as a possibility. A stratified cluster sample with random walks was used, with research areas first being stratified according to a rural-urban dimension and sub-counties, and interviews subsequently distributed according to the size of the strata. More specifically, 50 batches of 10 interviews were distributed in each research area according to the relative size of the strata (Ersanilli et al. 2011, 58) while a list of clusters (neighbourhoods, villages) was made for each stratum. After deciding on the number of clusters in each stratum, batches of 10 interviews were sampled in fixed intervals (Ersanilli et al. 2011, 39, 59–63; Ersanilli 2012, 9, 15). A random walk was carried out to select households. Within selected households (defined as "all persons who live under the same roof, normally eat together and have communal arrangements concerning subsistence and other necessities of life") respondents were randomly chosen (Ersanilli 2012, 11–17). The selected respondents were questioned face-to-face in the first half of 2011 with structured paper and pencil questionnaires. The selection of respondents in the research areas continued until 500 interviews were completed (Ersanilli 2012, 8–9, 19–20).
3 A selection probability weight was calculated for the within-household selection for each stratum (Ersanilli 2012, 26).

other country were also asked to which country they would prefer to go. The combination of these two questions resulted in a variable that measures the migration aspirations to Europe. Europe appeared to be the chosen destination of most individuals covered by this study.[4]

As already noted, the variables of interest in our quantitative analysis are the perceptions of the human rights situation in their own country versus the perceptions of the same in Europe, with the concept of human rights used being a broad one, including equality between men and women, poverty reduction measures by the government, the quality of health care and of schools, and also job opportunities. Several questions in the survey measured the *perception of human rights and democracy in Europe and their own country* (five questions for Europe and five questions for their own country)[5]: people were asked to express an opinion on whether they considered the equality between men and women, access to schools, quality of health care and governmental poverty reduction policies in their own country to be (very) good or (very) bad. The questions measuring the perception of human rights and democracy in Europe are coded from 0 (very bad) to 4 (very good). The questions measuring the perception of human rights and democracy in their own country are coded from 0 (very good) to 4 (very bad).

Another variable of interest tapping into the concept of broad human rights is the perception of job opportunities in Europe. This was measured with a statement whether or not according to the respondent 'it is easy to find a good job in Europe'. The answer was coded as one of five options: strongly disagree (0), disagree (1), neither agree nor disagree (2), agree (3) to strongly agree (4). People were also asked whether 'it is easy to find a good job in their country'. The answer was coded as one of five options: strongly agree (0), agree (1), neither agree nor disagree (2), disagree (3) to strongly disagree (4).

In addition, various variables controlling for socio-demographic characteristics of individuals were included, because they were considered very likely to have a significant link with migration aspirations and are therefore theoretically relevant: age, marital status, children, family migration experience, gender,

---

[4] The following countries are referred to as 'Europe' in this article: Austria, Belgium, Bulgaria, Belarus, Croatia, Cyprus, Czech Republic, Denmark, Europe, Finland, France, Germany, Greece, Hungary, Iceland, Ireland, Italy, Latvia, Lithuania, Luxembourg, Netherlands, Norway, Poland, Portugal, Romania, Russia, Slovakia, Spain, Sweden, Switzerland, the UK, Ukraine and Western Europe.

[5] The Cronbach alpha for the scale measuring human rights and democracy in Europe was 0.74. The Cronbach alpha or the internal consistency of the scale measuring these perceptions in their own country was 0.75.

years of education and material wealth (e.g. Carling 2002; Timmerman, De Clerck, Hemmerechts and Willems 2013b; Timmerman, Hemmerechts and De Clerck 2013a).[6]

For the qualitative data gathering, an interview guide had been developed as an instrument for the researchers, to ensure that none of the important issues to be discussed was left out of the conversation. The interview guide covered four pre-determined main topics: perceptions of life in the locality; perceptions of migration; imaginations of Europe; and personal migration aspirations. For each topic, suggested opening questions and a list of sub-topics was formulated. The interviews were recorded on tape and later transcribed, translated into English or French, and finally entered into NVivo and coded using a preset coding tree (De Clerck et al. 2011; De Clerck 2012).

---

[6] *Age* is a continuous variable measuring the age of respondents. We mean-centred the variable for the whole sample. A number of respondents in our sample were younger than 18 or older than 39. These were excluded from our analysis (119 respondents, including two missing). The *marital status* variable is coded 1 when respondents were unmarried, divorced, widowed or separated and coded 0 when respondents were married/monogamous, married/polygamous or living with partner/not married. The *children* variable is a dichotomous variable measuring whether respondents have at least one child (coded as 0). The variable is coded 1 when there are no children. In order to measure *family migration experience*, respondents had to indicate whether they "have any family members above 16 years old who are currently living in another country and who have been in contact with you at least once over the past 12 months." It is important to note that respondents also indicated whether they had recent contact with these family members or not. The variable was coded dichotomous (0 means no family migration experience, 1 means family migration experience). The *gender* variable has male as category 1 and female as category 0. The *years of education* variable is coded as 0 (no education, only Koranic school, only basic literacy or national language), 1 (pre-school in Morocco, Turkey and Senegal), primary school-old system in Turkey (1–5), primary education in Morocco and Senegal (2–7), primary school in Ukraine (1–4), lower secondary education in Morocco and Senegal (8–11), secondary school in Ukraine (5–9), upper secondary education in Morocco and Senegal (12–14), upper secondary school in Ukraine (until 2001) (5–11), upper secondary school (since 2001) (5–12), higher education in Morocco and Senegal (15–22), primary school in Turkey (2–9), lower secondary school-old system in Turkey (6–8), higher vocational school in Turkey (9–11), upper secondary school-old system in Turkey (10–12), upper secondary school-old system in Turkey (10–13), vocational school or ПТУ (10–13), polytechnic (until 2001) in Ukraine (11–14), polytechnic (since 2001) in Ukraine (13–16), university or polytechnic in Turkey (14–17), university in Ukraine (until 2001) in Ukraine (11–15), university (since 2001) in Ukraine or doctorate in Turkey and Ukraine (18–23). Furthermore, we created an index measuring the *material poverty* of respondents as a variable with principal component analysis (varimax rotation with Kaiser Normalization). The scale goes from high to low material wealth (0 to 4). The scale is internally consistent: the Cronbach alpha of the material poverty index computed for all countries together is 0.86. Finally, the *four countries* were coded in dummy variables: one for Morocco, Turkey, Senegal and one for Ukraine. We analysed the quantitative data with SPSS 21.

5 The Impact of Perceptions of Human Rights and Democracy on Migration Aspirations: Main Results

5.1 Insights Stemming from the Qualitative Data Collection

The qualitative cross-country data analysis revealed a general tendency among informants from Morocco, Senegal, Turkey and Ukraine to perceive the level of corruption in their own country much more negatively than corruption levels in Europe – that is, they regarded corruption to be far less common or even almost non-existent in Europe. There was a broad consensus among informants in Ukraine that horizontal and vertical corruption is widespread in their country. They often associated corruption with access to work, health care and education.[7]

> Now let's move on to the issue of corruption. This question may seem rather direct, but do you believe corruption is a problem here [in Ukraine]? Of course it is. It's everywhere, all around us. Even in hospitals we're told: buy us this or that, and we'll do what you want us to do. (Ukraine, Low Emigration Research Area, male, 23–30 age group, with migration aspirations)

The perception that there is widespread corruption in the home country and none, or far less, in Europe was shared by most of the informants interviewed in Turkey, Senegal and Morocco.

> Is there corruption here in Tinerhir? You can do nothing without corruption in Morocco, and especially in Tinerhir, because when you wait your turn in one of the government offices to get a document, you can see persons that come in later, yet, they go directly to the civil servant by jumping the queue because they know him or someone else in the office. The root of corruption is with the citizens themselves and with the civil servants. Because when you give *bakchich* to a civil servant, and someone else gives *bakchich* as well, that is how corruption is stimulated. The civil servants get used to receiving money before doing anything. (Morocco, High Emigration Research Area, male, 23–30 age group, with migration aspirations)

By contrast, views about the prevalence of corruption in Europe are more optimistic:

---

[7] The quotes in this chapter are translated from French (for Morocco and Senegal), Turkish and Ukrainian.

> These days you hear about insecurity, corruption, criminality ... do you think these things exist in Europe? No, from what I know, corruption, criminality and insecurity are much more present here in Africa then in Europe. In Europe, security is taken care of. (Senegal, Human Rights Research Area, male, 23–30 age group, without migration aspirations)

As mentioned before, human rights in the EUMAGINE project were not solely perceived in terms of political rights (corruption, safety and security, democracy, etc.), but also in terms of socioeconomic and cultural rights, such as quality of and access to social security, health care and education (De Clerck et al. 2012). Informants in all four research countries tended to perceive educational opportunities in their own country more negatively than those in Europe. Moreover, positive perceptions of educational opportunities in Europe (for either the informants themselves or for their children) were commonly cited as a reason for migrating to Europe, as illustrated by the following interview extract from Morocco:

> Which other motives may people have to migrate? Those who wish to ensure a good education for their children, take them abroad. Because, their schools are really well developed and equipped. (Morocco, High Emigration Research Area, female, 18–22 age group, without migration aspirations)

Qualitative data analysis illustrates that perceptions of educational opportunities in Europe are not the only factors in play, and that perceptions of gender equality in the home country and in Europe are deemed important as well. In general, gender equality was perceived to be less present at home than in Europe. Interview data from a number of informants show that a more positive perception of gender equality in Europe than in the home country was often cited as an incentive for migration to Europe.

> And over there in Europe, are men and women equal? Yes, there men and women are equal. Because a woman can do the same thing as a man. There, women are not beaten, they are not humiliated. Nor are the children. Yes, ... she is equal over there. Yes, sure, life is the same for men and for women there. Because they have the same rights. (Senegal, Low Emigration Research Area, female, 23–30 age group, with migration aspirations)

Interestingly, male informants appeared to largely share this perception of gender equality being greater in Europe than in their own country:

> Could you tell me something about the equality between men and women in Europe? Women in Europe find themselves in a good situation, she has the same rights as men, there is equality between the sexes. The situation of the woman over there is better than the situation of the Moroccan woman; she is well educated because of historical, economic and so-

cial reasons. Women in Europe can have the same job as men, maybe better even. Because over here, there is not yet sufficient confidence in the capability of women. (Morocco, High Emigration Research Area, male, 23–30 age group, with migration aspirations)

Clearly, the qualitative data analyses yielded new insights that, in turn, required closer scrutiny. They showed that migration aspirations are affected not only by perceptions of corruption levels but also by perceptions of specific other human rights and democracy-related aspects – in other words, educational opportunities and equal gender opportunities also impact positively on migration aspirations.

5.2 Insights Stemming from the Quantitative Analyses

Of the 8,000 respondents in the four countries, 3,605 reported having aspirations to migrate to Europe (compared with 3,629 who expressed no migration aspirations, the remainder aspiring to migrate elsewhere (720 respondents) or representing missing data (46 respondents) (weighted data).[8] By country, the results read as follows: in Morocco, 1,113 reported having aspirations to migrate to Europe (compared with 835 who expressed no migration aspirations, 51 respondents aspiring to migrate elsewhere and the rest missing); in Turkey, 644 respondents have migration aspirations to Europe (compared with 1,203 with no migration aspirations, 146 with migration aspirations to elsewhere and the rest missing); in Senegal, 519 respondents have no migration aspirations, 1,178 respondents have migration aspirations to Europe and 301 respondents have migration aspirations to elsewhere; in Ukraine, 1,072 respondents have no migration aspirations, 670 respondents have migration aspirations to Europe and 222 respondents have migration aspirations to elsewhere.

In the following analysis, we wish to investigate whether perceptions of human rights and democracy, as well as perceptions of job opportunities, are important to understand migration aspirations to Europe. In other words, are economic or democratic/human rights reasons important drivers of migration aspirations and, if so, which one is more important. Therefore, in the following model we do not take into account those aspiring to migrate to somewhere other than Europe (Table 1, n = 7127, unweighted total). Turkish respondents turn out to be least likely to aspire to migration to Europe, followed by respond-

---

[8] Individuals who reported a desire to migrate to a destination other than Europe were excluded from this part of the analysis.

Table 1: Migration aspirations to Europe: odds ratios and significance (Source: individual questionnaire (STUM20121001); weighted data)

	Model 1	
Variables	Odds ratio	Significance
Turkey	0.68	0.00
Senegal	2.16	0.00
Ukraine	0.84	0.06
Increasing material poverty	1.27	0.00
Age	0.98	0.00
Unmarried	1.54	0.00
No children	1.23	0.01
Gender	1.49	0.00
Family migration experience	1.47	0.00
Years of education	1.07	0.00
Years of education^2	0.996	0.00
Human rights & democracy in their own country	1.31	0.00
Human rights & democracy in Europe	1.44	0.00
Perception on job opportunities in their own country	1.19	0.00
Perception on job opportunities in Europe	1.16	0.00
Intercept	0.03	0.00

ents living in the Ukraine, Morocco and Senegal.[9] Looking more closely at the role of positive versus negative perceptions of the situation of human rights and democracy in Europe with regard to migration aspirations, we notice the following. Table 1 illustrates that respondents with a one-unit increase on the European human rights and democracy scale are 1.44 times more likely (in odds) to have migration aspirations to Europe than respondents with a more negative perception of European human rights and democracy (a one-unit increase on this scale indicates a more positive perception). A similar observation can be made by comparing the impact of positive versus negative perceptions of job opportunities in Europe on migration aspirations. In model 1, respondents with a one-

---

[9] We took Morocco as the reference category, yet taking Ukraine as the reference category resulted in the same conclusion. In a previous model, citizenship, other nationalities and the possession of a residence permit for another country were also included. These three variables did not have a significant effect on migration aspirations to Europe in the full model and were therefore excluded from the above model. We imputed all missing values with the multiple imputation technique (producing 10 imputed datasets) (Enders 2010). Only the missing values on the variable that measures age were not imputed because they were put as missing deliberately (people aged approximately less than 18 or more than 39 years).

unit increase on the European job opportunities scale are 1.16 times more likely (in odds) to have migration aspirations to Europe than respondents with a more negative perception of European job opportunities.[10]

This finding demonstrates not only that perceptions of human rights (defined as equality between men and women, quality of schools, access to health care and governmental poverty reduction policies) among respondents living in the selected research areas in Senegal, Turkey, Morocco and Ukraine are important in understanding migration aspirations, it also shows that these positive perceptions of human rights and democracy in Europe have a stronger relationship with – and thus play a larger role in – migration aspirations than perceptions of job opportunities in Europe.

6 Conclusion

Under the EUMAGINE project, the hypothesis was formulated that migration aspirations are affected by perceptions of democracy and human rights – broadly defined – while controlling for other relevant factors that are situated at the macro, meso and/or microlevels. Based on the analyses of data collected in accordance with quantitative and qualitative methodologies, we were able to confirm our hypothesis. As expected, migration aspirations are codetermined by additional factors situated at different social or societal levels. The EUMAGINE results demonstrate the importance of perceptions of human rights in explaining migration aspirations. They show that men and women are motivated not only by the economic opportunities that may come with migration but also, and more importantly, by perceptions of educational opportunities, access to health infrastructure, gender equality and governmental poverty reduction measures. There is a widespread view that political, economic and social rights are better guaranteed in Europe and that such free access to job opportunities, education or decent health is a precondition for the individual 'pursuit of happiness.' All in all, the results show how people coming from various cultural and religious backgrounds imagine themselves as having equal rights to any other human being, even though they were born in countries where the conditions needed to enjoy these rights are not always present. The global imaginary of human rights, which has now spread all over the globe, fuels the aspiration to migrate

---

10 In a previous model, citizenship, other nationalities and the possession of a residence permit for another country were also included (De Clerck et al. 2012). These three variables did not have a significant effect on migration aspirations to Europe in the full model and were therefore excluded from the above model.

to countries where rights are well-protected. Although the effective ability to migrate or move is highly unequally distributed, the human rights imaginary enables individuals to see mobility and the 'pursuit of happiness' as an inalienable right of every human being. To the extent that people see migration as a legitimate channel to gain access to democratic institutions, jobs and education, the imaginary association of Europe with human rights hence continues to impact and feed into the willingness and aspiration to migrate.

Bibliography

Alston, Philip, ed. 1999. *The EU and Human Rights*. Oxford: Oxford University Press.
Anderson, Christopher J., Patrick M. Regan, and Robert L. Ostergard. 2002. "Political Repression and Public Perceptions of Human Rights." *Political Research Quarterly*, 2:439–456.
Battistella, Graziano, 2005. *Human Rights of Migrants*. Quezon City: SMC.
Berriane, Mohamed, Mohammed Aderghal, Lahoucine Amzil and Abdellah Oussi. 2011. *Morocco Country and Research Areas Report*, EUMAGINE Project Paper 4, http://www.eumagine.org/outputs/PP4%20-%20Morocco%20Country%20and%20Research%20Areas%20Report%20-%20Final.pdf, accessed on 31 January 2013.
Bielefeldt, Heiner. 2006. "The Liberal Concept of Political Secularism." In *Between Cosmopolitan Ideals and State Sovereignty*, edited by Ronald Tinnevelt and Gert Verschraegen, 99–108. New York: Palgrave MacMillan.
Bommes, Michael. 2012. "Migration in Modern Society." In *Immigration and Social Systems. Collected Essays of Michael Bommes*, edited by Christina Boswell and Gianni D'Amato, 19–36. Amsterdam: Amsterdam University Press.
Boneva, Bonka S., and Irene Hanson Frieze. 2001. "Toward a Concept of a Migrant Personality." *Journal of Social Issues*, 57:477–491.
Bosniak, Linda. 2006. *The Citizen and the Alien: Dilemmas of Contemporary Membership*. Princeton: Princeton University Press.
Caloz-Tschopp, Marie-Claire, and Pierre Dasen, eds. 2007. *Mondialisation, Migration et Droits de l'Homme: Un Nouveau Paradigme Pour la Recherche et la Citoyenneté. Globalization, Migration and Human Rights: A New Paradigm for Research and Citizenship (Volume I and II)*. Brussels: Bruylant.
Carling, Jørgen. 2002. "Migration in the Age of Involuntary Immobility: Theoretical Reflections and Cape Verdian Experiences." *Journal of Ethnic and Migration Studies*, 1:5–42.
Carlson, Matthew, and Ola Listhaug. 2007. "Citizens' Perceptions of Human Rights Practices: An Analysis of 55 Countries." *Journal of Peace Research*, 4:465–483.
Checkel, Jeffrey.T. and Peter J. Katzenstein, 2009. "The politicization of European identities." In *European Identity*, edited by Jeffrey T. Checkel and Peter J. Katzenstein, 1–23. Cambridge: Cambridge University Press.
Christiansen, Thomas, Knud Erik Jørgensen and Antje Wiener. 2001. *The Social Construction of Europe*. London: Sage.
Christoffersen, Jonas, and Mikael R. Madsen, eds. 2011. *The European Court of Human Rights between Law and Politics*. Oxford: Oxford University Press.

Cohen, Joshua 2004. "Minimalism about human rights: The most we can hope for?" *The Journal of Political Philosophy*, 12:190–213.
Collyer, Michael. 2006. *How does a Culture of Migration Affect Motivations for Migration?* Paper presented at the IMISCOE conference on Poverty, Vulnerability and Migration Choice. Geneva, 18–19 May 2006.
De Clerck, Helene Marie-Lou. 2012. *First Qualitative Analysis*, EUMAGINE Project Paper 8, http://www.eumagine.org/outputs/Project%20Paper%208%20-%20First%20qualitative%20data%20analysis.pdf, accessed on 2 February 2013.
De Clerck, Helene Marie-Lou, Roos Willems, Christiane Timmerman, and Jorgen Carling. 2011. *Instruments and Guidelines for Qualitative Fieldwork*, EUMAGINE Project Paper 6B, http://www.eumagine.org/outputs/PP6B%20Instruments%20and%20guidelines%20for%20qualitative%20fieldwork.pdf, accessed on 3 March 2013.
De Haas, Hein. 2009. *Mobility and Human Development*. New York: United Nations Development Program.
De Haas, Hein. 2010. "The Internal Dynamics of Migration Processes: A Theoretical Inquiry." *Journal of Ethnic and Migration Studies*, 10:1587–1617.
De Teyssier, François and Gilles Baudier. 2006. *La Construction de l'Europe*. Paris: Presses Universitaires de France.
Demba, Papa Fall, María Hernández Carretero and Mame Yassine Sarr. 2011. *Senegal Country and Research Areas Report*, EUMAGINE Project Paper 2, http://www.eumagine.org/outputs/PP2%20-%20Senegal%20Country%20and%20Research%20Areas%20Report%20-%20Final.pdf, accessed on 5 May 2013.
Efionayi-Mäder, Denise, Milena Chimienti, Janine Dahinden and Etienne Piguet. 2001. *Asyldestination Europa – Eine Geographie der Asylbewegungen*. Zürich: Seismo.
Enders, Craig K. 2010. *Applied Missing Data Analyses*. New York: Guilford Press.
Ersanilli, Evelyn. 2012. *Survey Report*, EUMAGINE Project Paper 7, http://www.eumagine.org/outputs/PP7%20-%20survey%20report%20-%2020121001.pdf, accessed 6 June 2013.
Ersanilli, Evelyn, Jorg Carling and Hein De Haas. 2011. *Methodology for Quantitative Data Collection*, EUMAGINE Project Paper 6 A, http://www.eumagine.org/outputs/PP6 A%20Methodology%20for%20quantitative%20data%20collection%20-%20Final%20version.pdf, accessed on 7 July 2013.
Faist, Thomas. 2000. *The Volume and Dynamics of International Migration and Transnational Social Spaces*. Oxford: Oxford University Press.
Glendon, Marie-Ann. 2001. *A World Made New: Eleanor Roosevelt and the Universal Declaration of Human Rights*. New York: Random House.
Goss, Jon, and Bruce Lindquist. 1995. "Conceptualizing International Labor Migration: A Structuration Perspective." *International Migration Review*, 29:317–351.
Gregory, David. 2000. "Discourse." In *The Dictionary of Human Geography*, edited by Derek Gregory, Ron Johnston, Geraldine Pratt, Michael Watts, Sarah Whatmore, 166–167. Oxford: Blackwell.
Jacobson, David. 1997. *Rights Across Borders: Immigration and the Decline of Citizenship*. Baltimore MD: John Hopkins University Press.
Joppke, Christian. 2010. *Citizenship and Immigration*. Cambridge: Polity Press.
Korfalı, Deniz Karcı, Ayşen Üstübici and Helene Marie-Lou De Clerck. 2011. *Turkey Country and Research Areas Report*, EUMAGINE Project Paper 5, http://www.eumagine.org/out

puts/PP5 %20-%20Turkey%20Country%20and%20Research%20Areas%20Report%20-%20Final.pdf, accessed on 8 August 2013.
Koser, Khalid and Charles Pinkerton. 2004. *The Social Networks of Asylum Seekers and the Dissemination of Information About Countries of Asylum.* London: University College London.
Malmborg, Mikael Af, and Bo Stråth. 2002. *The Meaning of Europe: Variety and Contention Within and Among Nations.* Oxford: Berg.
Massey, Douglas S. 1998. "Contemporary Theories of International Migration." In *Worlds in Motion – Understanding International Migration at the End of the Millennium*, edited by Douglas S. Massey, Joaquin Arango, Graeme Hugo, Ali Kouaouci, Adela Pellegrino and J. Edward Taylor, 17–59. Oxford: Clarendon Press.
Madsen Mikael R., and Gert Verschraegen. 2013. "Making Human Rights Intelligible: An Introduction to Sociology of Human Rights." In *Making Human Rights Intelligible: Towards a Sociology of Human Rights*, edited by Mikael R. Madsen and Gert Verschraegen, 61–80. Oxford: Hart Publishing.
Meyer, John W., John Boli, George M. Thomas, and Francisco O. Ramirez. 1997. "World Society and the Nation-State." *American Journal of Sociology* 103:144–181.
Morris, Lydia. 2010. *Asylum, Welfare and the Cosmopolitan Ideal: A Sociology of Rights.* London: Routledge.
Morris, Lydia. 2013. *Human Rights and Social Theory*, New York: Palgrave MacMillan.
Morsink, Johannes. 1999. *The Universal Declaration of Human Rights: Origins, Drafting and Intent.* Philadelphia: University of Pennsylvania Press.
Moyn, Samuel. 2010. *The Last Utopia: Human Rights in History.* Cambridge, MA: Belknap Press.
O'Byrne, David. 2012. "On the Sociology of Human Rights: Theorising the Language-Structure of Rights." (Special Issue, The Sociology of Human Rights), *Sociology*, 46:829–843.
Pang, Ching Lin. 2007. "Chinese Migration to Belgium." In *Migration in a New Europe: People, Borders and Trajectories in the Enlarged EU*, edited by Ton van Naerssen, 87–110. Rome: International Geographical Union.
Schirmer, Jennifer. 1999. *The Guatemalan Military Project: A Violence Called Democracy*, Philadelphia: University of Pennsylvania Press.
Shamir, Ron. 2005. "Without Borders? Notes on Globalization as a Mobility Regime." *Sociological Theory*, 23:197–217.
Soysal, Yasmine. 1994. *Limits of Citizenship.* Chicago: University of Chicago Press.
Stråth, Bo. 2006. "Future of Europe." *Journal of Language and Politics*, 3:427–449.
Taylor, Charles. 2004. *Modern Social Imaginaries.* Durham: Duke University Press.
Timmerman, Christiane. 2008. "Marriage in a 'Culture of Migration': Emirdag Marrying into Flanders." *European Review*, 4:585–594.
Timmerman, Christiane, Petra Heyse and Christophe Van Mol. 2010. *Conceptual and Theoretical Framework Eumagine Research Project*, EUMAGINE Project Paper 1, http://www.eumagine.org/outputs/PP1%20-%20Conceptual%20and%20Theoretical%20Framework.pdf accessed on 9 September 2013.
Timmerman, Christiane, Kenneth Hemmerechts, and Helene Marie-Lou De Clerck. 2013a. *The Relevance of a 'Culture of Migration' in Understanding Migration Aspirations in Contemporary Turkey.* Paper presented at the Workshop: Aspirations and Capabilities in Migration Processes, convened by Jørgen Carling (PRIO), Mathias Czaika (IMI), and Hein

de Haas (IMI), January, http://www.imi.ox.ac.uk/workshop-aspirations-and-capabilities-in-migration-processes, accessed on 10 October 2013.

Timmerman, Christiane, Kenneth Hemmerechts, and Helene Marie-Lou De Clerck. 2013b. *The Relevance of 'Feedback Mechanisms' in Migration Impacted Regions in Relation with Changing Macro Socio-Economic Contexts. A Case Study on Moroccan and Turkish Emigration Regions*. Conference paper. Presented at the THEMIS conference "Examining Migration Dynamics: Networks and Beyond," Oxford University, 24–26 September.

Vollmer, Bastian, Yuriy Bilan, Iryna Lapshyna and SvetlanaVdovtsova. 2011. *Ukraine Country and Research Areas Report*, EUMAGINE Project Paper 3, http://www.eumagine.org/outputs/PP3%20-%20Ukraine%20Country%20and%20Research%20Areas%20Report.pdf, accessed on 11 November 2013.

Wilson, John and Sharon Millar. 2007. "Introduction." In *The Discourse of Europe: Talk and Text in Everyday Life*, edited by Sharon Millar and John Wilson, 1–16. Amsterdam: John Benjamins.

Ernst van den Hemel
Post-Secular Nationalism

The Dutch Turn to the Right & Cultural-Religious Reframing of Secularity

1 Introduction

When Geert Wilders wrote an open letter to Pope Francis in 2013, he not only reiterated well-worn images of the religious domineering Islam hovering threateningly over a vulnerable secular Western Europe, the Dutch populist politician also suggested that the modern secular values of tolerance and the separation of Church and State were the result of the "West's Christian Heritage" (Wilders 2013). He went on to make the corollary claim that it was necessary for "atheists and Christians" to unite in the struggle against Islam. This conflation of religion and secularity is part of a wider tendency in Western European right-wing populism. Although it is well known that these populist parties pit a secular self against the religious intolerance of 'others,' it is considerably less studied in what manner this discourse reframes the role secularity and religion play in the imagination of Western European nation states. Whether it is the PVV's insistence that atheism is a Christian value, PEGIDA's defense of the secular 'christlich-jüdisches Abendland' ('Judeo-Christian West'), Front National's insistence on *laïcité* as a hallmark of Christian culture, or UKIP's 'Christian Manifesto,' contemporary populism in Western Europe not only emphasizes the opposition between the secular West and Islam, it also focusses on the religious dimension of the secular West itself.

In this article I focus on the role of religion in populist constructions of secular national identity. At the moment of writing, populist right wing parties are in the process of garnering electoral and popular success in the Netherlands, Great Britian, Belgium and France. These parties challenge classical divides between progressive and conservative politics (cf. Oudenampsen 2018), but also between secular and religious divides (cf. Van den Hemel 2014). Particularly, I will argue in this article that a major aspect of populist discourse in Western Europe is not its theoretical or ideological coherence, but rather its attempt to reframe the backdrop against which religiosity and secularity are imagined. A major hypothesis of this paper is that Charles Taylor's notion of the social imaginary offers a productive approach to analyze this dimension of populist discourse.

I will first set the scene by describing some of the paradoxical effects of these discursive practices. After which I will address how Taylor's notion of the social imaginary might be better suited to approach the reframing of religion and secularity than other approaches that have been dominant in the analysis of the PVV. After having crafted a conceptual definition of 'post-secular nationalism,' I will elaborate on the two parts of this equation ('post-secular' and 'nationalist') by focusing on post-secular debates, I will illustrate how populist discourse challenges certain assumptions behind Taylor's approach to secularity. I will conclude by specifying the freshly coined definition of post-secular nationalism by comparing it to civil religion, speculating on the effects this discourse has for the imagination of national communities.

2 Setting the Scene: Atheism as a Sign of Judeo-Christian Superiority?

The Netherlands is often seen, by others but also by its inhabitants, as the epitome of secular, progressive, tolerant, pluriform nationhood (cf. Gregory 2013). The Netherlands is currently going through what commentators have called "a turn to the right" (cf. Mudde 2007). At the moment of writing, the Freedom Party (PVV) is the second largest party in the Netherlands. Notorious for a harsh stance on Islam and its concern with defending the cultural identity of Western-European societies, the PVV has been a forerunner in 21st century nationalist discourse. This development seems to be radically at odds with the image of the Netherlands as a progressive tolerant country. Commentators have identified a variety of backgrounds to these forms of nationalist discourse in the Netherlands, including the arrival, through migration, of religiously conservative newcomers in a secularized country (Buruma 2006; Aalberts 2012), a response to globalization and economic crisis (Barr 2009; Moffitt 2015) and the eternal appeal of manipulative, nihilist fascist-like discourse (Riemen 2010; Schaap 2012; Hainsworth 2008). In the study of Dutch and Western European populism the role of religion in secular national self-identification has been somewhat overlooked. For instance, a recent major literature review, outlining the major tenets in the study of populism does not mention religion and secularity in depth (Gidron and Bonikowski 2013). Approaches to the PVV, when they do mention phrases like 'Judeo-Christian' usually emphasize its paradoxical nature (Wallet 2012). As a result, an important dimension of PVV discourse has been somewhat overlooked. Let us sketch some examples:

In 2006, the PVV suggested to replace article 1 in the Dutch constitution (which outlaws discrimination) with an article that proclaims the primacy of 'judeo-christian-humanist tradition' in the Netherlands (PVV 2006). In parliament, the PVV explained its proposal by referring to the secular values that are anchored in Judeo-Christian roots: "separation of Church and State, the notion that man is the measure of all things, and the right to life and freedom in the present" (PVV 2006). In the explanation of this proposal, the PVV stated that it is only through an insistence on the cultural roots of Dutch culture that progressive accomplishments can be safeguarded. This proposal explicitly seeks to replace a juridical codification of equality with an emphasis on the cultural identity which is needed for this equality to function. 'Judeo-Christianity' functions here not as a reference to the practice of believers, but as a backdrop against which shared practices characteristic of Dutch culture became possible.

In 2010, prominent PVV-member Martin Bosma published his take on contemporary Dutch society: *De Schijn-Elite van de Valsemunters*. In his book Bosma states that: "Dutch citizens should cherish above all the Christian background of his country. Almost all our crucial accomplishments are connected to Christianity. Democracy, separation of Church and State, tolerance, but also values such as a work-ethic and efficiency. Those of us who have read Max Webers *The Spirit of Capitalism* know that our economic successes are linked to Christianity." (Bosma 2010, 68)[1]

Bosma concludes that *"the PVV is now the second largest Christian party of the Netherlands"* (69, italics mine). Again, presenting the PVV as a Christian party is somewhat of an innovation in the Dutch political landscape. For there are important differences between Christian-Democrats and PVV politicians. First of all, whereas traditional Christian Democrat parties tend to focus on issues such as family values, PVV claims atheism, gay marriage and feminism as accomplishments of Dutch Judeo-Christian culture. Secondly, there is a clearer link between faith and Christian-inspired politics in Christian-Democrat politics. This point was reiterated recently, in the general debate of the Dutch parliament for 2016. Wilders stated that the influx of Syrian refugees meant the cultural suicide of Christian values, and he was questioned by a number of Christian Democrat politicians about these Christian values. Asked why the references to Chris-

---

[1] "Met weinig zaken mag de Nederlander blijer zijn dan met de christelijke achtergrond van zijn land. Bijna al onze cruciale verworvenheden hebben een relatie met het Christendom. Democractie, scheiding van kerk en staat, tolerantie, maar ook waarden als vlijt en efficiency. Wie Max Webers *De geest van het kapitalisme en de protestantse ethiek* heeft gelezen weet dat ook onez economische successen een direct verband hebben met het Christendom." (Bosma 2010, 68).

tian values differ so much from what is usually understood by them, the PVV stated "one doesn't need to be Christian in order to cherish Christian values, millions of Dutch people do so."[2] These references to the Christian and Judeo-Christian background of the Netherlands have a number of things in common: secular values are associated with a religious-cultural background, progressive accomplishments are reframed as dependent on a culturalized religious identity, and a definition of religion is used which is no longer separate from secularity, but rather seems to be an integral part of it.

This takes place against the backdrop of a wider return of religious-cultural identification in Dutch society. Important precursors to the Dutch turn to the right, populist pioneer Pim Fortuyn and liberal Frits Bolkestein have referenced the importance of the religious-cultural roots of secularity (cf. Van den Hemel 2014). For instance, in an influential lecture, often seen as a starting point of the Dutch turn to the right, liberal politician Frits Bolkestein stated: "(...) humanism and Christianity have, after a long history that includes many black pages, brought forth a number of fundamentally important political principles, like the separation of Church and State, freedom of speech, tolerance and non-discrimination," Bolkestein proceeds to outline the necessity of a tougher standpoint on immigration and integration (Bolkestein 1992). In 2009, Bolkestein stated:

> The shared myth [of Christianity] is gone. And now the question is whether we can function without that myth. (...) we can say: 'hurray! We are no longer Christian!' but I wonder whether that attitude will be sufficient. I'm afraid not. Some intellectuals converted to Catholicism for that reason. For me that would be too artificial, because I am not a religious person, but culturally speaking, I am most certainly Christian. (Bolkestein 2009)

Similarly, Pim Fortuyn stated: "Problems concerning integration and mutual acceptance are centered on the relation between the dominant Judeo-Christian humanistic culture on the one hand and Islamic culture on the other. I consciously speak in the broad terminology of culture rather than of religion. One can leave a religion, as we can see happening massively in our country, a culture however, one cannot leave behind." (Fortuyn 2002, 83). In even wider circles, this discursive joining fits a seldomly highlighted dimension of the rhetoric with which conflicts between 'the West' and 'Islam' is outlined. For instance, already in Samuel Huntington's *A Clash of Civilizations?* we can find the following central quote (which is a paraphrase of Bernard Lewis): "This is no less than a clash of civilizations – the perhaps irrational but surely historic reaction of an ancient

---

[2] https://www.youtube.com/watch?v=TA7AyqBsJyg

rival against our Judeo-Christian heritage, our secular present, and the worldwide expansion of both" (Huntington, 1993: 32).

Whereas the clash of civilizations is often presented as secular, already in Huntington's famous phrasing of this struggle 'Judeo-Christian heritage' is fused with 'our secular present.' Such discourses do not fit in nicely with narratives that identify the populist turn as a secular reaction to the return of religion through migration. This is often the background against which the PVV is approached. See for instance the take of Ian Buruma on the Dutch turn to the right as he formulates it in his *Murder in Amsterdam: Liberal Europe, Islam and the Limits of Tolerance:* "[It is] a European civil war that has raged for many centuries, (...) the war between the ideal of universal rights and values versus the pull of the tribal soil (...) the spirit of faith versus enlightened self-interest" (Buruma 2007, 169). In contrast to this framing of the Dutch turn to the right, which sketches a backdrop of secularist universalism versus tribalist religiosity, the discourse mentioned above paints a considerably more complex picture. In opposition to 'Islam' which is perceived to be inherently non-secular and intolerant, we don't see a mobilization of universalist, Enlightenment reason, an invocation of the private role of religion, or the insistence of the separation of Church and State or any other classical definition of secularity but rather a localized, historically grown, and religiously-oriented cultural identity. Dutch Judeo-Christian culture is presented not only as the soil out of which tolerant, secular and inclusive culture arose, but insisting on the present character of secular, religious-cultural identity is seen as crucial to the maintenance of secular societies. By fusing together secular values and a religious-cultural heritage in this manner, all sorts of progressive values that, historically, one would not expect be connected to a religious past, such as feminism and gay rights, are presented as hallmarks of 'Judeo-Christian' superiority (cf. Van den Hemel 2014).

In short, the 'turn to the right' in the Netherlands was not merely an opposition between the secular, universalist, Enlightened West and the backward, tribalist, religious non-West. If the work of major Dutch players in the turn to the right (Bolkestein, Fortuyn, Bosma, and Wilders), international frameworks such as those of Samuel Huntington, as well as our cursory sketch of populist movements in other countries in Western Europe is anything to go by, the turn to the right is part of a broad re-negotiation of the interaction between religion and secularity.

A number of important questions arise: what is the use of religion in the construction of this national identity? Can we or should we, still call this religion? What implied definition of secularity is being used here? What could explain these seemingly paradoxical identifications? How are emancipatory practices reframed? From a perspective that sees secularity as a regulation of religious differences and religion as a rational choice for a dogmatic framework, the discursive practices of PVV (and other populist parties in Western Europe) are indeed nonsensical and contradictory. Yet, from a different methodological approach, new inroads can be taken. I hold that these discursive manoeuvres should be understood as part of a reframing of the imaginary backdrop against which is decided who can partake of Western secularity and who is excluded. In short, this discourse points to changes in the social imaginary of Western Europe.

3 Social Imaginary

According to Taylor, a social imaginary is defined as a "common understanding that enables us to carry out the collective pratices that make up our social life" (Taylor 2004, 24). In modern social imaginaries, a public sphere in which participants are equal and a self-governing people are crucial ingredients. To illustrate this, Taylor uses the example of a demonstration. In a protest, even antagonistic participants inhabit a shared framework; taking place in public spaces, "we are already in some kind of conversation with each other." In this manner, even a violent protest "figures the addressee as one who can be, must be, reasoned with" (Taylor 2004, 27). This sense of equality, in both the public sphere as well as within notions of the sovereignty of the people, does not need to be consciously held, it is rather part of a backdrop against which 'ordinary people' act and share commonality. Social imaginaries are different from social theory in important manners. Instead of a small minority who determines and masters social theory, social imaginary focuses on "the way ordinary people 'imagine' their social surroundings" which is carried in "images, stories and legends" (Taylor 2004, 23). This does not mean, according to Taylor, that there is no continuity between reflections on society and the way in which 'ordinary people' live in imagined, shared frameworks. Rather, there is a complex sense of interaction between, say, Grotius defense of natural law and a moral order broadly shared among citizens in modern, secular societies. In this manner, the implicit ways in which inhabitants of secular societies relate to each other is influenced by social theory, but no longer need the conscious theoretical reflection to be of effect. Taylor sketches the way in which social theory influences social imaginaries:

> What exactly is involved when a theory penetrates and transforms the social imaginary? For the most part, people take up, improvise, or are inducted into new practices. These are made sense of by the new outlook, the one first articulated in the theory; this out look is the context that gives sense to the practices. Hence the new understanding comes to be accessible to the participants in a way it wasn't before. It begins to define the contours

of their world and can eventually come to count as the taken-for-granted shape of things, too obvious to mention. (Taylor 2004, 29)

From this perspective, the PVV and other populist movements can be seen as part of shifts in modern self-understanding of secular societies. Populist parties don't just express the argument that Islam should reform, when stating that a first article of the constitution should state the supremacy of Judeo-Christian culture, the assumptions that determine the very fabric of the public sphere, and of the sovereignty of the people are addressed. Whereas for thinkers such as Huntington the opposition between Western, Judeo-Christian-secular culture was of a scholarly nature, it is now not uncommon to see atheism, feminism, gay rights, freedom of speech, separation of Church and State imagined as part of a Western sense of community in which the participation of people who don't share the cultural background is increasingly more difficult to imagine.

4 Post-Secular Nationalism

What this paper proposes is that movements such as the PVV can be sketched as part of an important contestation in the social imaginary of Western European states. This article furthermore proposes to call this particular contestation 'post-secular nationalism.' With post-secular nationalism I mean: a discursive reframing of imaginations of secular national identity in which the non-neutrality of secularity plays an important role. This has as its advantage that it allows for a differentiation between classical far right discourse, whilst allowing discussion of the future of religion and secularity in constructions of national identity. Finally, the word 'post-secular' also means to indicate the open-ended question that these discursive practices pose to scholars: are the words secular and religious suitable terms to describe these developments or are these terms themselves part of the ideological framework itself? In what follows I propose to further specify this role of religion in populist discourse by analyzing the 'post-secular' and 'nationalist' dimensions of this term.

4.1 Post-Secular Nationalism?

Under the influence of conflicts concerning secularity and religion in the 21st century, scholars have emphasized the need for revisiting the secularization narrative (Habermas 2008). An important impetus in this development has been the questioning of the assumptions behind what is recognized as religion and secularity (Asad 1993; Jakobsen and Pellegrini 2008), and scholars have focussed on how the concepts religion and secularity are part of a power discourse of its own (Fitzgerald 2000; Keane 2015). Against this backdrop the concept post-secular has come to stand for challenges concerning the continued presence in secular societies (Habermas 2008), but it has also come to stand for a series of questions concerning alternative conceptualizations of religion and secularity (cf. Gorski et al. 2012). Most relevant for this project is the rejection of secularity and religion as 'meta-categories' and a subsequent focus on how these terms are part themselves shape and regulate communities (cf. the definition of the post-secular as "a change in secular self-understanding" by De Vries (2006, 3). Instead of applying religion and secularity as meta-categories, scholars have aimed at developing an approach which locates religion and secularity in discursive practices: "the actual concrete meaning of whatever people denominate as 'religion' [should be] elucidated in the context of their particular discursive practices" (Casanova in: Calhoun, Juergensmeyer, Vanantwerpen, 63). This religion "beyond a concept," to borrow the title of a volume by Hent de Vries, allows for an interdisciplinary "bottom-up" approach to religion that can incorporate practices and objects that would normally fall outside of the frame of classical definitions of religion (De Vries 2008, 66; cf. Meyer 2012, 3). Instead of focusing on religion and secularity as stable meta-categories, religion and secularity are seen as discursive practices which shape and influence political reality.

There are good reasons to include the post-secular in the analysis of contemporary forms of nationalism: many of the post-secular academic diagnoses of the crises of secularism (it would be Protestant instead of universal in nature, its inclusive values would cater predominantly to the West, it would be inherently incapable of inclusive conceptualizations of the public sphere, to name but a couple of arguments), are actively embraced by movements such as the PVV: as we have seen, the nationalist politicians and thinkers mentioned above affirm explicitly that secularity is in crisis; they explicitly embrace the idea that its values are based on a biased and culturally determined take on religion; they simply acknowledge that indeed religious-secular identity means an a-priori exclusion of Islam, and so on. In short, a lot of the problems that have dominated post-secular scholarship play an active role in the new nationalist movements. As illustrated by the resurgence of Carl Schmitt in both the work of post-secular scholarship as well as of ideologues of the PVV (Bart Jan Spruyt), one can say that the crisis of secularism that Mahmood and Asad describe, resonates in the outright insistence of figures such as Spruyt, Bosma and Wilders that indeed, secular nations are in need of religious foundations. The shared albeit diametrically opposed, concerns with the crisis and the religious roots of secularism and with the problematic position of Islam within this religious-secular identity warrants the conclusion that post-secular nationalism is indeed an apt term to describe parties such as the PVV.

This also allows us to revisit critically some of the arguments put forward against the normative implications of Taylor's approach to the contemporary challenges to our secular age. Even though the notion of the social imaginary might be of use to sketch how the backdrop of secular identification changes, the larger historical framework in which Taylor identifies the social imaginary keeps in place identifications that might be considered problematic. As Taylor reaches the end of his monumental *A Secular Age*, he states: "it's not an accident that 'Christians' fall into similar deviations to those of 'secular humanists.' As I have tried to show throughout this book, we both emerge from the same long process of Reform in Latin Christendom. We are brothers under the skin." (Taylor 2007, 675)

Secular humanists and Christians are, in the end, "brothers under the skin," and they share the same challenges: "it appears a matter of who can respond most profoundly and convincingly to what are ultimately commonly felt dilemmas" (Taylor 2007, 675). Authors such as Talal Asad, Saba Mahmood, José Casanova and William Connolly have, in their own way, felt the need to not just describe the trajectory of the secular, but to criticize and challenge secularity as the "established unconscious of European culture" (Scott and Hirschkind 2006, 75). In a critical discussion of the aftermath of the Danish Cartoon crisis, Talal Asad analyzes the Regensburg lecture by Pope Benedict XVI in 2006. In this lecture, Benedict stated that Europe is a Christian continent, but, more importantly, that, unlike Islam, Christianity does not divorce reason from religion. In this manner, Benedict states: "the scientific ethos, (...) is the will to be obedient to the truth, and, as such, it embodies an attitude which belongs to the essential decisions of the Christian spirit" (Benedict 2006). Asad highlights that this equating of science with Christianity is part of a series of deeply problematic "religious roots without being religious" (Asad 1993, 54) which: "reinforces the existing distinction between the paradigmatically human and candidates for inclusion in true humanity who do not as yet own their bodies, emotions, and thoughts. It reinforces, in other words, the ideological status of European Muslims as not fully human because they are not yet morally autonomous and politically disciplined." (Asad 1993, 55/56).

Similarly, in Saba Mahmood's *Can Secularism be Otherwise: A Critique of Charles Taylors A Secular Age* (2010), Mahmood writes: "It seems that by delineating an account of Christian secularism that remains blind to the normative assumptions and power of Western Christianity, Taylor's invitation to interreligious dialogue sidesteps the greatest challenge of our time" (299).

4.2 Post-Secular Nationalism?

The post-secular nationalists' embrace of secular-religious values as central elements of national identity calls for an update of the often implicit secular approaches to nationalism. Without wanting to sketch the important and interconnected history of nationalism, secularism and religion, let me suffice here by stating that in the modernization-secularization thesis, the modern nation state is seen as both a replacement of religious fidelity as well as the instrument that, by keeping religion at bay, safeguards a peaceful and democratic public sphere. This narrative posits that nationalism as a movement and an ideology in particular, is inseparable from modernity. One of the central elements is the ongoing process of secularization – the idea that the rise of nationalism in the context of the rationalization of the world necessarily brings bout the decreased importance of religion. For instance, the much-cited Benedict Anderson states that the rise of the imaginary national communities was paired with a "secular transformation" simultaneous to the "ebbing of religious belief" (1991, 11).

With the advent of the tumultuous 21st century, scholars of nationalism have, and increasingly do so, pointed to the religious dimensions of nationalism itself. Frequently building upon the insight of Carl Schmitt that "all concepts of the modern state are secularized theological concepts" (Schmitt 2010, 36), or the permanence of the theologico-political (Lefort 2006), a number of contemporary scholars have argued for a renewed interest in the constitutive role of the religious in the secular nation state. As Roger Friedland states, a form of religion might be fundamental to all authority: "Faith, beyond reason and proof, thus undergirds the performativity of [any] authority, the saying so that makes it so" (2010, 97). Jan Assman highlights the religious dimension of national thought: "nationalism is (…) a political religion that does not tolerate other religions besides itself" (Assman 2005, 150). Jose Llobera even states that "nationalism is the god of modernity": "in modernity, nationalism has become a functional equivalent of religion: nationalism has become a religion – a secular religion where god is the nation" (1994, 143). Although a number of these approaches might risk blowing up the category religion so that any authority can be called religious, nonetheless a number of important developments have been made. This is also the standpoint of Jonathan Eastwood and Nikolas Prevalakis, who conclude an extensive survey of work on the notions nationalism, religion and secularization with the prediction "we have only begun to answer some of the fundamental questions that arise when one attempts to consider the multiple relationships that exist (and have existed) between nationalism, religious identity and alleged processes of secularization" (Eastwood and Prevalakis 2010, 91).

Contributing to this movement is the self-proclaimed goal of contemporary scholar Philip Gorski. Gorski has spent the largest part of his career analyzing the way in which secularism and early-modern nation states can be conceived of as disciplinary apparatuses (2000, 2003). After these critical approaches of the role of religion in the nation state, Gorski changed his approach with the advent of the post-Bush years in the United States. More specifically, Gorski saw in the rise of Obama empirical proof that civil religion is alive and kicking. In *Civil Religion Today* (2010) Gorski identified and praised the role of religion as cement for secular values in the 21st century. Philip Gorski has pointed out the need to rethink the role of religion in constructions of national communities. He suggests that there exist roughly three types of intertwinements of religious dimensions and the nation state: religious nationalism, liberal secularism and civil religion. "Religious nationalists," in Gorski's eyes, "advocate a total fusion between a religious creed and a political community" (Gorski 2010, 7). Examples would include the conservative right in the U.S, as well as a variety of historical attempts to construct a state out of believers of the same type. 'Liberal secularists' on the other hand, advocate total separation of the two spheres. The state should be fully neutral on religious grounds, and thus safeguard a tolerant society that provides equal opportunities to its citizens. Although Gorski clearly favours the ideals of liberal secularism, he also recognizes that the 21st century saw a crisis of these ideals. They are in need, according to Gorski, of a supplement, an ideology, a creed. Civil religion functions precisely in this manner. "Civil religionists, on the other hand, imagine [the domains of religious creed and political community] as overlapping." (2010, 7). Gorski states that the category civil religion might be better suited to both describe ongoing practices, as well as provide guidance on how to order a society:

> In short, civil religionists agree that a fair degree of institutional separation between church and state is salutary for both, the notion that religion can and should be kept out of politics or, for that matter that political commitments can somehow be 'neutral' and 'general' is rejected in favor of a robust pluralism in which citizens are free to deploy religio-ethical forms of argumentation and encouraged to do so. (Gorsli 2010, 10)

Civil religion is seen here not as a factor opposed to modern political functioning, nor as subservient to it, but as an active part of it. This use of the term civil religion as a productive part of modern communities, has its origins in the work of Jean-Jacques Rousseau. Rousseau, in his *Social Contract* speculated on the role of a civil religion that would be necessary to provide the 'sanctity of the social contract':

> The dogmas of civil religion ought to be few, simple, and exactly worded, without explanation or commentary. The existence of a mighty, intelligent and beneficent Divinity, possessed of foresight and providence, the life to come, the happiness of the just, the punishment of the wicked, the sanctity of the social contract and the laws: these are its positive dogmas. Its negative dogmas I confine to one, intolerance, which is a part of the cults we have rejected. (Rousseau 1997, 151)

It was this constructive, minimal and tolerant role of civic religion that Robert Bellah praised in his 1967 article *Civil Religion in America*. According to Bellah, America's civil religion, embodied by such documents as the Constitution and the Declaration of Independence, can be embraced next to one's personal religion. This 'common religion' ensured a tolerant public sphere, and curtailed religious extremism. The example that Bellah gives is the inaugural address of Kennedy, where as always, the mentioning of God frames the address, yet does not seem to be connected to the content of the address in any direct way. According to Bellah this minimal dimension ensures maximum participation. Bellah cites Dwight Eisenhower: "isn't Dwight Eisenhower reported to have said 'Our government makes no sense unless it is founded in a deeply felt religious faith—and I don't care what it is'?" (Bellah 1991, 170). Bellah concluded that civil religion "is a heritage of moral and religious experience from which we still have much to learn as we formulate the decisions that lie ahead" (1991, 186).

In light of Obama's rise to power and popularity, Gorski, who was a student of Bellah, stated that perhaps his mentor's notion of civil religion should be dusted again and taken off the shelf: "The American civil religion was alive, and, by November of 2008, very well indeed" (Gorski 2010, 2). Arising out of the reboot of civil religion in Obama's speeches, Gorski has argued for a positive revaluation of civil religion. Whereas liberal secularism might lack the 'glue' to make communities stick together, and religious nationalists smother a society into an aggressive monoreligious mixture, civil religion might offer the much-needed coherence of religious-secular societies. Gorski clearly advocates civil religion in times of post-secularity:

> I conclude on a normative note: The United States does have a civil religion. But *should* it have one? Does it *need* one? I have no reservations answering in the affirmative. (...) One of the fundamental challenges confronting all modern democracies, particularly diverse ones such as the United States, is achieving and maintaining the appropriate balance between pluralism and solidarity (Gorski 2010, 12).

Now the similarities with the post-secular nationalist discourse are apparent. Much like the civil religion Bellah and Gorski advocate, post-secular nationalists agree that religion is necessary for national communities. Also, in line with post-secular nationalists' view on religion, civil religion seems to be connected to a historical-cultural reference point rather than to a personal creed of choice. The post-secular nationalists would also emphasize that adherence to the religious roots of tolerance is needed in order not to become too passive so that religious radicals can undermine a pluriform society. Civil religionists, much like post-secular nationalists, would emphasize the role of religion as a moral compass in times of crisis. Yet at the same time, there are important differences between civil religion that binds a nation and what I propose to call post-secular nationalism.

To summarize, let us zoom in on the difference between civil religion and post-secular nationalism.

- The roots of post-secular nationalism lie in the conservative tradition,[3] whereas the roots of civil religion are connected to the Enlightenment tradition.[4]
- As illustrated by Pim Fortuyn's mentioning of the permanence of culture, as well as by the PVV's claim that Muslims inherently cannot be part of Judeo-Christian secularity, post-secular nationalists stress a culturalized notion of religion, in which one is born. As Fortuyn stated: one can leave or join a religion, a culture however, one cannot leave behind. Civil religion emphasizes that one can embrace the minimal civil religion next to one's own personal creed.
- As a result, the word civil religion has a strong artificial and state-oriented connotation, whereas the post-secular nationalist tradition tends to frame the religious roots of communities as an organically developed presence according to which the state should obey itself. As exemplified with PVV's proposal to change the Dutch constitution, and in contrast to the sacred status of the constitution in the U.S., the foundational documents of the Dutch state are not eternal objects of veneration, but should be formed to express a pre-existing religious-cultural identity.

5 Conclusion

In conclusion, let me reiterare the major points I have tried to make:
1. Instead of the frequently used tropes of fascism or radical secularism, contemporary populist movements can be characterized as post-secular. From the beginning these forms of nationalism have been different from far-right-

---

[3] This point can be made more explicit. For an analysis of the role of conservatism in the Dutch turn to the right, see Oudenampsen 2013.
[4] Cf. Rouner 1986.

ist positions in claiming secular, tolerant, progressive values, whilst differentiating themselves from the radical secularists by embedding these values in a culturalized notion of religious-secular citizenship (resulting in the construction of 'Judeo-Christian-Secularity'). The post-secular nationalist position is characterized by: a sketch of secular values as core components of national identity; an emphasis on the religious roots of these secular values; an emphasis on the cultural intransigence of this religious-secular citizenship. This position can be best approached not as a social theory, but as a reframing of social imagination.
2. Post-secular nationalism points to an uncomfortable dimension within larger narratives of secularism. These dimensions point to the urgent question that scholars such as Talal Asad and Saba Mahmood have posed: Can secularism be other-wise?
3. These dimensions ensure that there is an important difference with civil religion, whose advocates stress the universalizing, tolerant tendency of civil religion.

As an after-thought, I would like to problematize the notion of civil religion, lest the reader might think this article simply endorses civil religion over and against post-secular nationalism. Let us return shortly to the quote by Eisenhower that was mentioned by Bellah as an illustration of the inclusive nature of civil religion: "Our government makes no sense unless it is founded in a deeply felt religious faith—and I don't care what it is." This is often pointed out as being the basis of a non-secular yet inclusive presence of religion in the public sphere. Yet, the full quote reads: "Our form of government has no sense unless it is founded in a deeply felt religious faith, and I don't care what it is. With us of course it is the Judeo-Christian concept but it must be a religion that all men are created equal."[5] This full quote locates the civil religion, the 'us,' with a matter-of-factness within the Judeo-Christian tradition. The emphasis on equality leaves the door open to discursive claims that the Judeo-Christian tradition is the only faith that proclaim values such as equality.

Whether post-secular nationalism might be or should be opposed with a form of either national or international civil religion is a question that remains to be seen. Critics of post-secular nationalism quite often miss what makes post-secular nationalism effective. Seeing this movement as a post-secular nationalist, has the advantage of allowing us to see this movement as addressing and manipulating a collective imagination that underlies secular values.

---

5 See Silk 1984.

Having defined post-secular nationalism, the challenge becomes to formulate an updated approach to these matters, there is an urgent need to address the complicity of core notions of Western self-identification in the post-secular nationalist framework, just as there is a need to think of ways in which one can be feminist, pro-gay, anti-antisemitic, and even secular without being framed as examples and proponents of Judeo-Christian-secular superiority.

Bibliography

Aalberts, Chris. 2012. *Achter de PVV: Waarom Burgers op Geert Wilders Stemmen*. Delft: Eburon Uitgeverij.
Asad, Talal. 1993. *Genealogies of Religion: Discipline and Reasons of Power in Christianity and Islam*. Baltimore: Johns Hopkins University Press.
Barr, Robert R. 2009. "Populists, Outsiders and Anti-Establishment Politics." *Party Politics* 15 (1):29–48.
Bellah, Robert Neelly. 1992. *The Broken Covenant: American Civil Religion in Time of Trial*. Chicago: University of Chicago Press.
Benedict XVI. "Meeting With the Representatives of Science Lecture of the Holy Father, September 12th 2006." presented at the Regensburg Lecture, Aula Magna of the University of Regensburg, September 12, 2006. Website of The Vatican, accessed February 15th 2018.
Bolkestein, Frits. 1992. *Woorden Hebben hun Betekenis*. Amsterdam: Promotheus.
Bosma, Martin. 2010. *De Schijn-Elite van de Valsemunters*. Amsterdam: Prometheus.
Buruma, Ian. 2007. *Murder in Amsterdam: Liberal Europe, Islam, and the Limits of Tolerance*. London: Penguin Books.
Butler, Judith, Jürgen Habermas, Charles Taylor, Cornel West and Craig Calhoun. 2011. *The Power of Religion in the Public Sphere*. Edited by Eduardo Mendieta and Jonathan VanAntwerpen. New York: Columbia University Press.
Eastwood, Jonathan, and Nikolas Prevalakis. 2010. "Nationalism, Religion and Secularization: An Opportune Moment for Research." *Review of Religious Research* 52 (1):90–111.
Duyvendak, Jan Willem, Paul Mepschen and Evelien H. Tonkens. 2010. "Sexual Politics, Orientalism and Multicultural Citizenship in the Netherlands." *Sociology* 44 (5):962–979.
Fitzgerald, Timothy. 2000. *The Ideology of Religious Studies*. New York: Oxford University Press.
Fortuyn, Pim. 2002. *De Verweesde Samenleving: Een Religieus-Sociologisch Traktaat*. Uithoorn: Karakter.
Gorski, Philip. 2014. "Barack Obama and Civil Religion." In *Rethinking Obama. Political Power and Social Theory* 22:179–214. Bingley: Emerald Group Publishing.
Gorski, Philip. 2010. "Civil Religion Today." *Association of Religion Data Archives*.
Gorski, Philip S., and Jonathan VanAntwerpen, eds. 2012. *The Post-Secular in Question: Religion in Contemporary Society*. New York: New York University Press.

Gourevitch, Victor, Raymond Geuss, Quentin Skinner and Richard Tuck. 1997. *Rousseau: The Social Contract and Other Later Political Writings*. Cambridge: Cambridge University Press.
Gregory, Brad S. 2012. *The Unintended Reformation: How a Religious Revolution Secularized Society.* Cambridge, MA: Belknap Press.
Habermas, Jürgen. 2008. "Notes on Post-Secular Society." *New Perspectives Quarterly* 25 (4):17–29.
Hainsworth, Paul. 2008. *The Extreme Right in Europe.* London/New York: Routledge.
Houtman, Dick, and Birgit Meyer. 2012. *Things: Religion and the Question of Materiality.* New York: Fordham University Press.
Huntington, Samuel P. 1993. "The Clash of Civilizations?" *Foreign Affairs* 72 (3):22–49.
Jakobsen, Janet R., and Ann Pellegrini. 2008. *Secularisms.* Durham: Duke University Press.
Keane, Webb. 2007. *Christian Moderns: Freedom And Fetish in the Mission Encounter.* Berkeley: University of California Press.
Lefort, Claude. 2006. "Permanence of the Theologico-Political?" In *Political Theologies*, edited by Hent de Vries and Lawrence E. Sullivan, 148–187. New York: Fordham University Press.
Mahmood, Saba. 2010. "Can Secularism Be Other-Wise? A Critique of Charles Taylor's *A Secular Age*." In *Varieties of Secularism in a Secular Age*, edited by Jonathan VanAntwerpen, Michael Warner, and Craig Calhoun, 282–299. Cambridge, MA: Harvard University Press.
Moffitt, Benjamin, and Simon Tormey. 2014. "Rethinking Populism: Politics, Mediatisation and Political Style." *Political Studies* 62 (2):381–397.
Mudde, Cas. 2007. *Populist Radical Right Parties in Europe.* Cambridge: Cambridge University Press.
Mudde, Cas. 2013. "Three Decades of Populist Radical Right Parties in Western Europe: So What?" *European Journal of Political Research* 52 (1):1–19.
Oudenampsen, Merijn. 2018. *The Conservative Embrace of Progressive Values: On the Intellectual Origins of the Swing to the Right in Dutch Politics.* Dissertation, University of Tilburg.
PVV. 2006. "Algemene Opmerkingen Grondwet." Source: www.pvv.nl. Accessed February 15th 2018.
Riemen, Rob. 2010. *De Eeuwige Terugkeer van het Fascisme.* Amsterdam: Atlas-Contact.
Rouner, Leroy S. 1986. *Civil Religion and Political Theology.* Notre Dame University Press.
Schaap, Sybe. 2012. *Het Rancuneuze Gif: De Opmars van Onbehagen.* Budel: Damon.
Scott, David, and Charles Hirschkind. 2006. *Powers of the Secular Modern: Talal Asad and his Interlocutors.* Palo Alto: Stanford University Press.
Silk, Mark. 1984. "Notes on the Judeo-Christian Tradition in America." *American Quarterly* 36 (1): 65–85.
Spruyt, Bart Jan. 2005. *De Toekomst van de Stad: Over Geschiedenis en Politiek — een Boekenweekessay.* Zoetermeer: Boekencentrum.
Taylor, Charles. 2004. *Modern Social Imaginaries.* Durham: Duke University Press.
Taylor, Charles. 2007. *A Secular Age.* Cambridge, MA: Harvard University Press.
Van den Hemel, Ernst. 2013. "The Noble Lie: 'Judeo-Christian Roots' and the Rise of Conservative Nationalism in the Netherlands." In *Postsecular Publics: Transformations of*

Religion and the Public Sphere, edited by Rosi Braidotti, Eva Midden, and Bolette Blaagaard. New York: Palgrave.

Van der Brug, Wouter, Meindert Fennema, 2009. Sjoerdje van Heerden, and Sarah de Lange. "Hoe heeft het integratiedebat zich in Nederland ontwikkeld?" *Migrantenstudies* 25 (3):198–220.

Vries, Hent de. 2008. *Religion: Beyond a Concept.* New York: Fordham University Press.

Vries, Hent de, and Lawrence Eugene Sullivan. 2006. *Political Theologies: Public Religions in a Post-Secular World.* New York: Fordham University Press.

Wallet, Bart. 2012. "Zin en Onzin van de 'Joods-Christelijke Traditie.'" *Christen Democratische Verkenningen*, 100–109.

Wilders, Geert. 2013. "Open Letter to His Holiness Pope Francis." Source: www.geertwilders.nl. Accessed February 15th 2018.

List of Contributors

Hans Alma is extraordinary professor of Humanistic Studies at the Free University of Brussels (VUB), department of Philosophy and Ethics. Her main research interests are worldview pluralism and the role of imagination and art in people's search for meaning in life.

Christa Anbeek is professor of Remonstrant Theology at the Free University in Amsterdam. The main focus of her research is on the relationship between religions, philosophies and the meaning of life, especially with regard to the end of life or to serious life events.

Noel Clycq is visiting professor and holds the chair in 'European Values: Discourses and Prospects' at the Faculty of Arts, and is member of the Centre for Migration and Intercultural Studies (CeMIS), both at the University of Antwerp. His main research interests are socialization and identification processes in educational and family settings, with a focus on migration, diversity and Europe.

Saskia van Goelst Meijer is an independent scholar and ecological farmer. Her main research interests are contemporary nonviolence, sustainability and social change.

Ernst van den Hemel is a postdoctoral researcher at the Meertens Institute of the Royal Netherlands Academy of Arts and Sciences. His current research projects are 'The Heritagization of Religion and the Sacralization of Heritage in Contemporary Europe' and 'Populism, Social Media and Religion'.

Kenneth Hemmerechts is a postdoctoral researcher at the Free University of Brussels in Etterbeek (VUB) where he is currently working in the field of sociology of education. His previous work at universities in Belgium included research on migration, criminal recidivism, fraud, police capacity, employment and trade unionism, genocide and social theory.

Nicole L. Immler is associate professor of History and Cultural Studies at the University of Humanistic Studies in Utrecht. She specializes in memory culture, politics of recognition and transitional justice. Her present research 'Narratives of (In)Justice' studies how post-war and post-colonial memories affect each other, analyzing the implications of reparation claims for individuals and society.

Laurens ten Kate is associate professor of Philosophy and Religious Studies, and an endowed professor of Liberal Religion and Humanism, both at the University of Humanistic Studies, Utrecht. He publishes in the fields of philosophy of culture, religious studies and globalization theory. With Hans Alma, he has initiated and coordinates the international NWO-funded research consortium SIMAGINE, of which this book is a result.

Stijn Latré is a lecturer at Thomas More (University College of Applied Sciences) where he teaches courses in philosophy and religion. From 2009–2013, he worked at the University of Antwerp on a FWO research project entitled 'The End of Secularization?', studying proponents and critics of the classical secularization thesis.

Michiel Meijer is a postdoctoral researcher of the Research Foundation – Flanders (FWO) in the Department of Philosophy at the University of Antwerp. His research interests include (meta-) ethics, hermeneutics, and the philosophy of Charles Taylor. His current project is 'Moral Realism Without Moral Facts: A Hermeneutical Defense of Non-Naturalism.'

Joeri Schrijvers is an independent scholar. His main research interests are continental philosophy, contemporary philosophy of religion, and phenomenology.

Christiane Timmerman is research professor (ZAPBOF) and full professor at the University of Antwerp and director of the Centre of Migration and Intercultural Studies (CeMIS), which focuses on multidisciplinary research on migration, integration and ethnic minorities. She is/was coordinator/partner of several large (inter)national research projects and is member of the Board of Directors of the European Research Network on Migration, IMISCOE.

Robin Vandevoordt is a postdoctoral researcher at Oxford University's Refugee Studies Centre (RSC) and at the University of Antwerp's Centre for Research on Ecological and Social Change (CRESC). As a cultural and political sociologist, his main interests are in the lived experiences of forced migrants, civil humanitarianism and social theory.

Guido Vanheeswijck is full professor at the Department of Philosophy (University of Antwerp) and part-time professor at the Institute of Philosophy (Catholic University Louvain). His research is in the fields of philosophy of culture, philosophy of religion and metaphysics.

Gert Verschraegen is associate professor of Sociology at the University of Antwerp. His research interests are in the fields of social theory, sociology of human rights, cultural sociology and sociology of science.

Roos Willems is a Research Fellow in the Department for Social and Cultural Anthropology at the University of Leuven in Belgium. Her research interests include refugee and forced migration issues (mainly in an African context) as well as the topic of culture in development studies.

Index

actors 15, 168, 173, 178, 206 f., 212, 223
American revolution 145, 160
anekantavada 12, 95, 106 f., 109
Arendt, Hannah 100–102, 109, 126, 128, 130, 133 f., 229
articulation 3 f., 12, 53, 55, 57, 59–61, 65–67, 69 f., 73, 89, 95, 99–103, 109, 111, 113–115
Ayer, Alfred J. 33 f., 36 f.

Beiser, Frederick 25, 28
Bellah, Robert 128, 171, 258, 260
Berlin, Isaiah 4, 10, 23, 26, 31 f., 36–42, 44

Castoriadis, Cornelius 1 f., 11, 14, 21, 48 f., 51, 61, 64, 89 f., 125, 175, 177
Christendom (breakaway from) 146–150, 153, 249, 255
civil religion 16, 171, 180, 248, 257–260
Civil rights 224, 226
Collingwood, Robin George 4, 10, 23, 31–44
(Colonial) Reparation 194, 200–202, 205, 215, 217, 219
communitarian 155–156, 158
Compensation 9, 14 f., 193, 196, 200–203, 205, 208–210, 212, 215 f., 218 f.
contrast experiences 12, 57, 70, 95–97, 99 f., 102 f., 109 f., 114
Counter-Enlightenment 26, 40 f., 44, 63
court cases 196, 203, 206, 209 f., 212, 214, 218
Cross pressures 11, 48, 61, 64, 69, 96, 149, 162
cross-pressures 13, 86, 142, 162 f.
Cultural analysis 14, 66, 167–169, 181 f.
Cultural sociology 169, 182
Cultural theory 1

Democracy 2, 10, 15, 105, 143 f., 150–152, 177 f., 181, 223–225, 228, 230–235, 237–241, 249
Derrida, Jacques 13, 141–163

Dialogue 13, 15, 63, 73, 91, 98, 101 f., 113, 137, 141, 163, 198, 201, 203, 213, 215, 255
Diaspora 209, 215, 219
Dilthey, Wilhelm 35, 171
Dreyfus, Hubert 3, 9, 11, 29, 73, 76, 81, 83 f., 89
Durkheim, Emil 14, 168–173, 180, 184–186

Economic and social rights 201, 241
embodiment 12, 30, 114, 213
Enlightenment 26, 28, 40 f., 44, 54, 63, 144–146, 199, 251, 259
ethics 55, 74–76, 79–82, 84 f., 88, 101, 148, 155
Europe 15 f., 47, 143–147, 149, 151, 157, 196–199, 223–226, 228–231, 233–242, 247, 251 f., 255
Expressivist culture 11, 48, 53, 65, 89

Fink, Eugen 126, 132
Fortuyn, Pim 250 f., 259
Foundation 12, 25 f., 39, 41, 74–76, 79 f., 90 f., 120–122, 133 f., 150, 216, 223, 254
fragility 61, 64, 69, 74 f., 97, 102, 109
Fundamental rights 184, 225

Grondin, Jean 142, 161

Hamann, Johann Georg 10, 21, 23–29, 35, 39 f., 44
Hegel, Georg Wilhelm Friedrich 4, 23, 28, 30 f., 42, 69
Heidegger, Martin 10, 21, 23, 29, 31 f., 36, 43 f., 52, 54, 147, 162, 177
Herder, Johann Gottfried 4, 10, 23, 26, 28 f., 35, 39–41, 54, 91
Heritage 10, 15, 23, 123, 134, 145, 247, 251, 258
Human rights 6, 13–15, 65, 145 f., 148–156, 161, 167 f., 182–188, 193–199, 201–206, 209–220, 223–235, 237–242
Huntington, Samuel 250 f., 253

identity-politics 154 f., 157, 208
imagination 5, 9 f., 12, 16, 50, 52, 104 f., 109, 112, 114, 121–124, 131, 134, 136, 176 f., 216, 219, 230–232, 236, 247 f., 253, 260
Immanent frame 3, 11, 44, 47 f., 52, 64–69, 95, 104, 151, 153, 160, 162
International migration 230

Joas, Hans 6, 128, 184–187
judeo-christian 249
Justice 5–7, 12, 14, 31, 64, 69, 76, 89, 95, 114 f., 121, 160 f., 185, 195 f., 199–201, 206 f., 212 f., 215–219

Kant, Immanuel 10, 21–27, 35, 38 f., 44, 56, 60, 170
Karolis, Alexander 142, 162

Levinas, Emmanuel 152, 154

Merleau-Ponty, Maurice 10, 23, 29, 32, 36, 83–85
Migration 7, 9, 13–15, 121, 168, 177, 183, 188, 209, 224, 226, 228–236, 238–242, 248, 251
Migration aspirations 15, 224 f., 228, 230–241
Moore, George Edward 33, 35
moral re-orientation 12, 99 f., 102, 109
Multidirectional Memory 204, 213
Multiple modernities 21, 145

Nancy, Jean-Luc 119 f., 122, 126, 133–135, 137, 146–148, 154 f., 158–160, 162, 207
nationalism 15 f., 50, 122, 125, 156, 182, 225, 247 f., 253–257, 259–261
naturalism 43, 65, 76 f., 85 f.
Neo-positivism 43
Nietzsche, Friedrich 12 f., 63, 97, 119 f., 126–134, 137, 142, 148

objectivity 73–77, 79, 81, 88–91, 98, 101, 113
Ontology 11, 30 f., 42 f., 58, 60 f., 68, 74–77, 80–90

phenomenology 11, 74 f., 77, 80–84, 86–89, 98
philosophical anthropology 82, 86–89
Play 9, 12 f., 24 f., 35, 44, 57, 75, 96 f., 104 f., 111, 119 f., 125–127, 129–137, 153, 174, 199, 210, 215, 238, 241, 247, 253 f.
Pluralism 6 f., 12, 107, 119 f., 142, 215, 257 f.
Polanyi, Michael 29, 31, 43, 54
Pondaag, Jeffry 207–210, 212–214, 216
populism 7, 183, 247 f.
Postcolonial 196, 198
post-secular 16, 184, 248, 253–256, 258–261
Presuppositions 4, 26, 32–35, 37–43, 58

Rawagede 14, 193, 203–207, 210 f., 213, 216–218
realism 9, 11, 33, 61, 73 f., 76, 84, 87–91, 106, 156, 162
Recognition 63, 109, 113, 156, 179, 196, 198, 201 f., 207, 210, 216–219
religion 1, 5, 7, 10, 15 f., 26, 44, 49, 51 f., 65–69, 90, 95–98, 104, 110 f., 114, 122–124, 136 f., 143–147, 150, 157–159, 162, 169–171, 173, 176, 180, 182, 187, 196, 218, 223 f., 227, 247 f., 250–260
Russell, Bertrand 33, 35, 54

Sense 2, 5, 8 f., 12, 21 f., 25, 27, 31, 37, 40, 44, 52 f., 60, 66, 68 f., 77–79, 81, 83, 97–101, 103, 107, 109–112, 119–125, 132 f., 136 f., 143, 145, 147, 149 f., 156–158, 167–172, 174, 176–181, 183, 185–188, 193 f., 197 f., 201, 203, 205, 215, 219, 252 f., 258, 260
Smith, James K. A. 24, 81–83, 87, 153, 162
Social identity 180, 185
Social imaginaries 1–14, 21–23, 28, 30 f., 38, 41–45, 47–53, 55–58, 61, 63–65, 68, 70, 73–75, 79 f., 84, 88–91, 95 f., 100, 102–106, 109–112, 114 f., 119–125, 129, 132 f., 135–137, 142, 154, 157, 159, 163, 167, 169, 171 f., 175, 177–184, 188, 194–197, 214, 219, 225, 252
Social imaginary 1, 3 f., 6–8, 10 f., 14, 16, 22, 47–50, 52 f., 55, 64, 68, 90, 103, 111, 115, 124, 126, 150 f., 154 f., 160, 181,

184, 193–196, 214, 219, 225, 247f., 252f., 255
Social theory   52, 252, 260
sovereignty   50, 52, 145, 153f., 193, 206, 226, 229, 252f.
Space (social imaginary as)   9f., 12f., 22, 24, 43, 50, 56, 95, 103, 105, 108f., 113–115, 119f., 123, 125f., 129–133, 135–137, 157, 161, 178, 183, 185, 187, 195, 209, 212f., 225, 230, 252
Strong evaluation   8, 10–12, 48, 58–60, 65, 70, 73, 75–80, 87, 89, 96, 99–104, 109, 111, 113
Subtraction story   65
Super-diversity   3, 7, 9, 12, 48, 109, 119f., 122, 124, 169, 175

Taylor, Charles   1–5, 7, 9–14, 16, 21–24, 28–32, 36f., 39–45, 47f., 50–70, 73–91, 95–101, 103–105, 109, 112–114, 119–124, 128, 136, 141–155, 157–163, 167, 171, 175–181, 183f., 188, 194–199, 215, 218f., 224f., 227f., 247f., 252f., 255
Transcendence   3, 11, 13, 47, 64–70, 98, 122f., 136f., 142, 146, 151–153, 160, 163
Transcendental framework   11, 48, 55f., 58, 65
Transitional Justice   7, 14, 193f., 196, 199–202, 206, 209, 214f., 217–220
truth-seeking   12, 95f., 104–115

utopia   6, 14, 161, 194f., 197f., 214

Vico, Giambattista   35, 38–40

Weber, Max   14, 168, 171–173, 176, 249
Wilders, Geert   247, 249, 251, 254
Wittgenstein, Ludwig   3, 10, 21, 23, 29, 31, 43f., 47, 54, 177
World-play   5, 12f., 120, 126, 131–133
worldviewing   12, 95f., 109–111, 114f., 133, 135

Zegveld, Liesbeth   203, 209f., 212, 216

www.ingramcontent.com/pod-product-compliance
Lightning Source LLC
Chambersburg PA
CBHW031804220426
43662CB00007B/522